Financial Markets, Speculation, and Development

Abdorasoul Sadeghi · Hela Nammouri ·
Seyed Komail Tayebi

Financial Markets, Speculation, and Development

The Role of Monetary Policy in Emerging and Traditional Economies

Springer

Abdorasoul Sadeghi
Department of Economics
University of Tehran
Tehran, Iran

Hela Nammouri
ESDES
UCLy (Lyon Catholic University)
Lyon, France

Seyed Komail Tayebi
Department of Economics
University of Isfahan
Isfahan, Iran

ISBN 978-981-95-5894-0 ISBN 978-981-95-5895-7 (eBook)
https://doi.org/10.1007/978-981-95-5895-7

This Springer imprint is published by the registered company Springer Nature Singapore Pte Ltd.
The registered company address is: 152 Beach Road, #21-01/04 Gateway East, Singapore 189721, Singapore

Preface

The rapid transformations in global financial markets, particularly the emergence and expansion of cryptocurrencies, have redefined the role and function of financial markets in the contemporary economy. These phenomena, while transforming the structure of traditional financial intermediation, have also generated new incentives for speculative behavior and short-term profit-seeking, thereby altering investor behavior. Such developments have posed novel challenges to monetary policies at both national and international levels, ultimately affecting the trajectory of economic development.

Since World War II, the United States and the European counties have emerged as leading economic and political powers on the global stage. Their currencies—the U.S. dollar, the euro, and the British pound—have captured a significant share of global financial markets, reinforcing these countries' political influence worldwide. In contrast, other emerging powers, such as China, have not been able to achieve a comparable global market share for their currency, limiting their international political leverage.

Furthermore, the increasing share of cryptocurrencies in the global economy, given their potential as a store of value and means of payment, has raised concerns about the gradual erosion of the appeal of major global currencies and even gold. This, in turn, has sparked fears that global political powers, whose influence largely derives from their national currencies, may adopt suppressive approaches toward cryptocurrencies. This highlights a historical paradox: while governments have rarely attempted direct suppression of emerging technologies from the Industrial Revolution in the eighteenth century to the present century, cryptocurrencies could represent one of the first instances of such regulatory confrontation.

Despite the growing literature in finance, significant gaps remain in understanding the linkages between crypto, gold, bonds, major currencies, financial intermediaries, speculative incentives, and monetary policies. Most existing studies either focus on investor behavior in crypto markets or on macro-financial and monetary outcomes, without integrating these dimensions into a coherent framework. There is a clear need for research that examines these interconnections within both theoretical and empirical perspectives.

This book seeks to address this gap by employing analytical frameworks from to provide an integrated perspective on the interactions among financial markets, speculative motives, monetary policy, and economic development. In this book, we aim to complement the theoretical literature with empirical appendices, along with real-world examples where these theoretical concepts have occurred and been experienced. These complements of empirical appendices and real-world examples help provide a clearer and simpler understanding of the topics and concepts, confirming that the literature is not confined to academic frameworks, but rather it also takes place and unfolds in the real world, impacting developing, emerging, and developed economies.

The motivation for this book arises from the increasing complexity and interdependence of global financial markets, inflation-targeting monetary policy, behavioral area, sustainability of economic development, and the growing role of cryptocurrencies. Despite existing studies, the interaction between them remains insufficiently explored. We have considered the diversity of potential audience, which may include academic environments, institutional players such as governments and central banks, financial and monetary institutions, as well as various investors in financial markets. Therefore, an effort has been made to reduce the complexity of the concepts, making them easier to grasp and more relatable for the book's target audiences.

Chapter 1 focuses on financial markets and speculative incentives, employing statistical analysis to illustrate key dynamics. Chapter 2 explores the relationship between these financial markets and economic development. Chapter 3 introduces monetary policy into this relationship, examining how money flows between markets is influenced. Chapter 4 empirically evaluates the discussions from Chaps. 1–3 using complementary and appropriate empirical models. Graphs and statistical tables are presented to provide a clearer and more precise understanding of these complex interconnections. The rationale for including an extensive empirical chapter is to examine whether the expected relationships among financial markets, monetary policies, and economic development, as outlined in Chaps. 1–3, are consistent with real-world financial networks in both developed and emerging economies, providing a broader perspective. Chapter 5 consolidates the theoretical and empirical insights from the previous chapters, leading to conclusions and policy recommendations.

It is hoped that this work will contribute both theoretically and empirically to the literature while offering actionable insights for governments, policymakers, researchers, financial and academic practitioners. Given the breadth and dynamic nature of the topic, this book does not aim to cover all dimensions exhaustively but rather to open new avenues for future research in this rapidly evolving field.

Tehran, Iran Abdorasoul Sadeghi
Lyon, France Hela Nammouri
Isfahan, Iran Seyed Komail Tayebi

Competing Interests The authors have no competing interests to declare that are relevant to the content of this manuscript.

Contents

1 Financial Markets and Speculative Motivations 1
1.1 Introduction 1
1.2 National and Major Currencies 2
1.3 Gold Market 5
1.4 Financial Intermediaries 7
1.5 Bond Market 9
1.6 Crypto Market 11
1.7 Data Description 15
1.8 A Concise Distillation of the Discussions 17
1.9 A Brief Review of Empirical Studies 21
References 22

2 Financial Markets and Economic Development 25
2.1 Introduction 25
2.2 Economic Development 26
2.3 Financial Intermediaries and Economic Development 29
2.4 National Currency and Economic Development 31
2.5 Bond Market and Economic Development 33
2.6 Gold, Crypto, and Economic Development 37
2.7 A Concise Distillation of the Discussions 44
2.8 A Brief Review of Empirical Studies 45
References 47

3 Monetary Policy and Financial Markets 51
3.1 Introduction 51
3.2 Interest Rate Policy and Economic Development 52
3.3 Interest Rate Policy and National Currency 54
3.4 Interest Rate Policy and Gold 56

3.5 Interest Rate Policy and Banking Sectors 58
3.6 Interest Rate Policy and Stock Markets 63
3.7 Interest Rate Policy and Bond Markets 65
3.8 Interest Rate Policy and Crypto Markets 66
3.9 A Concise Distillation of the Discussions 67
3.10 A Brief Review of Empirical Studies 68
References 69

4 Empirical Appendix 73
4.1 Introduction 73
4.2 Connections Between Financial Markets 75
4.2.1 Empirical Results—TVP-VAR Models 77
4.3 Speculation, Interest Rate Policy, and Financial Markets 91
4.3.1 Empirical Results-Historical Volatility 96
4.3.2 Empirical Results-Dynamic Correlations 106
4.4 Economic Development and Financial Markets 120
4.4.1 Empirical Results-Markov Switching Models 123
4.5 Supplementary Results 131
References 134

5 Conclusion and Policy Implications 135
5.1 Introduction 135
5.2 Conclusion 136
5.3 Policy Implications 138

About the Authors

Dr. Abdorasoul Sadeghi holds a Ph.D. in Monetary Economics from Shiraz University and a postdoctoral fellowship at the University of Tehran. His research spans institutional, financial, monetary, and development economics, with a particular emphasis on analytical and policy-oriented inquiry. He has published in highly ranked, internationally recognized journals and serves as a reviewer for several top-tier global journals. His work reflects a sustained commitment to rigorous scholarship and the advancement of economic research.

Prof. Dr. Hela Nammouri is an Associate Professor of Finance and leads the "Green Finance & Innovation" research axis at ESDES Business School (UCLy) in Lyon, France. She holds a Ph.D. in finance from University of Paris-Saclay (University of Évry–Val-d'Essonne). Her research focuses on green finance, behavioral finance, and financial markets, using quantitative and econometric methods. Her work has appeared in international peer-reviewed journals, including the Journal of Economic Dynamics and Control, Energy Economics, Applied Economics, and Finance Research Letters. She also serves as an Associate Editor at Research in International Business and Finance and reviews for leading journals.

Prof. Dr. Seyed Komail Tayebi is a Professor of International Economics and Econometrics at the Department of Economics, University of Isfahan, Iran. He is also serving as the Director, Center of Excellence for International Economics (CEIE), University of Isfahan and the Editor-in-Chief of the International Economics Studies. He received his PhD from University of Wollongong, Australia in 1996. During 2005–2006, he was a visiting professor at the Southern Methodist University (SMU), Dallas, USA. He was also appointed as a distinguished professor in the country by the Ministry of Science, Research and Technology in 2007. Professor Tayebi has been a member of Asia Pacific Economic Forum (AFEF) since 2002, being appointed as the APEF president in 2008 and 2009. He has also been a member of Association of Korea Economic Studies (AKES) since 2010. Prof. Tayebi has presented and published his research extensively in international conferences and journals in the areas of international trade and economic integration, modeling financial crisis, micro-econometrics, SMEs, and technology spillovers. He is one of the most accomplished economists of Iran, and academic leader with rich and diverse experience in international economics and its linkages to promote R&D, technology, and scientific spillovers.

Professor Tayebi is now serving as the President ECO Science Foundation (ECOSF). With more than 25 years of international development and a long-standing commitment to socio-economic development of the ECO region, Prof. Tayebi brings a unique set of knowledge, wealth of experience, and academic excellence to lead ECOSF into the future.

Chapter 1
Financial Markets and Speculative Motivations

1.1 Introduction

In mainstream economics, the flow of money across different markets—from equities and bonds to national and major currencies, gold, and commodities—plays a decisive role in shaping trends and price fluctuations. These shifts are not solely driven by fundamental economic factors; rather, short-term expectations, collective behavior, and speculative motives also influence them. Investors naturally seek to maximize the returns on their resources; as Adam Smith noted, individuals pursue their own self-interest, and although their primary goal may not be collective welfare, the overall outcome of such behavior can ultimately benefit society as a whole.

Accordingly, investors constantly evaluate the conditions of various markets, aiming to select those that, based on their forecasts, promise the highest returns. National and major currency markets, bonds, equities, bank deposits, gold, and, more recently, cryptocurrencies, all have the capacity to become target markets for the flow of money. Their common feature is the potential for speculative incentives arising from price volatility and capital gains. Nevertheless, each of these markets has its own strengths and weaknesses, which can affect the flow of money between them and generate different impacts on the nominal and real sectors of the economy.

This raises a critical question: will the flow of money absorbed in these markets be directed toward productive investments and support for developmental projects, or will it merely fuel short-term speculative gains? The importance of this question lies in the fact that the mobilization of financial resources across markets, through its influence on the availability of stable funding, can directly affect realized investment and, ultimately, the path of economic development. For this reason, the dynamics of money flows have become a central theme in the literature on financial development. Therefore, this chapter addresses each of these markets and their respective strengths and weaknesses, which may either diminish or enhance their attractiveness to money flows. Accordingly, this chapter not only builds on the book's theoretical framework but also includes a brief overview of recent empirical findings. This addition supports

A. Sadeghi et al., *Financial Markets, Speculation, and Development*,
https://doi.org/10.1007/978-981-95-5895-7_1

the theoretical discussion and enriches the overall literature, helping readers more easily understand how money flows between markets.

1.2 National and Major Currencies

The foreign exchange market is an international market where different currencies are traded, and it plays a key role in the global financial system, with a significant turnover. In this turnover, many participants are involved, the most important of which are central banks, commercial and investment banks, multinational corporations, funds, and retail traders. The value of the national currency is influenced by various factors, such as domestic and global inflation rates, liquidity volume, domestic and foreign investments, economic growth, and global demand. As a result, exchange rates can experience significant fluctuations depending on economic and political conditions. Such volatility may create speculative incentives for short-term gains. This phenomenon is particularly pronounced in some developing economies, where a gap exists between official and market exchange rates, thereby increasing its significance. For example, in countries like Iran, Venezuela, and Cuba, multiple exchange rates make capital gains from currency transactions considerable, thereby enhancing incentives for short-term speculative profits in the foreign exchange market.

Furthermore, if a fixed exchange rate system is in place and the central bank is unable to provide the necessary foreign currency resources to meet existing demand and support the target exchange rate, these speculative incentives can further widen the gap between official and market rates through the creation of artificial demand. Consequently, developmental projects and productive investments that rely on foreign currency resources may be adversely affected.

In economies where both final consumer goods and production inputs heavily depend on imports, various sectors, such as production, consumption, and services, are highly sensitive to price fluctuations in the currency market. This price sensitivity, and the resulting increase in inflation, in turn affects the value of the national currency and therefore the exchange rate. Thus, a cyclical interaction emerges among speculative incentives, inflation, and exchange rates in the currency market, which can influence the overall development process.

In this context, Iran has consistently been an interesting case for studying the effects of speculative profit motives in the foreign exchange market. Following the political changes in 1979, the Iranian economy has continuously faced challenges arising from exchange rate gaps, i.e., the existence of multiple currency rates. For instance, Sadeghi et al. (2024) empirically examined the price sensitivity of various sectors of the Iranian economy, including production, consumption, and services, to exchange rate shocks (the Iranian rial against the U.S. dollar). Their findings indicate that all commodity groups, encompassing housing, healthcare, services, food items, as well as consumer and producer price indices, are significantly affected by exchange rate shocks originating from both domestic sources and external sources.

Additionally, statistical reports published by the Central Bank of Iran show that the gap between exchange rates has been continuous and substantial.

An interesting observation from the statistical data in Table 1.1 is the significant reduction in the gap between exchange rates following the implementation of the currency unification policy in 2002, a narrowing that continued until 2010. However, after the imposition of international economic sanctions in 2011, which reduced the Central Bank of Iran's foreign exchange resources due to limitations on oil exports, this policy—despite nearly a decade of relative success—ultimately failed. According to development literature, the pass toward sustainable development can be negatively affected by speculative incentives in financial markets like the national currency market, as these incentives reduce motives for productive investment and increase inflation through artificial demand. The empirical findings, which a summary of them is provided at the end of this chapter, support our initial discussion regarding the susceptibility of key economic indicators to cyclical interactions among speculative motives, inflation, and exchange rates in the foreign exchange market.

On the global scale, there is an organized market for interactions among major international currencies, commonly known as the "Forex" market. Volatility in these currency relationships can draw a significant part of money flow toward speculative profits. Purchasing and holding major currencies as assets has long been a preferred strategy for investors to preserve value amid domestic and global volatility and uncertainty. For instance, currencies such as the U.S. dollar, Japanese yen, and Swiss franc are consistently chosen by investors as hedges against risks arising from global political and economic shocks. Central banks in various economies also hold major global currencies, including the U.S. dollar, euro, British pound, Japanese yen, and Swiss franc, as reserves to support their domestic currency and overall economy.

The strength of major currencies lies in their global acceptance as a medium of exchange and their central role in international payments. However, a key weakness of these currencies is the possibility of unlimited issuance, which exposes them to inflationary risks. Since monetary policies are generally coordinated with governments' fiscal objectives, and governments require sufficient financial resources to achieve these objectives, one of the most accessible options is the unlimited printing of currency. This policy increases liquidity volume through the monetary base and enables governments to partially cover budget deficits via inflationary taxation and reduction in the value of principal and interest rate of sold government bonds. Consequently, due to the vulnerability of currencies to inflation and their potential role in covering government budget deficits, investors generally become more cautious. Hence, given the limitations of major currencies as a store of value in inflationary environments, investors consistently apply risk management when allocating investments to such assets.

As discussed, exchange rates are influenced by multiple factors, including the monetary base, inflation, political, security, and economic shocks, net exports, economic growth, and monetary and fiscal policies. These influences generate significant volatility in the currency market, creating incentives for short-term speculative profits. At the same time, because both the nominal and real sectors of the economy

Table 1.1 Official and market rates of Iran's currency against the U.S. dollar in 1974–2024

Years	OER	MER	GER
1974	68	68	0
1975	68	68	0
1976	68	68	0
1977	71	71	0
1978	71	71	0
1979	70	100	30
1980	70	141	71
1981	71	200	129
1982	80	270	190
1983	84	350	266
1984	87	450	363
1985	92	580	488
1986	88	614	526
1987	77	742	665
1988	70	991	921
1989	69	966	897
1990	72	1207	1135
1991	67	1412	1345
1992	68	1420	1352
1993	1458	1498	40
1994	1653	1806	153
1995	1750	2635	885
1996	1750	4036	2286
1997	1754	4446	2692
1998	1755	4782	3027
1999	1755	6468	4713
2000	1755	8634	6879
2001	1755	8131	6376
2002	1755	7925	6170
2003	7958	7991	33
2004	8282	8323	41
2005	8719	8747	28
2006	9023	9042	19
2007	9195	9226	31
2008	9285	9357	72
2009	9574	9667	93
2010	9920	9979	59
2011	10,339	10,601	262

(continued)

Table 1.1 (continued)

Years	OER	MER	GER
2012	10,962	13,568	2606
2013	12,260	26,059	13,799
2014	21,253	31,839	10,586
2015	26,509	32,801	6292
2016	29,580	34,501	4921
2017	31,389	36,440	5051
2018	34,214	40,453	6239
2019	42,000	228,809	186,809
2020	42,000	245,428	203,428
2021	42,000	309,650	267,650
2022	42,000	388,320	346,320
2023	42,000	504,040	462,040
2024	547,829	771,700	223,871

Note: The value of the Iranian national currency against the U.S. dollar represents the foreign exchange rate. OER and MER show official and unofficial (market) exchange rates, respectively. GER suggests differences or gaps between official and unofficial exchange rates. Necessary to say that the gaps between OER and MER were zero within 1974–1979. The dataset released in Iran's central bank was used

can be negatively affected by exchange rate fluctuations, the stability of the currency market is a key concern in central banks' monetary policies and government support measures. This advantage reduces investment risk in these currencies, strengthens the incentives to purchase and hold them in asset portfolios, and channels a portion of money flows into the foreign exchange market.

1.3 Gold Market

Gold has always been regarded as one of the possible components in investors' asset portfolios. Unlike many other assets, it does not lose value in the face of inflation; rather, its value often increases in inflationary environments. For this reason, gold holds a superior position compared to major global currencies and the holding of national currency. In contrast to national and major currencies, where central banks may cover a part of government budget deficits through increased money printing, thereby creating the risk of depreciation for currency holders, investors in gold are not exposed to such risks. Their holdings cannot be transformed into a tool for financing fiscal deficits.

Beyond its resilience to inflation, gold also becomes particularly attractive to investors during times of global political, security, and economic shocks. While most major currencies tend to depreciate under such conditions, certain exceptions exist: currencies such as the U.S. dollar, the Japanese yen, and the Swiss franc often experience increased demand during crises, moving in tandem with gold. This co-movement has led to the U.S. dollar, the yen, the franc, and gold being regarded as safe-haven assets. Nevertheless, although such major currencies are recognized as safe-haven currencies, the possibility of their unlimited printing and their potential use as instruments to cover government budget deficits can still limit this capacity. Put differently, in inflationary contexts and amid geopolitical, security, or economic concerns, gold functions as a shield for preserving investors' wealth, thereby attracting greater capital inflows.

Nevertheless, the gold market is highly sensitive to fluctuations in inflation rates and to monetary policy decisions. Specifically, when major central banks, such as the Federal Reserve, the European Central Bank, the Bank of England, and the Bank of Japan, pursue contractionary monetary policies aimed at reducing inflation, gold tends to display vulnerability. Consequently, investors must consistently monitor economic conditions in leading global economies, as well as the broader geopolitical environment. In response to inflation dynamics, global and domestic monetary policies, and episodes of political instability, the gold market is subject to volatility, which in turn creates opportunities for short-term speculative gains.

To classify theoretically, the classical approach to gold emphasizes its value-preserving advantage and, consequently, its definition as a safe-haven asset in inflationary environments characterized by uncertainty and instability. The macroeconomic perspective on gold relates to changes in its demand during economic cycles, financial crises, and interest rate policies of the central banks of major global economies. From a financial perspective, the focus lies on its potential for risk hedging and portfolio diversification for investors. Another important dimension that significantly expands the role of the gold market concerns its advantages within the international monetary system and its geopolitical implications, which manifest in political instruments such as sanctions, wars, and other geopolitical crises.

With a brief historical overview, gold has played a central role in the international monetary system for centuries, serving both as a medium of exchange and a store of value. Historically, the gold standard, which emerged in the nineteenth century, linked national currencies directly to a fixed quantity of gold. Under this system, the value of a currency was defined by the amount of gold it represented, ensuring price stability and limiting governments' ability to expand the money supply arbitrarily. The gold standard contributed to long-term monetary stability and facilitated international trade by providing a predictable framework for currency conversion. However, it also imposed significant constraints on monetary policy, particularly during economic crises, as governments could not adjust the money supply freely to respond to shocks.

The interwar period illustrated the limitations of the gold standard, as global conflicts and economic instability forced temporary suspensions and adjustments. Following World War II, the Bretton Woods system established a new international monetary framework in which the U.S. dollar was pegged to gold at a fixed rate of $35 per ounce, while other currencies were pegged to the dollar. This system stabilized exchange rates, promoted international trade, and created the International Monetary

Fund (IMF) to oversee monetary cooperation. Nevertheless, the growing imbalance between U.S. gold reserves and dollar liabilities ultimately led to the suspension of the dollar-gold convertibility in 1971, marking the end of the Bretton Woods gold standard.

In the modern era of major currencies, central banks and institutional investors continue to hold significant gold reserves as a hedge against currency depreciation and financial instability. Gold remains a strategic asset for managing systemic risks, diversifying reserves, and providing stability during periods of geopolitical uncertainty or financial market turbulence. Comparisons with other reserve assets, such as the U.S. dollar, euro, and the Japanese yen, highlight gold's enduring role as a "safe-haven" asset in the global financial system.

1.4 Financial Intermediaries

The banking network and the stock market have significant latent capacity to absorb the flow of money. Since the central role of financing in developing, emerging, and developed economies lies with the banking system and the stock market, government and central bank support is one of the major advantages of financial intermediaries. In other words, monetary and fiscal policymakers always consider the stability of the banking network and the stock market when designing their policies. Consequently, investors who include corporate stocks and bank deposits in their asset portfolios are continuously reassured that the stability of these financial intermediaries is important to governments and central banks, which reduces investment risk.

For example, after the shock caused by the global spread of COVID-19, stock markets initially faced a substantial decline in value due to massive stock sell-offs driven by concerns over company closures. Stock markets in Wall Street, the European Union, Oceania, the United Kingdom, and East Asian economies lost a significant portion of their value. Banking networks also faced liquidity challenges. As a result, central banks, in coordination with governments, prioritized restoring stability in stock markets and banking networks in their policies. These policies not only restored pre-COVID-19 stability to stock markets and banking networks but also led to remarkable growth.

The interest rate on bank deposits is a key factor that investors consider when deciding to deposit funds in the banking system. Central bank policies aim to maintain a balance between nominal interest rates and inflation. Therefore, in most economies, the real interest rate on bank deposits is not high enough to attract risk-tolerant investors; rather, risk-averse investors are typically drawn to bank deposits.

Investing in stock markets requires access to political information and economic knowledge. Investors need to be able to make low-error predictions about the future performance and profitability of the companies whose shares they intend to buy. Additionally, due to the negative sensitivity of stock markets to political shocks, staying informed about political developments is another essential requirement for investing in the stock market.

One of the advantages of stock markets that increases their attractiveness to investors is their relatively low vulnerability to inflation compared to other markets. In inflationary environments, stock markets usually experience significant growth. One reason is the reduction of real interest rates on bank loans, which lowers borrowing and debt costs for companies, thereby reducing the financial burden. However, the negative cost effects of inflation on purchased raw materials can negatively impact company performance.

There may be competition among financial intermediaries to draw the flow of money by offering financial services and investment opportunities. In many countries, such competition has existed, and the financial system has shifted from being bank-centric to stock market-centric. One factor driving this transformation has been the provision of some traditional banking services through stock markets, such as raising funds via fixed-income funds.

Since one of the shared roles of banking networks and stock markets is financing, financing through one can affect the other. If bank deposits decline, companies may face financing difficulties due to the banking network's reduced lending capacity, negatively impacting investment and economic activity. However, the stock market can compensate for reduced bank lending capacity, caused by declining deposits, by providing financing through equity issuance and investor purchases. Nevertheless, for companies highly dependent on bank financing, this negative impact from declining deposits cannot be fully offset by the stock market.

Another perspective views competition among financial intermediaries as essential for their positive impact on economic growth. Lack of competition and over-concentration on either the stock market or the banking sector may result in poor-quality services and limited access to alternative financing for productive economic activities. Conversely, financial intermediaries can complement each other: bank investments in stock markets and channeling bank deposits to companies in the stock market can work synergistically. Banks can positively contribute to stock market development by offering their financial assets as equities. In turn, the growth and development of stock markets, facilitating the supply and demand of bank shares, increases the value of banking equities, demonstrating a positive influence from stock markets.

Accordingly, fluctuations in bank deposits and stock markets can affect each other. However, without a clear outlook for banking performance and the profitability of listed companies, investors may lose interest, impeding the financing of productive investment projects. Financial intermediaries are also affected by economic conditions, as company revenues change with economic booms and recessions, impacting stock markets positively or negatively. Likewise, interest rates are influenced by economic conditions, affecting incentives for lending or borrowing and thus for bank deposits. Changes in economic growth also alter available resources for investing in deposits or stocks, and influence corporate returns and bank profitability, impacting share supply and bank lending behavior.

As discussed, inflation can have a double-edged effect on stock markets: positively, by raising product prices and reducing real financing costs through bank loans, and negatively, by increasing raw material costs. Another channel for transmitting the effects of inflation is through real interest rates, as borrowing and lending incentives depend on them, affecting the appeal of bank deposits and access to funds for companies listed on the stock market. Another potential channel includes increased uncertainty from higher inflation, which may reduce investment, as noted by Friedman (1977), or create unrealized profits due to higher taxes, as stated by Feldstein (1980). Tobin (1965) also argues that inflation can positively affect stock markets by reducing money's purchasing power—a view echoed by Fisher (1930) as well as Gavriilidis and Kgari (2016), emphasizing the potential of stock market investment to hedge against purchasing power risk. Overall, among various markets, stock markets and gold are more attractive for investment in inflationary environments.

Another potential effect is that inflation may reduce deposit incentives due to economic uncertainty. Changes in inflation also affect household purchasing power, possibly increasing the need for cash to buy desired goods, influencing long-term deposit decisions. Thus, in high-inflation economies, financial intermediaries' capacity to finance productive economic activities may decline, often affecting the private sector. Inflation also impacts the real value of corporate contracts and debt, influencing stock markets: The real value of the debts and the nominal receipts specified in contracts are reduced, impacting company revenues. Financial intermediaries may, in turn, influence inflation: Banking networks through liquidity volume and stock markets through wealth effects: Changes in expected returns alter household income and consumption, influencing aggregate demand and inflation.

As discussed, investing in stock markets requires economic knowledge and access to political information globally. Stock markets are affected by various factors, the most important of which are economic, political, and security instabilities, interest rate policies, and uncertainty, causing volatility and speculative motives. However, government and central bank support reduces these risks. Like stock markets, investing in bank deposits involves risk. Real deposit interest rates are influenced by inflation fluctuations and monetary policies aligning nominal interest rates with inflation. Hence, in inflationary economies with sticky nominal rates, there is a risk of deposit value erosion over time.

1.5 Bond Market

Bonds are financial instruments used for financing. These securities are issued by governments, corporations, and various institutions at a predetermined interest rate. Financing is achieved when investors, who are generally risk-averse, purchase these bonds. For the issuer, bonds entail interest expenses, while for the buyers they generate interest income. A question constantly raised for bond buyers is whether the inflation rate will decrease or increase. This is because, in the event of rising inflation and the central bank's failure to adopt a corresponding interest rate policy, the real value of the principal amount of the purchased bonds along with the interest rate allocated to them will decline over time, which will consequently reduce the attractiveness of these bonds for investors.

The major turning points in the issuance of bonds occurred during the seventeenth and eighteenth centuries. In this period, European governments engaged in prolonged and costly wars and made extensive use of bonds as a means of financing their military expenditures. The establishment of the Bank of England in 1694 marked another milestone in the history of bonds, as the institution played a pivotal role in organizing and issuing government securities.

In the nineteenth century, with the expansion of the Industrial Revolution and the growing financial needs of both governments and corporations, bonds were widely employed to fund the development of railways, large-scale industries, and infrastructure projects. During the same era, corporate bonds expanded alongside government bonds, enabling major companies to raise financial resources from the public through bond issuance.

In the modern era, new forms of bonds have emerged, most notably green bonds, which aim not only to provide financing but also to support environmentally and socially sustainable projects. Today, bonds constitute an integral part of global capital markets, serving as one of the most important financing instruments for both governments and the private sector.

Investment in the bond market is mostly included in the asset portfolios of primarily risk-averse investors. Although the yield rates of these bonds are significantly affected by inflation rate fluctuations, monetary policies related to adjusting the nominal interest rates allocated to these bonds against inflation volatility can have a substantial impact on investment incentives and risk acceptance in this market. On the other hand, since financing through bonds can play a significant role in solving liquidity problems, this market is usually supported by governments and central banks, leading to the consideration of its stability in policies. This advantage helps reduce investment risk in the bond market.

Governments, industries, and various companies can raise the desired financial resources by issuing bonds. Companies, depending on their targeted projects, if they consider the likelihood of success and profitability of their investment plans to be considerable, offer attractive interest rates to investors in order to encourage them to purchase bonds by lowering investment risk through this policy. However, governments face more limitations in this regard. This is because financing through bond issuance shapes indebted governments' future obligations, which are usually managed by increasing taxes or printing money, thus involving the welfare conditions of society in part of the principal and interest payments of these bonds. In other words, unlike company financing through bond issuance, which involves a limited and specific segment of society, government financing through bonds affects a significant portion of the country's population.

Moreover, given the openness of a considerable part of global economies and the resulting interdependence among economies, government financing through bond issuance, especially in major global economies such as the United States, the European Union, and the United Kingdom, can also implicate the global community in the consequences arising from how the principal and interest of these bonds are repaid.

1.6 Crypto Market

In 2009, a new form of asset known as Bitcoin was introduced and launched. Initially, it was not considered to have an important place in the global economy and was regarded as a fleeting phenomenon, incapable of competing with established assets such as major global currencies, gold, bonds, bank deposits, and corporate stocks, nor of being included in investors' portfolios. Given the novelty of this type of assets, this chapter places particular emphasis on its underlying literature and examines it from multiple perspectives.

Over time, some of Bitcoin's unique advantages began to emerge in certain technologically advanced regions of the world, encompassing the United States, the Eurozone, and East Asia, attracting increasing attention. The first and most significant of these advantages is Bitcoin's limited and predetermined supply, capped at approximately 23 million coins. This scarcity makes Bitcoin particularly attractive in inflationary environments. By contrast, as previously discussed, major global currencies are vulnerable to inflation, with their unlimited printing by central banks amplifying this weakness. In other words, Bitcoin's fixed and limited supply grants it the capacity to serve as a store of value, a feature that has proven highly appealing to investors. In fact, Bitcoin's store-of-value function parallels that of gold in inflationary contexts, a common advantage shared by both assets.

With respect to major global currencies, the absence of central bank independence and the weakness of inflation-targeting policies, which are meant to confine inflation within certain bands, reduce their ability to serve as a store of value in inflationary environments. This shortcoming diminishes their standing relative to gold and Bitcoin in the eyes of investors.

Another major advantage of Bitcoin lies in its use as a powerful means of payment that does not require intermediaries. Prior to Bitcoin, payments were always processed through intermediaries. Moreover, access to full transaction details also depended on the involvement of such intermediaries, typically the banking system. Bitcoin, however, enables both payments and the recording of transaction details without intermediaries. The elimination of intermediaries from payment processes thus represents a fundamental innovation that Bitcoin and other cryptocurrencies have introduced to the global economy.

By comparison, major global currencies, though powerful as a payment mechanism on a worldwide scale, rely heavily on intermediaries. Yet, as noted earlier, their susceptibility to inflation undermines their store-of-value capacity. Gold, while robust in preserving value during inflationary periods, no longer serves as a significant medium of exchange in today's global economy, given the far stronger alternatives offered by major currencies and cryptocurrencies. Bitcoin, by contrast, combines the benefits of both—a reliable store of value in inflationary contexts and a powerful, intermediary-free payment instrument. Together, these features give cryptocurrencies an extraordinary competitive edge against traditional assets like gold and major currencies.

The emergence of Ethereum, the second-largest cryptocurrency, has further amplified interest in digital assets. Ethereum has introduced a platform that enables the execution of smart contracts, capturing the attention of industries worldwide. Through smart contracts, the role of intermediaries in economic activities is considerably diminished, and in many cases eliminated altogether, thereby introducing a new form of disintermediated economy to the global stage. Unlike the conventional economy, where intermediaries play a central role, the growing adoption of smart contracts is expected to significantly reduce the share of intermediaries in the global economy. Among the most affected is the banking sector, whose position is increasingly threatened as smart contracts become mainstream.

This threat became more pronounced in 2020 with the introduction of the Solana and Binance Smart Chains, which have facilitated faster and lower-cost transactions. Beyond payments, it also provided real-time access to complete transaction details, eliminating the need for intermediaries to finalize payments or supply information. Prior to the Solana and Binance Smart Chains, Ethereum faced criticism for its slow transaction speeds and high fees, but competition among blockchain networks has mitigated these weaknesses.

Importantly, the trend of reducing intermediaries is not confined to banking; it threatens virtually all intermediaries in today's conventional economy. To clarify this concept, let us consider some everyday examples. Imagine you are an artist, such as a painter or musician. In the traditional economy, bringing your artwork or music to market requires navigating several intermediaries. First, you must register your work through a legal intermediary. Next, you must engage another intermediary to display your painting in galleries or to secure licenses for your music's distribution. Finally, a different intermediary handles the financial aspects of your sales and income.

By contrast, with the advent of smart networks such as Ethereum, Solana, and Binance, artists and musicians can tokenize their work directly, without reliance on various intermediaries, at minimal cost and time. Moreover, they can instantly showcase their work to a global audience and even organize auctions in real time without any intermediary involvement. In today's intermediary-driven world, such processes often take days, weeks, or even months, and incur substantial costs, not to mention the frequent requirement for physical presence. In a disintermediated world powered by cryptocurrencies and smart contracts, all these processes can be executed almost instantly, provided there is access to a computer, tablet, or smartphone and a reliable internet connection.

As this discussion illustrates, we live in a world dominated by intermediaries, where countless professions must engage with them at considerable cost of time and money. Yet, intermediaries in fields such as insurance, transportation, real estate, intellectual property registration, digital gaming, movie distribution, and telecommunications face profound disruption from crypto technologies, disruption that poses an existential threat to their traditional business models.

The advantages of the new economy, following the expansion of the role of cryptocurrencies, can be summarized as follows:

- Reduction of costs

- Increased speed in completing various processes
- Time efficiency and savings
- Elimination of intermediaries
- Decentralized financial systems
- Reduced need for physical presence
- Real-time recording of details and information transparency without intermediary intervention
- Decrease in crimes related to forgery and data manipulation
- Fast and easy access to information

A decentralized financial system is a financial framework that operates without intermediaries, thereby reducing both time and costs. In other words, unlike the conventional financial system, no single central financial institution governs or controls the entire network. Furthermore, individuals can access details of transactions executed within this decentralized network, thereby adding transparency and traceability to its advantages.

In simple, easy-to-understand, and straightforward language, such decentralized systems are built on blockchains—a chain of interconnected blocks. To validate transactions, a network of computers with significant computational power work to solve unique cryptographic puzzles that enable the execution of these transactions. Once a solution is reached, the relevant transaction is validated and recorded within a block. These blocks are linked sequentially to preceding and subsequent ones and stored across multiple computers named Nodes. As a result, all information on the blockchain is replicated and redistributed across the network. Given that transaction data is encrypted and distributed simultaneously across numerous machines, manipulation, deletion, or hacking becomes exceedingly difficult, which grants the system a high level of security.

Decentralized finance (DeFi) is just one of the capacities enabled by the crypto industry, something that once seemed like a dream for societies weary of intermediaries. Although these capacities have not yet been fully realized, considering the relative youth and short history of this industry, there is strong optimism that, over time and with the resolution of current challenges, they will increasingly become operational.

One of the principal barriers to the expansion of decentralized systems worldwide lies in governments and central banks of major global economies. Their national currencies play a dominant role in global trade and serve as instruments of geopolitical power. For example, the global political influence of the United States, the European Union, and the United Kingdom is directly tied to the prominent role of the U.S. dollar, the euro, and the British pound in the world economy. These powers leverage their currencies' dominance in international trade to coerce rival states by threatening restrictions on access to the global financial system built around these currencies.

The U.S. sanctions on Iranian oil exports exemplify this dynamic. The United States effectively presented China, Iran's largest oil importer, with two options: (1) comply with sanctions and cease importing Iranian oil or (2) ignore the sanctions and continue imports, while facing restrictions on access to the U.S. dollar and the unified global financial system. It is clear that China could not risk such restrictions, as its global trade depends heavily on access to the U.S. dollar—the world's most dominant currency.

A similar situation applies to Russia: prior to its invasion of Ukraine, the United States, United Kingdom, and EU threatened Russia with severe sanctions, which underscored the vulnerability of Russia's economy to such financial pressures. These cases demonstrate that the political influence of major global powers rests significantly on their currencies' dominance in global trade. It is therefore unlikely that such powers will easily allow cryptocurrencies to erode the role of their currencies in the global economy. Yet, in terms of both payment functionality and store-of-value capacity, Bitcoin, Ethereum, Solana, and Binance have the potential to surpass major currencies of global powers.

Fortunately, while writing this book, the United States, as the world's largest economy and the strongest currency, has abandoned its suppressive approach toward cryptocurrencies and is instead embracing this technology. The President of the United States, President Trump, has focused on the goal of transforming the country into a global hub for cryptocurrencies, aiming to place coins such as Bitcoin, Ethereum, Solana, Cardano, and Ripple on the Federal Reserve's balance sheet. This could mark the greatest historical milestone for the industry and steer Western economies away from repressive policies.

If we set aside these external barriers, such as sanctions policies, and focus on the industry's internal challenges, one of the most significant criticisms concerns the highly unequal distribution of Bitcoin and Ethereum coins. A considerable share of these assets is concentrated in the hands of individuals or institutions known as "whales." These whales can, in effect, act as unofficial central banks: by releasing large quantities of coins onto the market at chosen times, they can influence prices dramatically. Such large sell-offs cause sharp volatility, heightening uncertainty for investors while simultaneously fueling speculative activity. In this way, unequal distribution undermines the store-of-value function of cryptocurrencies, arguably one of their greatest strengths, which positions them as serious competitors to both gold and major currencies. Ultimately, this imbalance risks prioritizing the interests of whales over those of ordinary holders.

Turning to an intra-industry perspective: as discussed, Bitcoin's fixed and limited supply underpins its strong store-of-value feature. Ethereum, on the other hand, has distinguished itself as the second-largest cryptocurrency by introducing a platform for smart contracts, thus laying the foundation for disintermediation in the global economy. This innovation has rapidly increased Ethereum's attractiveness compared to Bitcoin. Nevertheless, Ethereum has faced criticism due to its high supply, making it more vulnerable to inflation than Bitcoin and undermining its store-of-value capacity. To address this issue, Ethereum's creator, Vitalik Buterin, implemented an update in 2021 that introduced a mechanism for "burning" a significant number of coins. As a result, Ethereum's inflationary vulnerability stemming from unlimited supply is no longer as pronounced, restoring confidence in its potential as a store of value.

Another unresolved criticism of Ethereum is its high transaction fees, which make its network costly to use. This shortcoming has fostered healthy competition within the industry, fueling greater innovation and dynamism. In 2020, Binance and Solana launched their Smart Chains, which surprised the market by offering faster transactions at significantly lower costs compared to Ethereum. Between 2021 and 2024, Binance and Solana Smart Chains attracted considerable investor interest and substantial capital inflows. Moreover, many emerging tokens have opted to launch on the Binance and Solana networks rather than Ethereum. This competitive edge has prompted Ethereum's developers to focus on increasing speed and reducing fees. Such healthy competition has historically driven technological innovation, accelerated problem-solving, and promoted dynamism—trends clearly visible in the cryptocurrency industry. Beyond Bitcoin, Ethereum, Solana, and Binance, other coins such as Cardano and Ripple have also drawn significant investor attention, benefiting from the transparency and competitive environment that characterize the sector.

1.7 Data Description

Considering the literature of this chapter, which focuses on the advantages and risks of investing in each target market and may incentivize speculative behavior aimed at short-term profits, this section examines volatility in the financial networks of the United States, the United Kingdom, Germany, and Japan, encompassing stock, national currency, gold, Bitcoin, and bond markets. As shown in Figs. 1.1, 1.2, 1.3, and 1.4, and as discussed, Bitcoin exhibits significant volatility across the financial networks of all four countries. This statistical evidence supports our discussion regarding the negative impact of the unequal distribution of coins on Bitcoin's store-of-value function. Such unequal distribution has generated considerable volatility in the crypto market, making it an attractive arena for short-term speculative gains. In other words, institutions and individuals holding substantial amounts of these coins always have the incentive to inject volatility into the market by releasing significant portions at opportune times, thereby realizing short-term profits.

Despite the appeal of speculative activities, there are also considerable medium- and long-term investments in this market, indicating its potential capacity to attract longer-term capital. Among major currencies, stock and bond markets, which benefit from government and central bank support due to their impact on both nominal and real sectors of the economy, major currencies and stock markets exhibit lower volatility in all four countries. While major currencies, as previously discussed, may be vulnerable to inflation and partially to government budget deficits through money printing, the currencies of the United States, the United Kingdom, Germany, and Japan, representing the largest shares in the global economy, benefit from central bank monetary policies that limit inflation volatility within defined ranges, thereby strengthening their store-of-value function and reducing their fluctuations.

Gold, as depicted in Figs. 1.1, 1.2, 1.3, and 1.4, shows lower volatility compared to other markets, consistent with its store-of-value characteristics. Meanwhile, bond

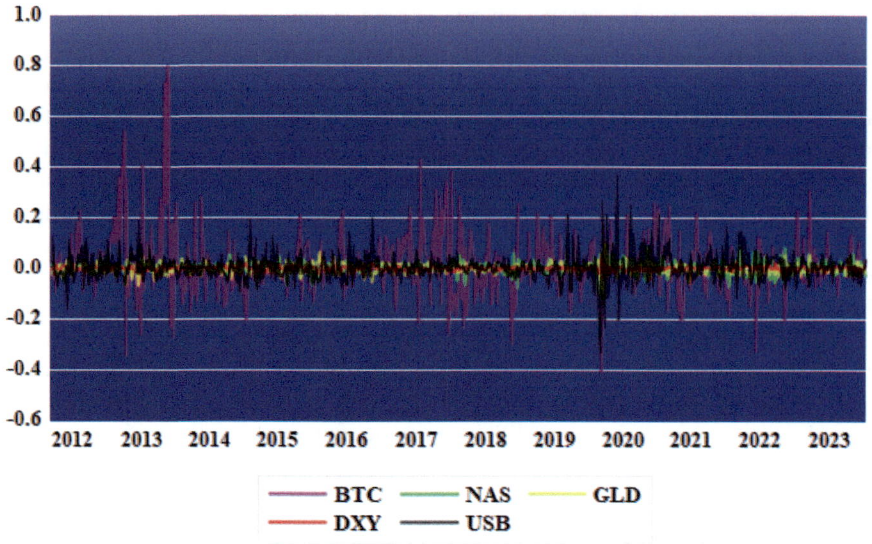

Fig. 1.1 U.S. financial network for weekly time series, March 2012—December 2023. (*Note*: Percentage changes in the price of Bitcoin [BTC], the U.S. stock market index, NASDAQ-100 [NAS], gold [GLD], the U.S. Dollar Index [DXY], and the 10-year U.S. Treasury yield [USB]. The percentage changes of each market are distinguished by different colors within ranges highlighted in white. Data are sourced from the time series published on www.investing.com)

yields in the financial networks of the United States and the United Kingdom display relatively calm fluctuations. However, in the financial networks of Germany and especially Japan, bond yields exhibit relatively higher volatility during certain periods. In Japan, for instance, bond yield volatility increased after the central bank adopted negative interest rates in 2016.

Moreover, in the financial networks of all four countries, changes in central bank interest rate policies have triggered significant fluctuations in bond yields. For example, during the COVID-19 pandemic in 2020, the unprecedented reduction of interest rates, approaching zero in the United States, the European Union, and the United Kingdom, led to notable volatility in bond markets. Following the development of COVID-19 vaccines and the subsequent unprecedented tightening of monetary policy, interest rates surged over a nine-month period after 2022—rising from zero to 5.5% in the United States, 5.25% in the United Kingdom, and 4.5% in the EU—resulting in greater sensitivity in bond markets compared to other markets.

During 2016 and 2019, coinciding with the United Kingdom's Brexit process, bond markets experienced significant volatility in Germany and the United Kingdom. Notably, this volatility was concentrated in specific periods marked by either strong monetary policies or major global political events such as Brexit, while remaining relatively calm at other times. In contrast, Bitcoin volatility has not been limited to specific periods but has consistently demonstrated significant fluctuations.

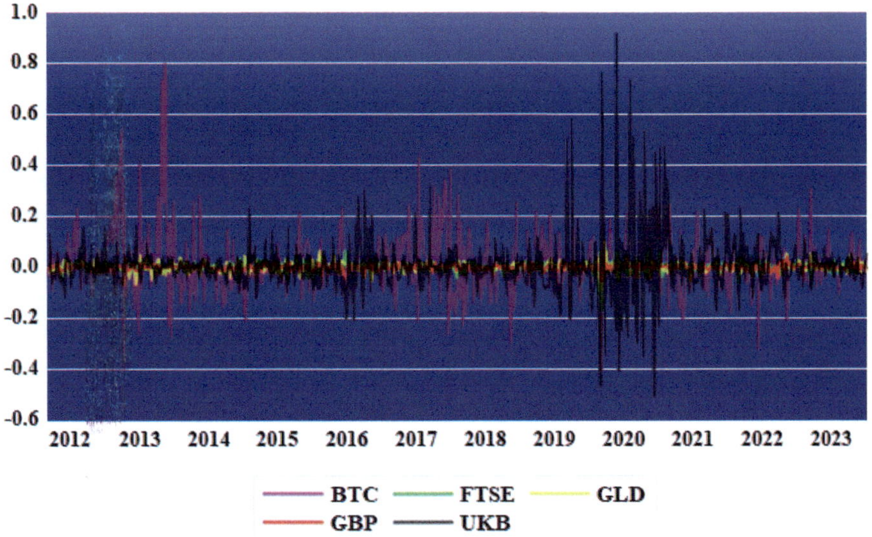

Fig. 1.2 U.K. financial network for weekly time series, March 2012—December 2023. (*Note*: Percentage changes in Bitcoin [BTC] prices, the U.K. stock market index, FTSE-100 [FTSE], gold [GLD], the British pound against the U.S. dollar [GBP], and the 10-year U.K. Treasury yield [UKB]. The percentage changes of each market are distinguished by different colors within ranges highlighted in white. Data are sourced from the time series published on www.investing.com)

1.8 A Concise Distillation of the Discussions

Various markets can serve as channels for absorbing the flow of money. Financial intermediaries—the stock market and the banking network—alongside national and major currencies, gold, bonds, and cryptocurrencies, are among the markets that have consistently been considered potential components of investors' portfolios.

What these markets share in common is that, due to inflation fluctuations and monetary policies, an important amount of money can flow into them as speculative profit-seeking incentives increase. In this regard, risk-averse investors typically avoid engaging in speculative activities, as such activities require economic expertise and up-to-date political knowledge at both domestic and global levels, which strongly influence the mentioned markets. Risk-averse investors usually prefer mid- to long-term investment horizons and opt for markets with relatively lower price volatility.

Based on statistical evidence and historical trends, it has been established that the cryptocurrency market exhibits significant price volatility, making it an attractive destination for liquidity from speculators and short-term risk-tolerant investors. In contrast, stocks, bonds, national and major currencies, which play a crucial role in financing and economic stability, tend to experience comparatively lower levels of price fluctuation. As such, they attract risk-averse investors with mid- to long-term

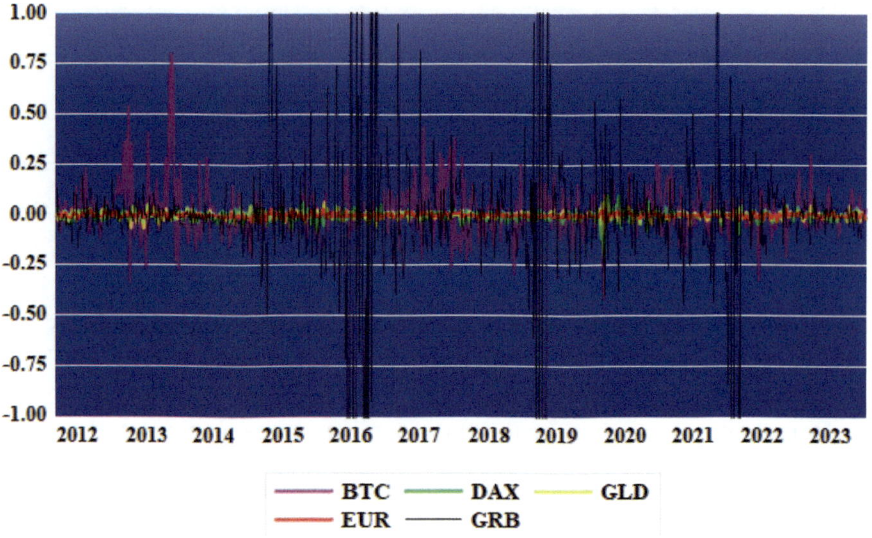

Fig. 1.3 The German financial network for weekly time series, March 2012—December 2023. (*Note*: Percentage changes in Bitcoin [BTC] prices, the German stock market index [DAX], gold [GLD], the euro against the U.S. dollar [EUR], and the 10-year German Treasury yield [GRB]. The percentage changes of each market are distinguished by different colors within ranges highlighted in white. Data are sourced from the time series published on www.investing.com)

perspectives and are less appealing to short-term speculative activities or risk-seeking investors.

One important point to consider regarding the crypto market is that while its high price volatility may encourage speculative motivations for short-term gains, its relatively modest market value of around $4 trillion, compared to gold's $20 trillion, combined with its broader potential, has drawn significant long-term investor interest. This potential includes serving as a powerful payment instrument, a substantial store of value, a network for executing smart contracts, and a means of disintermediating the economy. Consequently, the market has witnessed a notable upward trend in long-term investment attention, particularly marked by the increasing presence of institutional investors.

As discussed, each of these markets has its own strengths and weaknesses that affect their attractiveness to investors and the volume of money flowing into them. These can be summarized as follows:

Major Currencies:

– Means of payment on a global scale (Advantage)
– Store of value in inflationary environments, provided central bank independence and inflation-targeted monetary policy (Advantage)
– Unlimited issuance potential due to lack of supply ceiling (weakness)

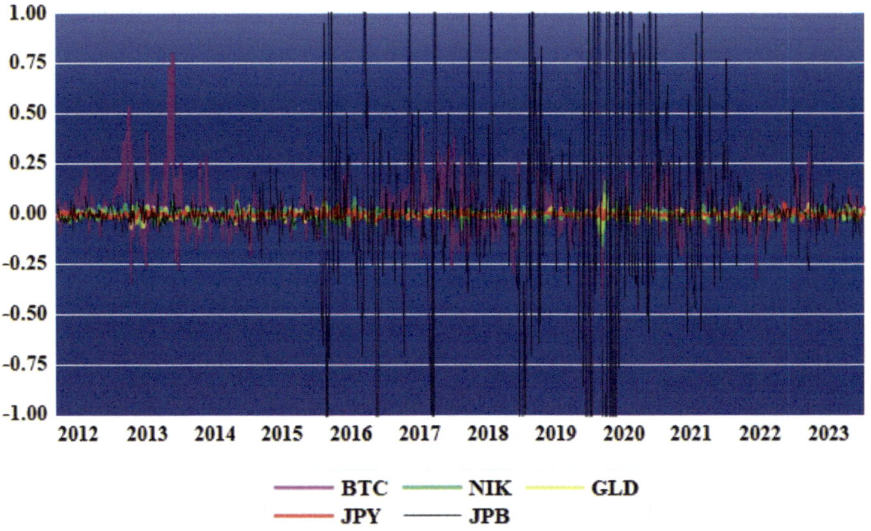

Fig. 1.4 The Japanese financial network for weekly time series, March 2012—December 2023. (*Note*: Percentage changes in Bitcoin [BTC] prices, the Japanese stock market index, Nikkei-225 [NIK], gold [GLD], the Japanese yen against the U.S. dollar [JPY], and the 10-year Japanese Treasury yield [JPB]. The percentage changes of each market are distinguished by different colors within ranges highlighted in white. Data are sourced from the time series published on www.investing.com)

- Government and central bank support (Advantage)
- Recognition on the balance sheet of central banks (Advantage)
- Weak store of value in inflationary environments if central bank independence is lacking and governments use money printing to cover budget deficits (Weakness)
- Vulnerability to global economic and political shocks (Weakness)
- High sensitivity to monetary policy (weakness)

Gold:

- Declining role as a payment means due to stronger competitors such as major currencies and cryptocurrencies (Weakness)
- Store of value in inflationary environments (Advantage)
- Store of value during global political and economic shocks (Advantage)
- Recognition on the balance sheet of central banks (Advantage)
- Vulnerability to interest rate hikes (Weakness)

Stock Market:

- Wide range of options given the large number of listed companies (Advantage)
- Government and central bank support (Advantage)
- Relatively low vulnerability to inflation (Advantage)

- Requires economic knowledge and access to domestic and international political information (Weakness)
- Subject to taxation (Weakness)
- Vulnerability to global economic and political shocks (Weakness)
- High sensitivity to monetary policy, given the dual impact of interest rates (Weakness)

Bank Deposits:

- Government and central bank support (Advantage)
- Lower investment risk compared with other markets (Advantage)
- Exempt from taxation (Advantage)
- Attractive to risk-averse investors due to guaranteed fixed interest returns (Advantage)
- Low appeal to risk-lover investors due to lower annual returns compared with investments in other asset classes (Weakness)
- Vulnerability to inflation (Weakness)
- Lack of attractiveness in financially repressed economies, i.e., sticky nominal deposit interest rates (Weakness)
- High sensitivity to monetary policy (Weakness)

Bond Market:

- Risk reduction in non-inflationary environments (Advantage)
- Attractive to risk-averse investors due to guaranteed returns (Advantage)
- Government and central bank support (Advantage)
- Reduction in real debt burden (principal and interest) for issuers in inflationary environments (Advantage)
- Vulnerability to inflation (Weakness)
- High sensitivity to monetary policy (weakness)

Crypto Market:

- Strong means of payment (Advantage)
- Store of value in inflationary environments (Advantage)
- Healthy intra-industry competition (Advantage)
- Rapid technological development (Advantage)
- Recognition on the balance sheet of central banks (Advantage)
- Unequal distribution of coins (Weakness)
- Strong government and central bank support for major currencies (Weakness)
- Vulnerability to global economic and political shocks due to unequal coin distribution (Weakness)
- Potential sensitivity to monetary policy due to financing needs for development projects (Weakness)

– Adverse impact on sustainable development due to high energy consumption (Weakness)

1.9 A Brief Review of Empirical Studies

This section provides a brief review of the empirical literature from recent years that focuses on the relationships among the target markets discussed in this chapter. Reviewing this empirical literature alongside the theoretical foundation upon which this book is based can serve as a complement to the theoretical discourse, enriching the overall literature. Furthermore, it facilitates readers' understanding of the philosophy behind the flow of money between markets, simplifying its complexities.

Bond and stock markets: Considering the strengths and weaknesses of the stock and bond markets that were previously discussed in this chapter, there may be a connection between the stock and bond markets, complementary or substitute in drawing the flow of money. As noted, in general, risk-averse investors are typically attracted to the bond market, and risk-loving investors to the stock market. Therefore, there is the possibility of spillovers between the two markets. In some empirical studies, such as Zhang et al. (2025), Grossmann and Ngo (2025), Mensi et al. (2022), and Dong et al. (2023), the relationships between these two markets have been confirmed.

Stock and major currency markets: Many export-oriented corporations or those reliant on importing raw materials are potentially affected by the volatility in the national currency market. Therefore, national currency and stock markets can be connected to each other. In some empirical studies, such as Nong (2024), Sadeghi et al. (2023), and Syarif et al. (2021), this relationship was observed.

Gold, stock, bond, and currency markets: Given the appeal of gold in inflationary environments and times of instability, and the weakness of national currencies in such contexts, it is unexpected the mutual influence between them. Similarly, the stock market usually becomes more attractive during inflationary periods but loses its appeal in times of instability. The bond market is also highly sensitive to inflation and instability. Therefore, the flow of money between these markets and their mutual influence can be expected. There have been some empirical findings confirming these relationships: Connections among stock, bond, and national currency markets by Jiang et al. (2022), Liu (2022), and Wu et al. (2021); between gold and stock markets by Shakeel et al. (2023); among gold, bond, and stock markets by Dutta et al. (2021) and Ma et al. (2021); among national currency, stock, and gold markets by Sujit and Ray (2023).

Crypto, gold, stock, bond, and major currency markets: Considering the potentials of Bitcoin, which include serving as store of value, means of payment, and reducing the role of intermediaries in the conventional economy, its relationship with stock, bond, gold, and national currency markets is not surprising, and thus money flow between them can be expected. These potentials and relationships were confirmed in some empirical studies: Bitcoin's serving as a safe haven for global risk by Chibane and Janson (2025); Bitcoin's serving as a hedge for inflation by Liu and Valcarcel (2024); Bitcoin's serving as a safe-haven asset akin to gold by Jin and Tian (2024); crypto's serving as a portfolio diversification and a hedge for the risk of investing in other markets by Tiwari et al. (2019); connections between stock and crypto markets by Parrondo and Sala (2025) as well as Li et al. (2025); between national currency and crypto by Palazzi et al. (2021) and Iyer (2022); among national currency, crypto, and stock markets by Nadirgil (2025); among BTC, gold, and stock markets by Younis et al. (2025), Feder-Sempach et al. (2024), Jia et al. (2023), and Oosterlinck et al. (2023); among bond, gold, and crypto markets by Wang et al. (2022).

References

Chibane, M., & Janson, N. (2025). Is Bitcoin the best safe haven against geopolitical risk? *Finance Research Letters, 74,* Article 106543.

Dong, X., Xiong, Y., Nie, S., & Yoon, S. M. (2023). Can bonds hedge stock market risks? Green bonds vs conventional bonds. *Finance Research Letters, 52,* Article 103367.

Dutta, A., Bouri, E., & Noor, M. H. (2021). Climate bond, stock, gold, and oil markets: Dynamic correlations and hedging analyses during the COVID-19 outbreak. *Resources Policy, 74,* Article 102265.

Feder-Sempach, E., Szczepocki, P., & Bogołębska, J. (2024). Global uncertainty and potential shelters: Gold, bitcoin, and currencies as weak and strong safe havens for main world stock markets. *Financial Innovation, 10*(1), 67.

Feldstein, M. (1980). Inflation and the stock market. *The American Economic Review, 70*(5), 839–847.

Fisher, I. (1930). *The theory of interest Macmillan.* Macmillan.

Friedman, M. (1977). Nobel lecture: Inflation and unemployment. *Journal of Political Economy, 85*(3), 451–472.

Gavriilidis, K., & Kgari, L. M. (2016). Stock returns and inflation: The case of Botswana. In *Handbook of Frontier Markets* (pp. 27–38). Academic Press.

Grossmann, A., & Ngo, T. (2025). The stock market reaction to bond refinancing issues with and without senior debt. *Journal of Corporate Finance, 91,* Article 102746.

Iyer, T. (2022). *Cryptic connections: Spillovers between crypto and equity markets.* International Monetary Fund.

Jia, Z., Tiwari, S., Zhou, J., Farooq, M. U., & Fareed, Z. (2023). Asymmetric nexus between Bitcoin, gold resources and stock market returns: Novel findings from quantile estimates. *Resources Policy, 81,* Article 103405.

Jiang, Y., Wang, J., Ao, Z., & Wang, Y. (2022). The relationship between green bonds and conventional financial markets: Evidence from quantile-on-quantile and quantile coherence approaches. *Economic Modelling, 116,* Article 106038.

Jin, C., & Tian, X. (2024). Enhanced safe-haven status of Bitcoin: Evidence from the Silicon Valley Bank collapse. *Finance Research Letters, 59,* Article 104689.

Li, J. C., Xu, Y. Z., Tao, C., & Zhong, G. Y. (2025). Multi-period impacts and network connectivity of cryptocurrencies to international stock markets. *Physica A: Statistical Mechanics and its Applications, 658,* Article 130299.

Liu, J., & Valcarcel, V. J. (2024). Hedging inflation expectations in the cryptocurrency futures market. *Journal of Financial Stability, 70,* Article 101205.

Liu, M. (2022). The driving forces of green bond market volatility and the response of the market to the COVID-19 pandemic. *Economic Analysis and Policy, 75,* 288–309.

Ma, R., Sun, B., Zhai, P., & Jin, Y. (2021). Hedging stock market risks: Can gold really beat bonds? *Finance Research Letters, 42,* Article 101918.

Mensi, W., Shafiullah, M., Vo, X. V., & Kang, S. H. (2022). Spillovers and connectedness between green bond and stock markets in bearish and bullish market scenarios. *Finance Research Letters, 49,* Article 103120.

Nadirgil, O. (2025). Dynamic transmissions between green and technology stocks, ETFs, commodities, crypto and fiat currencies throughout the global turbulences. *Journal of Cleaner Production,* 145002.

Nong, H. (2024). Connectedness and risk transmission of China's stock and currency markets with global commodities. *Economic Change and Restructuring, 57*(1), 5.

Oosterlinck, K., Reyns, A., & Szafarz, A. (2023). Gold, bitcoin, and portfolio diversification: Lessons from the Ukrainian war. *Resources Policy, 83,* Article 103710.

Palazzi, R. B., Júnior, G. D. S. R., & Klotzle, M. C. (2021). The dynamic relationship between bitcoin and the foreign exchange market: A nonlinear approach to test causality between bitcoin and currencies. *Finance Research Letters, 42,* Article 101893.

Parrondo, L., & Sala, C. (2025). Connectedness between traditional finance, cryptocurrencies and DeFi in the post COVID period. *Finance Research Letters,* 106897.

Sadeghi, A., Marzban, H., Samadi, A. H., Azarbaiejani, K., & Rostamzadeh, P. (2024). Inflationary effects of the foreign currency shocks with different sources: The response of monetary policy in a developing economy. *Iranian Economic Review, 28*(3), 695–729.

Sadeghi, A., Tayebi, S. K., & Roudari, S. (2023). Financial markets, inflation and growth: The impact of monetary policy under different political structures. *Journal of Policy Modeling, 45*(5), 935–956.

Shakeel, M., Rabbani, M. R., Hawaldar, I. T., Chhabra, V., & Zaidi, F. K. (2023). Is there an intraday volatility spillover between exchange rate, gold and crude oil? *Journal of Open Innovation: Technology, Market, and Complexity, 9*(3), Article 100094.

Sujit, K. S., & Ray, S. (2023). Linear and nonlinear asymmetric relationship in crude oil, gold, stock market and exchange rates: An evidence from the UAE. *Resources Policy, 83,* Article 103633.

Syarif, M., Indrijawati, A., Adam, P., & Saidi, L. O. (2021). The causal relationship between exchange rates and bond yield in Indonesia. *Iranian Economic Review, 25*(1), 167–178.

Tiwari, A. K., Raheem, I. D., & Kang, S. H. (2019). Time-varying dynamic conditional correlation between stock and cryptocurrency markets using the copula-ADCC-EGARCH model. *Physica a: Statistical Mechanics and Its Applications, 535,* Article 122295.

Tobin, J. (1965). Money and economic growth. *Econometrica: Journal of the Econometric Society,* 671–684.

Wang, Y., Lucey, B. M., Vigne, S. A., & Yarovaya, L. (2022). The effects of central bank digital currencies news on financial markets. *Technological Forecasting and Social Change, 180,* Article 121715.

Wu, C. C., Chen, W. P., & Korsakul, N. (2021). Extreme linkages between foreign exchange and general financial markets. *Pacific-Basin Finance Journal, 65,* Article 101462.

Younis, I., Naeem, M. A., Shah, W. U., & Tang, X. (2025). Inter-and intra-connectedness between energy, gold, Bitcoin, and Gulf cooperation council stock markets: New evidence from various financial crises. *Research in International Business and Finance, 73,* Article 102548.

Zhang, F., Ma, Y., Liu, X., & Zhou, X. (2025). Revisiting the hedging and safe haven roles of gold: Evidence from quantile-on-quantile approach. *The North American Journal of Economics and Finance,* 102516.

Chapter 2
Financial Markets and Economic Development

2.1 Introduction

Economic development is one of the constant pillars of macroeconomic planning across different political structures. Access to adequate financial resources is a prerequisite for achieving a suitable level of investment and economic growth, and sustaining this growth is essential for attaining long-term economic development. Consequently, the mobilization of financial resources across different markets has been strongly emphasized in the literature on financial development, as financial markets play a decisive role in attracting money flow and allocating it to various sectors of the economy.

As discussed in the previous chapter, different markets can serve as target markets for absorbing the flow of money. The type of activities into which the attracted financial resources are injected is a critical factor in shaping the process of economic development. Investment in these markets may be directed purely toward short-term speculative gains, or it may take the form of medium- and long-term productive investments. Funds mobilized in stock markets, bank deposits, and bonds can be allocated to research and development projects as well as productive economic activities. On the other hand, financial markets that are attractive due to high capital returns arising from significant price volatility are also prone to unproductive activities such as speculation aimed at profit-making. Severe price fluctuations can generate systemic risks in financial markets, while unproductive investment may exert a detrimental impact on sustainable growth.

However, given their substantial competitive potential, these markets are also capable of attracting long-term capital, thereby competing with financial intermediaries and bond markets in absorbing the flow of money. In this context, the cryptocurrency market possesses sufficient appeal for investors motivated by short-term speculative gains. Nonetheless, investment in this market, considering its relatively small market capitalization compared to rival markets, may also be pursued with alternative objectives, such as preserving and enhancing asset value over time with

A. Sadeghi et al., *Financial Markets, Speculation, and Development*,
https://doi.org/10.1007/978-981-95-5895-7_2

a medium- to long-term outlook, thereby generating positive effects on the process of economic development.

Therefore, key indicators of economic development, such as inflation, investment, and gross domestic product (GDP), may be influenced by liquidity flows across these markets, which will be addressed in this chapter. Accordingly, the theoretical foundations of the relationship between economic development and each of the target markets will be explored separately, followed by a brief review of recent empirical studies that can complement the theoretical literature, making it more comprehensible and enriched. A comparative analysis is one of the objectives pursued in this chapter, as it can provide clearer insights into the relationships among different markets and their implications for economic development.

2.2 Economic Development

Economic development is the process leading to more resources and choices for a society, which is shown by GDP growth and capital formation. In other words, it is sustainably structural changes improving income and standards of living. According to the neoclassical growth theory, first introduced by Ramsey (1928) and later expanded by Solow (1956), the rate of investment plays a central role in driving economic growth, particularly in situations where economies face limitations in resource allocation. Romer (1990) further emphasizes that capital formation is a fundamental determinant of sustained growth, similarly.

Prescott (2016) highlights the significance of saving–investment decisions within the framework of the neoclassical growth model. Economic development, on the other hand, is commonly assessed through macroeconomic indicators such as gross domestic product, investment levels, and overall stability, which are classified by the World Bank as key measures of development. Ensuring the fulfillment of certain prerequisites can facilitate and accelerate the process of economic development. One of the most crucial prerequisites is maintaining consistent access to financial resources, which are essential for achieving adequate capital formation and economic growth, as emphasized in neoclassical theory. In this context, financial markets assume a particularly vital role in mobilizing and channeling these resources.

Economic development encompasses a wide range of dimensions, though the focus here is on a specific and limited aspect of it. Broadly, economic development is defined as the level and diversity of resources, along with their efficient distribution. In other words, the overall level of economic development is largely determined by access to financial resources, since these resources influence both the pace of progress toward economic goals and the degree of vulnerability reduction. Beyond the diversity of resources, factors such as the variety of goods and services, consumer purchasing power, access to employment opportunities, educational attainment, and income levels also play an integral role in defining economic development. The combination of these elements enhances the quality and standard of living, fosters greater innovation by creating motivation, and reduces incentives for migration, thereby ensuring the sustained positive impact on the domestic economy.

Financial development, as a crucial dimension of economic development, is primarily associated with its potential impact on capital formation, economic growth, and inflation. It mainly includes the expansion of the banking sector and stock markets, as emphasized in the studies by Levine (1997) and Beck and Levine (2004). Over time, however, with the quantitative and qualitative evolution of other forms of assets, financial development has come to encompass additional financial markets that can absorb liquidity, including gold, bonds, currency units, and cryptocurrencies.

While achieving adequate investment growth and a desirable level of gross domestic product is recognized as an essential prerequisite for economic development, inflation remains another key macroeconomic indicator that plays a central role in the development process. This centrality arises from its potential impact on production, consumption, liquidity flows across markets, financial development, and foreign trade.

More explicitly and in greater detail, the impact of inflation on the process of economic development can occur through the following channels:

- Production costs, driven by the effect of inflation on wages and the price of domestic and imported raw materials
- Financing costs through bank loans and bonds
- The real value of revenues from the sale of final products
- Consumer purchasing power
- Wage purchasing power, labor productivity, and incentives for innovation and productive activities
- Financing of productive investments
- Speculative incentives in markets with high price volatility, and consequently, the reallocation of financial resources across markets
- The relative prices of domestic versus foreign goods and the resulting effect on net exports
- Heightened uncertainty within the economic environment

Beyond the list above, our primary emphasis lies on specific channels of influence, which will be discussed in detail. Revenue generation from renewable resources, such as human capital, is considered a substitute for income derived from non-renewable natural resources. What makes human resources particularly significant in relation to economic growth is their productivity. As Barro (1999) considers human capital as a determining element for development process in neoclassical growth theory. In this regard, wage purchasing power is a key factor with substantial potential influence on labor motivation and, consequently, on productivity. This becomes especially important in economies where nominal wage rigidity is embedded in labor contracts: In such contexts, inflation has a significant effect on the real purchasing power of wages, as well as on the motivation and productivity that stem from it.

This issue becomes even more critical in developing economies, where, unlike developed or emerging economies, labor unions and professional associations have not yet reached adequate quantitative and qualitative maturity. As a result, they lack the institutional capacity and bargaining power to safeguard workers' real purchasing power against inflationary fluctuations or to adjust nominal wages accordingly. Therefore, alongside the gradual strengthening of institutions, which requires both qualitative and quantitative development supported by long-term planning, it is essential to use available tools to control inflation volatility and ensure stability, thereby protecting or enhancing the purchasing power of wages. This, in turn, sustains labor motivation and productivity.

Beyond its impact on labor incentives and productivity, high inflation volatility can also generate extraordinary capital gains in financial and commodity markets. This often diverts a considerable portion of financial resources into unproductive economic activities, such as short-term speculation in volatile markets, rather than directing them toward long-term, productive investments. In contrast, channeling these resources into markets that support productive investments helps lay the groundwork for sustainable and desirable economic growth.

In this regard, the expansion of the bond market—alongside financial intermediaries such as stock markets and the banking system—plays a critical role. These markets can absorb financial resources and allocate them to research and development (R&D) sectors as well as productive economic activities, while preventing the diversion of funds into speculative, non-productive pursuits. This requirement, often referred to as financial development, is strongly emphasized in the economic development literature. In essence, financial development increases the relative attractiveness of productive sectors over unproductive ones, thereby restraining the growth of non-productive segments of the economy.

Sustainable economic development, which ensures the continuity of desirable long-term growth, also hinges on environmental and climate considerations. Economic activities can potentially cause harm to the environment and climate conditions. Thus, while desirable economic growth remains central to economic planning, its sustainability over the long term, affecting the quality of life of future generations, requires the preservation of a healthy and stable natural environment. For this reason, development-oriented programs increasingly integrate the potential risks of environmental and climate-related damages into their macroeconomic policy frameworks, as highlighted by the United Nations' Sustainable Development Goals (UN SDGs).

Here, too, the significance of financial markets and their role in financing becomes evident. If the Paris Agreement's 2 °C temperature threshold, requiring US$53 trillion in clean energy-related investments by 2035 (International Energy Agency [IEA]), i.e., annually four to five trillion dollars, is to be achieved, sufficient financing must be found to support clean products. Green bonds have been defined for this purpose and to facilitate the transition from fossil fuels to clean energy.

2.3 Financial Intermediaries and Economic Development

Corporate financing in different economies is primarily undertaken through the banking system and the stock market. The relative dominance of each financial intermediary varies across economies. Generally, financing systems in high-income countries are market-based, while in developing countries they tend to be bank-based. Financial intermediaries have the capacity to positively influence investment and economic growth by efficiently mobilizing and allocating financial resources to productive investments. This capacity is realized through their role in:

- Enhancing transparency and reducing information asymmetry
- Facilitating transactions
- Supporting risk management
- Reducing the costs of accessing investment opportunities
- Financing of productive investments

Beyond these, financial intermediaries play additional roles that remove barriers to investment, accelerate its process, and foster economic growth, as highlighted by Greenbaum et al. (2019) and Levine (1992):

- Lowering the costs of transferring financial resources
- Channeling savings into investments
- Facilitating domestic and especially international trade
- Providing access to and assessment of information related to investors, borrowers, and firms
- Evaluating economic projects

These functions are particularly critical for small enterprises, which typically lack adequate access to such tools. To illustrate, the process of channeling financial resources through the banking sector can be explained simply: An entrepreneur intends to engage in a productive economic activity but lacks sufficient resources. On the other side, a saver possesses resources but seeks returns without directly engaging in risky or time-intensive activities. The bank, acting as an intermediary, after reviewing the relevant information:

- Ensuring the feasibility of the borrower's project and their capacity to repay the loan with interest rates
- Channeling savings into investments

Guarantees depositors that they will receive returns consistent with the interest rate. By establishing this channel of interaction, the bank aligns the interests of the investor, the borrower, the banking system, and the real sector of the economy, resulting in mutual gains.

In the stock market, firms issue shares purchased by investors. The raised capital is directed toward developmental projects and other productive economic activities, with a portion of the resulting profits allocated to shareholders. Thus, financing through both banks and stock markets benefits investors, financial intermediaries, firms, and ultimately the real economy.

In the development literature, this process is referred to as financial resource mobilization. In the absence of financial intermediaries or in cases where resource mobilization is weakened, the following risks can undermine investment and negatively impact economic growth:

- Failure to secure the required financial resources
- Excess cash hoarding during recessions
- Potential default on loans
- Failure of economic projects to materialize

When financial resources are directed toward productive, innovation-driven economic activities, the positive impact of financial intermediaries on growth is amplified. By assessing firms' conditions and providing investors with access to their performance and outlook, intermediaries reduce investment risk. Ultimately, investments are channeled into firms with favorable prospects, benefiting investors, firms, and the real sector alike. The critical role of financial intermediaries in fostering investment and growth, through their traditional functions of mobilizing and allocating resources and other mechanisms discussed above, was emphasized by Schumpeter (1954) and McKinnon (2010).

In sum, the continuous mobilization of sufficient resources by financial intermediaries can drive desirable growth in productive investment and gross domestic product, both of which are prerequisites for economic development. Moreover, channeling liquidity into financial intermediaries rather than speculative markets reduces artificial demand, thereby easing inflationary pressures. With lower inflation, workers' purchasing power improves, which in turn enhances their motivation and productivity. Consequently, development driven by human capital becomes more attainable. Therefore, here we observe a beautifully intricate chain of relationships.

That said, it is not possible to speak with certainty about the precise effects financial intermediaries may have on the real sectors of an economy, which ultimately shape economic development. While expectations regarding the influence of financial sector development on investment and growth are generally positive, empirical findings reveal mixed outcomes. For example, Benczúr et al. (2019), analyzing the relationship between growth and financing through banking, stock markets, and debt instruments in 23 EU and OECD countries, found that bank- and debt-based financing had negative effects on growth, whereas stock market financing had positive effects. Conversely, Sadeghi et al. (2023) reported positive effects of both banking sector and stock market development, even in a developing economy such as Iran, which lacks advanced financial markets. Thus, the development of financial intermediaries across different economies may yield divergent outcomes and does not necessarily guarantee positive results.

In theory, financial intermediaries are expected to have a positive impact; however, in practice, outcomes may differ. For this reason, there is always an empirical appendix to theoretical discussions, allowing for the assessment of whether theories hold true in reality. This approach is also followed in this book, which includes an empirical supplement to the theoretical literature discussed in Chaps. 1 through 3. This point is particularly important for students of economics and finance, who need a solid grasp of theoretical knowledge, as it can also have practical applications.

2.4 National Currency and Economic Development

The inherent role of the foreign exchange market in the economic environment includes the following:

- Facilitating international trade and investment by providing liquidity and reducing transaction costs, thereby contributing to economic growth
- Supporting the effectiveness of monetary policies and overall economic stability and resistance
- Attracting foreign capital by providing transparency and predictability, which are essential for sustainable economic development
- Reducing uncertainty for businesses and investors, fostering long-term economic growth, by enabling hedging against currency risks

Regarding the effects of exchange rate changes on economic growth, existing views are often conflicting. For instance, some perspectives regard an increase in the exchange rate negatively. A depreciation of the national currency can increase uncertainty in the economic environment, which, through higher inflation rates and rising relative prices, negatively affects investment and economic growth, as highlighted by Singleton (1987).

Some perspectives hold that an increase in the exchange rate can lead to higher bank savings, which in turn fosters capital accumulation, investment, and economic growth. The most notable example is China, which implemented this policy and achieved high economic growth. Other Asian economies, such as South Korea, Malaysia, and Thailand, have also employed similar policies, resulting in significant growth in both GDP and savings rates. In this context, a monetary policy aimed at increasing the exchange rate, which enhances the international competitiveness of domestic goods and raises the cost of imports, leads to growth in net exports and domestic savings. With rising savings, domestic resources for financing investments expand.

Another perspective suggests that the impact of changes in the national currency's value on investment and economic growth depends on the economic structure. In other words, the export orientation of domestic firms and their reliance on imported raw materials can shape how exchange rate changes affect investment and growth. Additionally, the volume of imported final consumption goods can significantly influence this effect. Since GDP equals the sum of consumption, investment, government spending, and net exports:

$$\frac{GDP}{P} = \frac{C}{P} + \frac{I}{P} + \frac{G}{P} + \frac{X - M}{P} \tag{2.1}$$

Considering the sensitivity of consumption, net exports, and domestic and foreign investments to exchange rate changes; since many final consumer goods and technologies are imported, or domestic production relies on imported raw materials, and that the outlook of the national currency's value also affects the attraction of both domestic and foreign investment, the gross domestic product is influenced by the exchange rate. Therefore, the impact of exchange rate changes depends on the degree of firms' reliance on imported raw materials and the share of export products in their production baskets.

Conversely, according to Eq. (2.1), the value of the national currency can also be influenced by investment, economic growth, and the general price level. This is because net exports, and thus the supply and demand for domestic currency relative to foreign currencies, are affected by these economic indices.

Regarding the relationship between exchange rates and inflation, the degree of firms' dependence on imported raw materials, as well as the volume of imported final consumption goods in household consumption baskets, can transmit the inflationary effects of exchange rate changes to domestic prices. This phenomenon is known as the "exchange rate pass-through effect." This effect is crucial because it links the domestic economy to external shocks, thereby potentially transmitting the inflationary consequences of exchange rate fluctuations to export goods, imported goods, and overall consumer and producer price indices.

Some historical events support or refute the inflationary effects of currency shocks. For example, the sharp depreciation of the British pound following the 2008–2009 global financial crisis and after the Brexit referendum in January 2016 led to substantial price increases. Conversely, the appreciation of the pound during 2013–2015 did not translate to domestic price increases. After the global financial crisis, the twelve countries that were formerly part of the Soviet Union experienced high domestic inflation following significant exchange rate increases, prompting monetary policy adjustments in some of these countries to mitigate inflationary effects. The severe expansionary monetary policies, i.e., interest rate cuts to near-zero levels, implemented by European, British, and East Asian economies in the aftermath of the COVID-19 outbreak, which led to a significant depreciation of currencies such as the euro, the pound, the yen, and the yuan, resulted in unprecedented inflation rates across the Eurozone, the United Kingdom, and East Asian economies.

The transmission of inflationary effects from exchange rate hikes can be complete or partial. Sticky nominal prices prevent the full transmission of exchange rate-induced inflation to prices in the short term. Another reason is that some firms adjust their prices within specific time periods, while others do so at different intervals. In other words, not all firms change their prices simultaneously, as highlighted by Walsh (2010). Another reason for incomplete pass-through mainly observed in emerging and developed economies is the strengthening of domestic goods markets and their alignment with consumer preferences after structural reforms, which reduced import dependence.

Another factor influencing the impact of exchange rate changes on domestic prices is the share of tradable goods in consumer and producer baskets. Firms with a high proportion of imported raw materials or intermediate goods in production pass-through exchange rate changes more strongly to their prices. This affects not only producer and consumer price indices but also foreign trade by influencing the relative price of domestic versus foreign goods and thereby the competitiveness of domestic products in international markets. In contrast, domestically produced non-imported goods are less sensitive to exchange rate changes.

As discussed in Chap. 1, national and major currency markets are prone to speculative capital inflows driven by profit opportunities. Speculative activities require awareness of economic and political conditions, as well as low-error forecasts, since misjudgments lead to losses rather than gains. Therefore, speculative activities in markets susceptible to economic factors such as GDP growth, inflation, foreign exchange reserves, and liquidity volume generally attract risk-tolerant rather than risk-averse investors.

In developing economies with gaps between official and market exchange rates, i.e., multiple exchange rates, speculative incentives in the foreign exchange market are heightened. Capital attraction in different markets is linked to their risk levels. Investors are willing to assume higher risk in a market if expected returns are higher. If investors perceive that the profits of speculation in the foreign exchange market exceed those from other markets, they will allocate more capital to this market. This becomes even more significant considering the importance of exchange rates to foreign investors. Foreign capital inflows, which enable continuous capital formation and innovative investment expansion, are a key indicator in the economic development literature. Given that indicators affecting economic development are sensitive to currency market fluctuations, holds key importance in the path to economic development.

2.5 Bond Market and Economic Development

Financing R&D projects and other productive investments is considered a necessary condition for achieving economic development. In this context, financing through bond issuance has always attracted the attention of both companies and governments. As discussed in Chap. 1, what becomes particularly important regarding bond issuance is the repayment of the principal and the interest rate allocated to these bonds. For governments, this issue has consistently posed a challenge, given that it also affects social welfare. A key concern regarding government financing through bond issuance is that governments may raise tax rates to repay the principal and interest rates or reduce the real value of sold bonds by printing more money and the resulting inflation. Increasing tax rates can impose financial burdens on different sectors of the economy, particularly the production sector, negatively affecting investment and economic growth. However, if governments finance repayments from alternative sources, or if repayment through taxes is carefully balanced and occurs after the economic projects yield results and the overall economic situation improves, such concerns can be mitigated.

A major advantage of financing through bond issuance for both companies and governments is the reduction in the real value of debt in inflationary environments. While this decline in debt value is beneficial for bond issuers, it represents a significant risk for individuals and institutions that allocate capital to purchase these bonds. However, this concern is more relevant in economies experiencing significant fluctuations in inflation rates, where inflation-targeting policies fail to stabilize the economy. Furthermore, if a repression approach toward nominal interest rates is pursued, without adjusting them in line with inflation fluctuations, the decline in debt value can inflict greater losses on bondholders. In most developed and emerging economies, interest rate repression is not practiced; instead, inflation-targeting monetary policies manage inflation fluctuations within a specific range, ensuring price stability. Therefore, investors in these economies face minimal risks concerning inflation volatility.

Moreover, since the overall economic situation depends on access to financial resources, governments and central banks often support the bond market. Such support, combined with inflation-targeting monetary policies, significantly reduces investment risk in the bond market. However, it should be noted that due to the proportional relationship between nominal interest rates and inflation rates maintained by emerging and developed economies' central banks, the returns in the bond market are typically less attractive to risk-seeking investors compared to other markets.

Another notable aspect of the bond market is its low appeal for speculative profit-seeking, given the limited volatility in non-inflationary environments. Therefore, if the bond market is sufficiently attractive for long-term investment, it can reduce short-term speculative incentives in parallel markets. As a result, economic development can benefit positively, as attracting capital to markets that support R&D and other productive projects can favorably influence investment and economic growth. Additionally, avoiding liquidity absorption into speculative activities, which could create artificial demand pressures, affecting prices and inflation volatility, prevents non-augmenting effects on inflation, thereby supporting the development process.

Hence, financing through bond issuance can be considered an alternative to bank- and stock market-based financing. According to World Bank statistics, the most developed bond markets are in the United States, China, the European Union, and the United Kingdom, holding the largest market values. As shown in Table 2.1 and Fig. 2.1, the development of the bond market's role in financing has followed a steep upward trend in the United States and China, while Germany and Japan have experienced a steadier increase. Reports from the European Central Bank indicate that bond financing has expanded significantly in the Eurozone; by the third quarter of 2023, the proportion of financing through bonds for non-financial companies reached 20%.

Figures 2.3, 2.4, and 2.5 show that the banking sector plays a larger role in financing in Germany, Japan, and China compared to the stock market. Nevertheless, the stock market's role in financing has also followed an upward trend in Japan and China. In contrast, as shown in Fig. 2.2 and Table 2.1, in the United States, the development of the stock market's share in financing significantly surpasses that of the banking sector, highlighting the centrality of the stock market in the U.S. financial

Table 2.1 The share of stock markets, bonds, and bank deposits in the United States, China, Germany, and Japan from 2000 to 2020

JP			GR			CN			US		
B	STO	DEP	B	STO	DEP	B	STO	DEP	B	STO	DEP
0.0100	0.49	2.25	0.026	0.93	1.39	0.00006	0.62	1.18	0.03	2.91	0.55
0.0127	0.38	1.45	0.029	0.66	1.38	0.00090	0.34	1.19	0.05	1.97	0.56
0.0112	0.41	1.4	0.025	0.41	1.36	0.00300	0.22	1.28	0.03	1.56	0.57
0.0101	0.51	1.45	0.023	0.40	1.33	0.00200	0.23	1.36	0.03	1.40	0.57
0.0071	0.70	1.44	0.013	0.41	1.31	0.00188	0.26	1.29	0.03	1.56	0.58
0.0092	0.89	1.48	0.014	0.45	1.25	0.00607	0.17	1.22	0.02	1.98	0.60
0.0086	1.19	1.49	0.023	0.65	1.17	0.00455	0.42	1.19	0.03	2.21	0.62
0.0121	1.43	1.46	0.011	0.95	1.16	0.00522	1.77	1.16	0.03	2.96	0.66
0.0117	1.21	1.55	0.018	1.11	1.19	0.01215	0.84	1.11	0.03	3.20	0.68
0.0147	0.73	1.76	0.032	0.52	1.13	0.02687	1.53	1.35	0.04	2.37	0.63
0.0121	0.74	1.78	0.015	0.43	1.06	0.01987	1.35	1.37	0.04	2.39	0.61
0.0109	0.69	1.82	0.015	0.41	1.05	0.02300	0.88	1.33	0.03	2.63	0.59
0.0113	0.53	1.83	0.028	0.35	1.03	0.03709	0.58	1.39	0.05	1.99	0.59
0.0145	1.16	1.79	0.026	0.35	0.99	0.03934	0.80	1.44	0.05	1.97	0.58
0.0121	0.98	1.73	0.027	0.32	0.97	0.05984	1.14	1.51	0.04	2.22	0.59
0.0116	1.25	1.60	0.027	0.43	0.94	0.05546	3.55	1.68	0.05	2.27	0.61
0.0144	1.04	1.57	0.026	0.32	0.92	0.06388	1.62	1.79	0.05	2.25	0.64
0.0186	1.17	1.56	0.029	0.42	0.91	0.04172	1.39	1.81	0.05	2.04	0.63
0.0207	1.25	1.52	0.033	0.40	0.91	0.03972	0.94	1.86	0.03	1.61	0.63
0.0247	0.99	1.53	0.032	0.34	0.97	0.04112	1.27	1.96	0.04	1.09	0.64
0.0286	1.25	1.70	0.032	0.47	0.96	0.04402	2.15	2.18	0.07	1.21	0.74

Note: DEP, STO, and B show, in order, the ratios of bank deposits, the value of shares traded in the stock market, and government and corporate bonds to gross domestic product. For this statistical information, the time series of financial development indicators from the World Bank was used. US, CN, GR, and JP represent the United States, China, Germany, and Japan, respectively

system. Conversely, in China and Japan, the financial system remains bank-centric. These observations pertain to emerging and developed economies, where:

- Mature markets
- The absence of financial repression—adjusting nominal interest rates according to inflation fluctuations
- Limiting inflation volatility by inflation-targeting monetary policies distinguishes them from developing economies.

By comparison, for developing economies like Iran, which have historically faced nominal interest rate repression and negative real interest rates on bank deposits and loans, the financial system has been bank-based. However, as shown in Fig. 2.6, the role of the stock market in financing has followed a steep upward trend since 2013, reducing its gap with the banking sector. As Fig. 2.6 illustrates, the weight of the stock market in financing has approached that of the banking sector significantly.

As discussed at the beginning of this chapter, economic development is sustainable when it lies at the core of planning efforts, particularly in countries with high fossil fuel consumption, where significant environmental and climatic damages may occur.

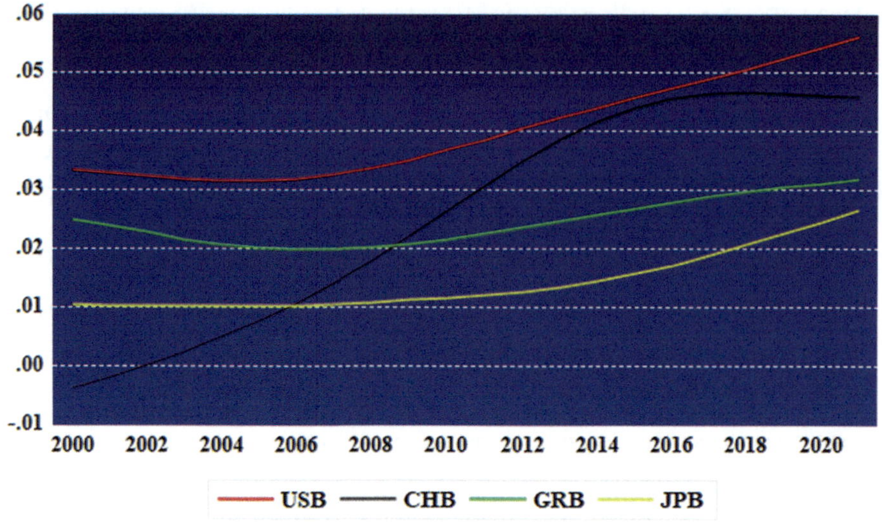

Fig. 2.1 Trend related to the share of bond markets in the economies of the United States, China, Germany, and Japan from 2000 to 2020. (*Note*: To cycle out and extract the trend component of the ratio of bonds issued by governments and corporations to GDP, the Hodrick-Prescott filter was applied using series related to the World Bank's financial development indicators. It should be noted that, to eliminate the impact of the COVID-19 shock on the development of the bond market's role, statistical data from 2021 to 2023 were not used)

The substitution of fossil fuels with clean renewable energy has been defined as one of the sustainable development objectives in developed economies such as the United States. As previously noted, financing development projects is a fundamental prerequisite for their initiation, implementation, and eventual success. Accordingly, green financing and its development have emerged as key policy instruments aimed at replacing fossil fuels with clean renewable energy.

Green financing, which includes the issuance of bonds related to companies involved in such projects, has been one of the approaches that has experienced considerable growth over the past decade and has received support from various societal bodies, governments, and central banks. This is because the quality of life and living conditions for future generations, who are the children of the present generation, are closely linked to the success of these development initiatives. This financing tool has gained popularity among individuals concerned with environmental and climate issues. Therefore, the significance of environmental and climatic considerations in the process of sustainable economic development has facilitated the growth of the green bond market. According to Fig. 2.7, the development of the green bond market has been highest in the Eurozone, followed by the Asia–Pacific region, and North America, with the Eurozone showing a substantial lead over other regions globally.

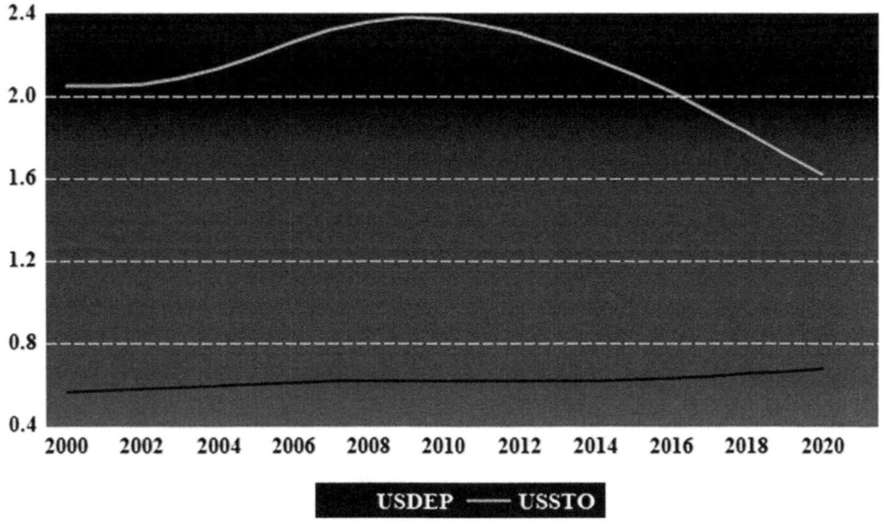

Fig. 2.2 Trend related to the development of the role of the stock market and the banking network in the US economy, 2000–2020. (*Note*: To cycle out and extract the trend component of the ratio of shares traded in the US stock market and bank deposits to GDP, the Hodrick-Prescott filter was applied using series related to the World Bank's financial development indicators. It should be noted that, to eliminate the impact of the COVID-19 shock on the development of the role of the stock market and the banking network, statistical data from 2021 to 2023 were not used)

2.6 Gold, Crypto, and Economic Development

Case by case, the relationship between gold and economic development follows this path:

- Being included in central banks' balance sheets for economic stability and resilience
- Serving as financial backing to counter economic and political shocks
- The impact of gold mining on sustainable development

Gold plays a pivotal role in enhancing the resilience of national currencies and broader macroeconomic stability. As a reserve asset in central bank balance sheets, gold provides a hedge against inflation, currency depreciation, and external shocks. In periods of economic or geopolitical uncertainty, gold reserves act as a stabilizing buffer, enabling governments to maintain liquidity, mitigate exchange rate fluctuations, and secure international creditworthiness. Moreover, by diversifying reserve portfolios beyond foreign currencies, gold reduces systemic vulnerability to global financial crises. In this regard, gold not only functions as a strategic financial safeguard but also reinforces macroeconomic resilience, supporting the long-term stability and credibility of national economies.

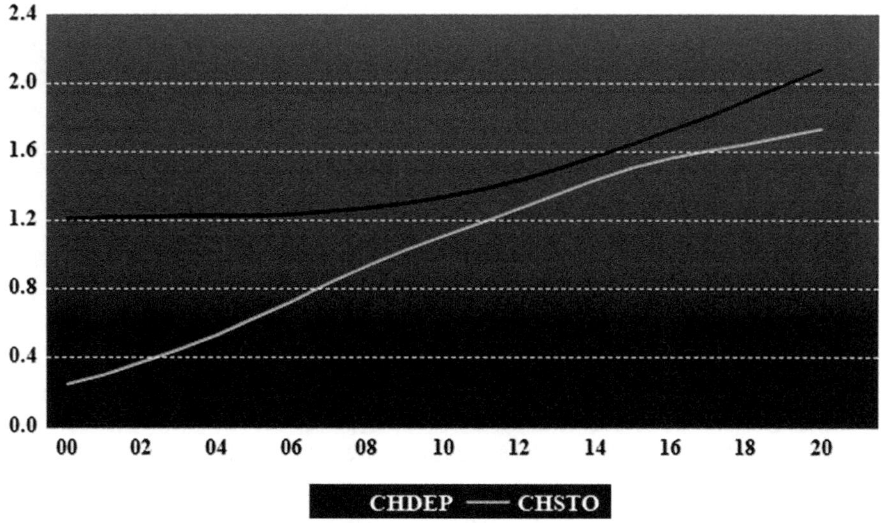

Fig. 2.3 Trend related to the development of the role of the stock market and the banking network in the Chinese economy, 2000–2020. (*Note*: To cycle out and extract the trend component of the ratio of shares traded in the Chinese stock market and bank deposits to GDP, the Hodrick-Prescott filter was applied using series related to the World Bank's financial development indicators. It should be noted that, to eliminate the impact of the COVID-19 shock on the development of the role of the stock market and the banking network, statistical data from 2021 to 2023 were not used)

This is why gold, as one of the various forms of assets, has consistently attracted the attention of diverse groups of investors due to its appeal, which stems from its capacity as a store of value. This includes central banks of global economies as well. Given that during global shocks—whether economic, political, or security-related—gold not only shows resilience but also experiences a significant increase in global demand, central banks across different economies, whether large or small in terms of global influence, pay considerable attention to it.

The role of gold as a store of value during global instability is unrivaled in a world with diverse asset types. Only cryptocurrencies, such as Bitcoin, can potentially compete with gold in this regard. Cryptocurrencies, in theory, have the capacity to store value during global instability like gold, but these capacities have not yet fully materialized. Unequal distribution of these coins is one factor limiting this potential, as discussed in Chap. 1. Moreover, the cryptocurrency industry is still nascent, and given the long and millennia-old history of gold, it will take considerable time for cryptocurrencies like Bitcoin and Ethereum to establish themselves as reliable stores of value during global instability on par with gold in the eyes of investors.

The vulnerability of economies to cross-border and global shocks remains a major barrier to economic development. Among various asset types, gold currently has the capacity to provide a certain level of resilience to economies against such shocks by serving as backing for national currencies. In other words, gold can mitigate the

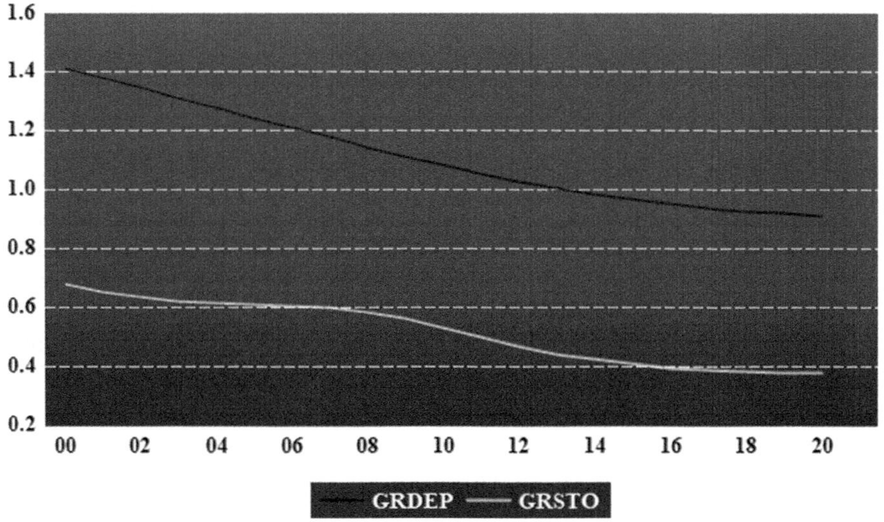

Fig. 2.4 Trend related to the development of the role of the stock market and the banking network in the German economy, 2000–2020. (*Note*: To cycle out and extract the trend component of the ratio of shares traded in the German stock market and bank deposits to GDP, the Hodrick-Prescott filter was applied using series related to the World Bank's financial development indicators. It should be noted that, to eliminate the impact of the COVID-19 shock on the development of the role of the stock market and the banking network, statistical data from 2021 to 2023 were not used)

potential spillover effects of these shocks on the domestic economy and strengthen economic resilience.

Nevertheless, despite these advantages, there are also some drawbacks regarding the relationship between gold and sustainable development, stemming from environmental damage caused by gold extraction. Gold mining, while contributing to economic growth and national revenues, imposes significant environmental costs that directly challenge the principles of sustainable development. The process of extraction often involves large-scale land disturbance, deforestation, and habitat fragmentation, leading to the degradation of ecosystems and loss of biodiversity. Furthermore, the use of toxic substances such as cyanide and mercury in gold processing introduces severe risks to soil and water resources, with long-term consequences for both human health and ecological integrity.

From a sustainability perspective, these environmental externalities undermine the intergenerational equity principle, as they compromise the ability of future generations to access clean water, fertile land, and intact ecosystems. Additionally, gold mining generates substantial greenhouse gas emissions and tailings waste, exacerbating climate change and creating persistent sources of environmental hazards.

The alignment of gold mining practices with sustainable development therefore requires an integrated approach that combines cleaner extraction technologies, regulatory enforcement, the use of renewable energy sources in mining operations

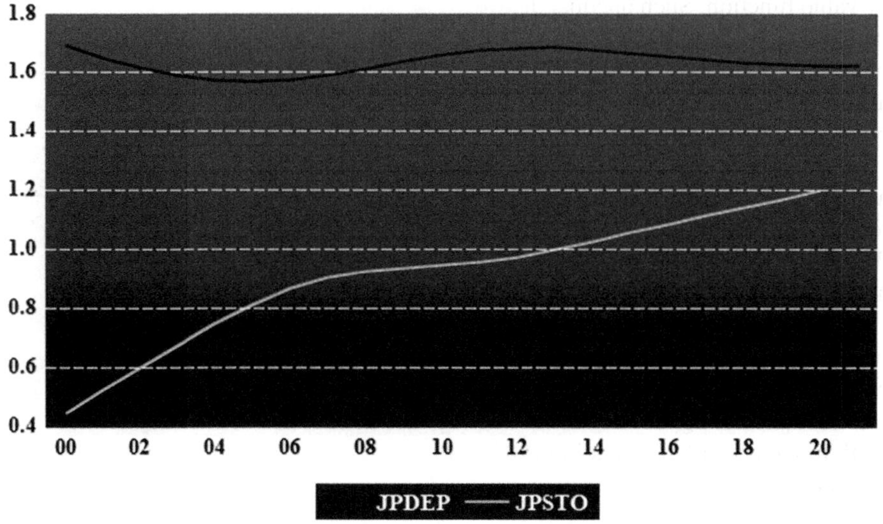

Fig. 2.5 Trend related to the development of the role of the stock market and the banking network in the Japanese economy, 2000–2020. (*Note*: To cycle out and extract the trend component of the ratio of shares traded in the Japanese stock market and bank deposits to GDP, the Hodrick-Prescott filter was applied using series related to the World Bank's financial development indicators. It should be noted that, to eliminate the impact of the COVID-19 shock on the development of the role of the stock market and the banking network, statistical data from 2021 to 2023 were not used)

contributing to minimizing long-term degradation and reducing carbon emissions, and socio-economic considerations. Integrating environmental costs into economic assessments of gold production ensures that the pursuit of short-term economic gains does not erode long-term social and ecological resilience. In this sense, the environmental dimension of gold mining is not merely a technical concern but a structural determinant of whether the sector can contribute positively or negatively to sustainable development.

Over time, a new form of asset has emerged, which, while similar to other asset types, such as major currencies and gold, also presents distinct differences. This new asset class is cryptocurrencies. As discussed in Chap. 1, Bitcoin and Ethereum, the first and second largest cryptocurrencies, serve both as powerful payment means and as adequate stores of value in inflationary environments. The cryptocurrency industry, with its ambitious goal of removing intermediaries from the economy, has attracted global attention. The current world we live in is heavily dependent on intermediaries; many processes require their involvement. As the saying goes, life's wheels do not turn without intermediaries.

Eliminating intermediaries can impact economic development through various channels. Increasing the speed of processes and saving time and financial costs are among the most important factors affecting development once intermediaries are removed. Cryptocurrencies like Ethereum, Solana, and Binance have realized this

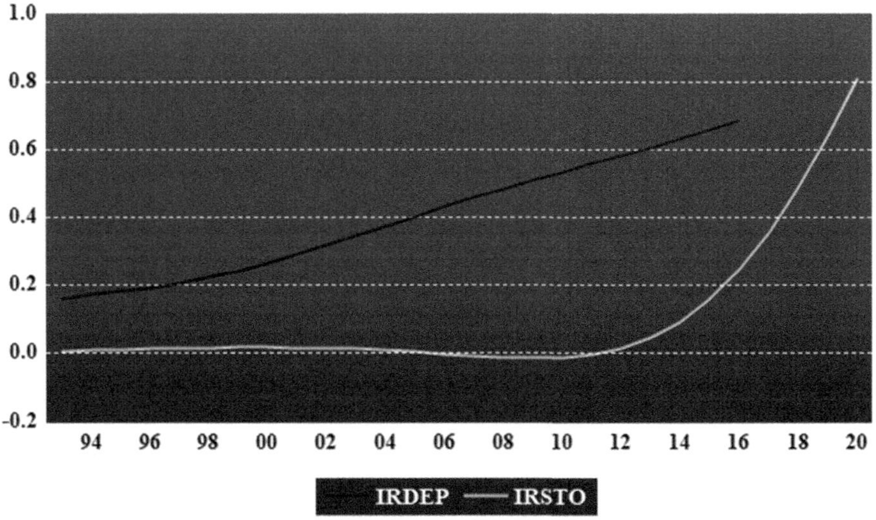

Fig. 2.6 Trend related to the development of the role of the stock market and the banking network in the Iranian economy, 1993–2020 and 1993–2017, respectively. (*Note*: To cycle out and extract the trend component of the ratio of shares traded in the Iranian stock market and bank deposits to GDP, the Hodrick-Prescott filter was applied using series related to the World Bank's financial development indicators. It should be noted that, to eliminate the impact of the COVID-19 shock on the development of the role of the stock market and the banking network, statistical data from 2021 to 2023 were not used. Moreover, statistical data on bank deposits were not available for the years 2018–2020)

vision by providing platforms for smart contracts, bringing the idea of intermediary-free transactions into practice. This infrastructure can significantly affect the development process. The innovation of executing and recording smart contracts is not limited to specific professions; it can cover all businesses and the economy at large.

For instance, initiating an investment in a specific economic sector—including obtaining legal permits, attracting investors, registering labor contracts, handling payments, insurance, advertising, and delivering final products—can all be executed through smart contracts on these platforms without intermediaries and with minimal time and cost. In contrast, in the current world, these processes require significant time, financial resources, and physical presence, as multiple intermediaries are involved at various stages:

- Legal intermediaries
- Insurance companies
- Raw material suppliers
- Market intermediaries for final products
- Banking network
- Intellectual property registration
- Advertising
- Labor contract registration intermediaries

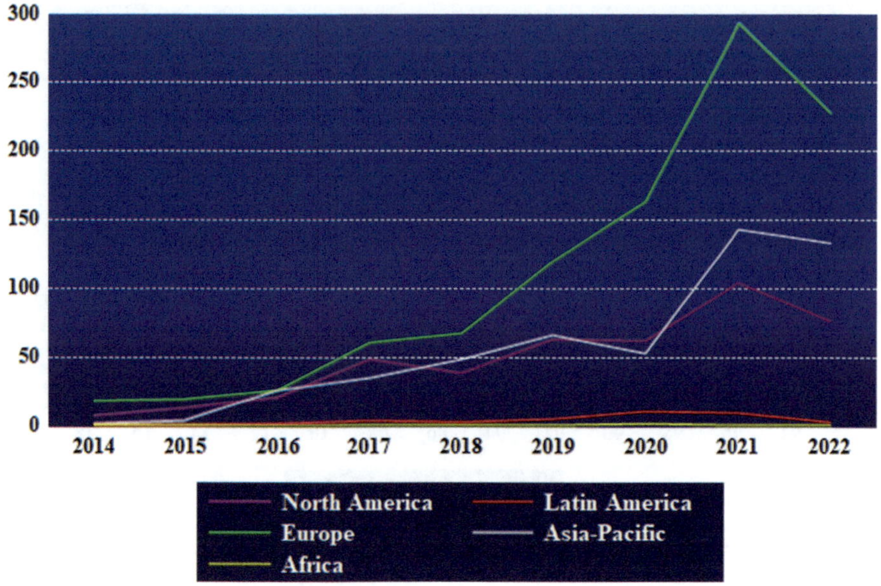

Fig. 2.7 Green bond market development in different regions of the world, 2014–2022. (*Note*: Time series data published on the website www.climatebonds.net were used)

– Investor agreement intermediaries
– Auctions and tenders
– Trade exhibitions
– Customs

Through the Ethereum, Solana, and Binance smart networks, all the above steps only require high-speed internet and access to a smartphone or computer, with no need for physical presence and involvement of intermediaries. Consequently, accelerating the execution of processes while reducing financial and time costs can meaningfully impact economic development. This is particularly significant for small businesses and entrepreneurs who may lack the skills to deal with intermediaries. The friction caused by intermediaries often delays or obstructs project completion. Furthermore, innovations in technology no longer require multiple intermediaries for recording, presenting, and executing processes. These innovations can quickly attract financing through smart contract registration and facilitate rapid global market exposure via the cryptocurrency industry.

One notable criticism arising from intra-industry weaknesses, which may negatively affect sustainable development through environmental damage, is the high energy consumption in the mining and transaction stages. Unlike gold, which is physically extracted, Bitcoin mining requires electricity to perform extremely complex computations to generate the 16-digit codes associated with each coin. These computations are carried out continuously on advanced computing machines, resulting in substantial energy consumption. As Yuan et al. (2022) note, this energy usage is equivalent to the annual energy consumption of a country like Norway.

Therefore, given the emphasis on sustainable development and reducing environmental harm, Bitcoin has faced significant criticism. However, due to the competitive and dynamic nature of this industry, cryptocurrencies are moving toward solutions that improve energy efficiency. This shift mainly affects the transaction verification stage rather than mining. Since a substantial portion of Bitcoin, approximately 19.8 million out of the total 21 million coins, has already been mined, the high energy consumption for mining will not continue indefinitely, as only about 1.2 million coins remain to be mined. Regarding transaction verification, Ethereum's shift from a proof-of-work (PoW) to a proof-of-stake (PoS) system marks a turning point in reducing energy consumption. In PoS, an individual's likelihood of successfully validating transactions depends on the amount of their staked capital. While a minimum stake is required, there is no upper limit. Therefore, those who stake more capital have a higher chance of transaction validation. In contrast, under PoW, it was the complex computational machines that increased one's probability of transaction verification, leading to high energy consumption.

The topic concerning the capacities of the crypto market to play a significant role in the development process, which has been addressed in this section, holds key importance and must be taken seriously. This is closely related to the very nascent nature of this market. The realization of many of these competitive capacities, which possess considerable potential to influence the economic development process, particularly through the elimination of numerous intermediaries within the current conventional economic environment, began in 2020.

The introduction of smart networks such as Solana and Binance, alongside the Ethereum smart network, which has faced and continues to face criticism regarding its processing speed and high fees, as discussed, has been effectively addressed by the Solana and Binance smart networks, offering high speed coupled with low fees for processes. This has facilitated the serious development of the industry and the potential to eliminate intermediaries not only within the current centralized financial system but also across various economic sectors and professional fields where intermediaries are involved.

On the other hand, for reasons discussed in Chap. 1, many central banks of major world economies have consciously and voluntarily refrained from embracing this industry and have not yet initiated formal coexistence with it. It is only in the current year, 2025, that the United States, under the leadership of President Trump, has formally begun laying the groundwork for this coexistence. Therefore, to fully realize the potential impact of this market on economic development, it will take at least another decade before the effects of this market can be realized and manifested in the real world. Nevertheless, since 2015, following the introduction of Ethereum, the market has attracted significant attention and has begun to draw part of money flow toward itself, with this influx intensifying since 2020 and especially in 2025. Thus, the current economic development effects of this market can be expected primarily through its influence on the money flows circulating among markets that are poised to play a role in economic development.

2.7 A Concise Distillation of the Discussions

Continuity in access to sufficient financial resources to achieve an adequate level of realized investments and economic growth is one of the prerequisites for achieving economic development. Therefore, the flow of money among various markets is of considerable importance. If this money flow is absorbed by financial intermediaries in the stock market and the banking network, or in the bond market, it can support R&D and other productive investments, provided there is no misallocation, leading to positive effects on the economic development process. In other words, flowing money into these markets may solve liquidity problems in the production sectors and facilitate the implementation of development projects.

Investment in the cryptocurrency market, if undertaken with a medium- to long-term perspective rather than speculative motives for short-term profits, can contribute to the development of the cryptocurrency industry and the possibility of eliminating intermediaries in the economy. This can accelerate the investment process, enable the implementation of development projects, significantly reduce costs, and save time. Entrepreneurship and the development of small businesses are among the sectors that can be notably influenced by the growth of the cryptocurrency industry. Similarly, investment in the gold market, if approached with a medium- to long-term view, can provide a suitable store of value for economies during periods of political, economic, and security instability, thereby reducing investment risk and increasing the economy's resilience against various shocks through backing.

Regarding the harmful environmental effects of gold and cryptocurrency mining, which undermine sustainable development, these impacts can be minimized through technological innovations, regulatory and supportive measures within companies and governments, and social responsibility. This is clearly evident in the cryptocurrency industry and its internal competition, which has, to some extent, contributed to improving this issue.

If price fluctuations in the targeted financial markets, national and major global currencies, bonds, stocks, gold, and cryptocurrencies are significant, the capital gains generated in these markets can increase speculative motives for profit-making. Consequently, the flow of money is attracted toward short-term speculative activities in these receptive markets instead of being allocated to development projects and investments with medium- and long-term perspectives. This not only negatively impacts investment and economic growth but, through the creation of artificial demand, can also lead to inflationary pressures that cause further volatility in inflation rates. Inflation rate volatility, in addition to increasing speculative incentives across various markets, negatively affects the purchasing power of wages, and thus impacts the motivation and productivity of the workforce and human capital, key factors in the R&D growth, which can adversely affect the economic development process.

As a result, considering the discussions presented in this chapter, the capacities of financial markets and the flow of money among them, given that each of them, alongside their advantages, may also pose challenges to development and its sustainability, can significantly influence the path to sustainable development.

2.8 A Brief Review of Empirical Studies

This section offers a brief review of recent empirical studies that examine the relationships between target markets and economic development discussed in this chapter. Integrating this empirical evidence with the theoretical framework underpinning this book can enhance the theoretical discussion and provide a richer perspective. Moreover, it helps readers grasp the underlying principles of how money flows between markets influence economic development, making these complex dynamics easier to understand.

Bonds and economic development: Given the capacities of the bond market in influencing economic development, as discussed in the theoretical literature of this chapter, the existence of a relationship between this market and economic development is expected in empirical studies: The relationship between bonds and inflation was addressed by Nneka et al. (2025), Bok et al. (2025), and Kamal et al. (2025); between bonds and economic growth by Petlele and Buthelezi (2025), Nguyen and Duong (2025), Liu et al. (2025), and Fang et al. (2025); between green bonds and sustainable development by Sadeghi et al. (2025), ElBannan and Löffler (2024), Zhang (2024), and Meng et al. (2024); expanding the role of bonds in financing by Equiza-Goñi (2023), and Lichtenberger et al. (2022).

Financial intermediaries and economic development: Taking into account the capacities of the banking sector and the stock market, particularly in financing and mobilizing financial resources, as previously discussed in the theoretical literature of this chapter, similar to the bond market, the relationship between these financial intermediaries and economic development can be expected in empirical studies: The relationship between financial intermediaries and inflation was addressed by Humpe et al. (2025), Thorbecke (2025), Ghossoub (2023), and Sadeghi et al. (2022); between financial intermediaries and economic growth by Farah et al. (2025), Nuta et al. (2025), Cisse et al. (2025), Zhang et al. (2025), and Meniago et al. (2025).

National currencies and economic development: Considering the theoretical literature that highlights the potential of the foreign exchange market in influencing both the nominal and real sectors of the economy, which was addressed in this chapter, especially regarding the economy's resilience to external and internal shocks and the attractiveness of the domestic economy in attracting both foreign and domestic investments, confirming the relationship between this market and economic development in empirical studies is not unexpected: The relationship between national currencies and inflation was addressed by Matsvai (2025), Iorngurum (2025), Lama et al. (2025), Iorngurum (2025), Sadeghi et al. (2024), and Beirne et al. (2024); between national currencies and economic growth: Sheykhi et al. (2025), Ridhwan et al. (2024), Doojav et al. (2024), Iqbal et al. (2023), Olamide et al. (2022), and Arthur and Addai (2022).

Gold and economic development: Regarding the potential of gold to play a key role in the path toward development, which was previously examined in the theoretical literature of this chapter—especially in providing a shield against inflation, depreciation of the national currency, external shocks, internal uncertainties, and environmental damages—one can expect the existence of a relationship between this market and economic development in empirical studies: The influence of gold on inflation was met by Ergül and Karakaş (2024), Valadkhani and O'Mahony (2024), Do et al. (2023), and Valadkhani et al. (2022); The influence of gold on the real sectors of the economy by Haroon and Hayyat (2025), Soltani and Abbes (2025), Mensah et al. (2025), Ngene et al. (2025), and Zhang et al. (2025); Connection between gold and environment damages by Gasparinnetti et al. (2024), Laker (2023), Meutia et al. (2023), and Ouoba (2023).

Cryptocurrencies and economic development: Considering the competitive capacities of the crypto market, as discussed in the theoretical literature of this chapter, the most significant of which include the elimination of various intermediaries in the current conventional economic structure, a store of value, a robust payment means with notable processing speed and low fees, a platform capable of processing smart contracts, and a decentralized financial system, one can anticipate a relationship between this market and economic development. A key point in this regard, which was also highlighted in this chapter, relates to the nascent nature of this market. Its serious development began around 2020, following the introduction of coins such as Solana and Binance and the maturation of their smart contract networks alongside Ethereum.

Therefore, in this short-term period—during which many central banks and major global economies have yet to fully embrace the industry, and an acceptable coexistence has not yet been established—it is unrealistic to expect the full realization of this industry's potential impacts on economic development in the real world. Hence, the influence of this market on economic development can only be anticipated through its effect on the flow of money among financial markets, which themselves hold significant potential to impact economic development. Accordingly, this section briefly refers to several empirical studies that have examined the relationship between this market and other financial markets, as well as addressed the competitive capacities of the crypto market potentially influencing the path toward economic development: Crypto's environmental damages by Bajra et al. (2024), Zribi et al. (2023), and Xiao et al. (2023); Bitcoin's serving a store of value by Majumder (2025) and Baur et al. (2024); Bitcoin's serving a hedge for inflation and for the risk of investing in other markets by Choi and Shin (2022) and Chemkha et al. (2021), respectively.

Connection between Bitcoin and stock markets by Wang et al. (2024), Bazán-Palomino (2023), as well as Ivanovski and Hailemariam (2023); between Bitcoin and gold by Čeryová and Árendáš (2025), Bouzguenda and Jarboui (2025), and Oosterlinck et al. (2023); between Bitcoin and major currencies by Pastpipatkul and Ko (2025), Aliu et al. (2024), Aliyev and Eylasov (2025), and Abid et al. (2023); between Bitcoin and bonds by Liu and Yuan (2024), Bouteska et al. (2024), and Lee et al. (2023).

References

Abid, I., Bouri, E., Galariotis, E., Guesmi, K., & Mzoughi, H. (2023). Bitcoin vs. fiat currencies: Insights from extreme dependence and risk spillover analysis with financial markets. *International Review of Financial Analysis, 90,* 102806.

Aliu, F., Asllani, A., & Hašková, S. (2024). The impact of bitcoin on gold, the volatility index (VIX), and dollar index (USDX): Analysis based on VAR, SVAR, and wavelet coherence. *Studies in Economics and Finance, 41*(1), 64–87.

Aliyev, F., & Eylasov, N. (2025). The impact of Nasdaq100, US dollar index and commodities on cryptocurrency: New evidence from Augmented ARDL approach. *Economics Letters,* 112191.

Arthur, B., & Addai, B. (2022). The dynamic interactions of economic growth, foreign direct investment, and exchange rates in Ghana. *Cogent Economics & Finance, 10*(1), 2148361.

Bajra, U. Q., Rogova, E., & Avdiaj, S. (2024). Cryptocurrency blockchain and its carbon footprint: Anticipating future challenges. *Technology in Society, 77,* Article 102571.

Barro, R. J. (1999). Notes on growth accounting. *Journal of Economic Growth, 4,* 119–137.

Baur, D. G., Karlsen, J. R., Smales, L. A., & Trench, A. (2024). Digging deeper-Is bitcoin digital gold? A mining perspective. *Journal of Commodity Markets, 34,* Article 100406.

Bazán-Palomino, W. (2023). The increased interest in Bitcoin and the immediate and long-term impact of Bitcoin volatility on global stock markets. *Economic Analysis and Policy, 80,* 1080–1095.

Beck, T., & Levine, R. (2004). Stock markets, banks, and growth: Panel evidence. *Journal of Banking & Finance, 28*(3), 423–442.

Beirne, J., Renzhi, N., & Panthi, P. (2024). Exchange rate pass-through in emerging Asia and exposure to external shocks. *Economic Analysis and Policy, 81,* 1608–1624.

Benczúr, P., Karagiannis, S., & Kvedaras, V. (2019). Finance and economic growth: Financing structure and non-linear impact. *Journal of Macroeconomics, 62,* Article 103048.

Bok, B., Mertens, T. M., & Williams, J. C. (2025). Macroeconomic drivers and the pricing of uncertainty, inflation, and bonds. *Journal of Financial Economics, 172,* Article 104130.

Bouteska, A., Hassan, M. K., Rashid, M., & Bilgin, M. H. (2024). The dynamics of bonds, commodities and bitcoin based on NARDL approach. *The Quarterly Review of Economics and Finance, 94,* 58–70.

Bouzguenda, M., & Jarboui, A. (2025). Quantile connectivity between cryptocurrency, commodities, gold and BRICS index: What is the best investment strategy? *Eurasian Economic Review, 15*(1), 125–161.

Čeryová, B., & Árendáš, P. (2025). Time-varying relationship and diversification between sin stocks, Bitcoin and gold. *International Review of Financial Analysis,* 104533.

Chemkha, R., BenSaïda, A., Ghorbel, A., & Tayachi, T. (2021). Hedge and safe haven properties during COVID-19: Evidence from Bitcoin and gold. *The Quarterly Review of Economics and Finance, 82,* 71–85.

Choi, S., & Shin, J. (2022). Bitcoin: An inflation hedge but not a safe haven. *Finance Research Letters, 46,* Article 102379.

Cisse, B. A., Teme, A., Keita, S., & Sönmez, Y. (2025). Macroeconomics dynamics: Exploring the impact of stock market development on economic growth in mali. *SN Business & Economics, 5*(3), 21.

Do, M. D., Tran, T. D., Nguyen, H. N., Le, N. M., & Ninh, D. H. (2023). Is gold an inflation hedge in Vietnam? A non-linear approach. *Cogent Economics & Finance, 11*(2), 2244857.

Doojav, G. O., Purevdorj, M., & Batjargal, A. (2024). The macroeconomic effects of exchange rate movements in a commodity-exporting developing economy. *International Economics, 177,* Article 100475.

ElBannan, M. A., & Löffler, G. (2024). How effectively do green bonds help the environment? *Journal of Banking & Finance, 158,* Article 107051.

Equiza-Goñi, J. (2023). Euro area inflation linked debt: An evaluation. *Economics Letters, 232,* Article 111363.

Ergül, Ö., & Karakaş, T. (2024). Analysis of the relationship of gold prices with inflation and bitcoin in the post-tapering period. *Borsa Istanbul Review, 24*(4), 797–805.

Fang, Y., Liu, Y., Yang, Y., Lucey, B., & Abedin, M. Z. (2025). How do Chinese urban investment bonds affect its economic resilience? Evidence from double machine learning. *Research in International Business and Finance, 74,* Article 102728.

Farah, A. A., Mohamed, M. A., Ali Farah, M., Yusuf, I. A., & Abdulle, M. S. (2025). Impact of Islamic banking on economic growth: A systematic review of SCOPUS-indexed studies (2009–2024). *Cogent Economics & Finance, 13*(1), 2490819.

Gasparinnetti, P., Bakker, L. B., Queiroz, J. M., & Vilela, T. (2024). Economic valuation of artisanal small-scale gold mining impacts: A framework for value transfer application. *Resources Policy, 88,* Article 104259.

Ghossoub, E. A. (2023). Economic growth, inflation, and banking sector competition. *Economic Modelling, 129,* Article 106528.

Greenbaum, I., Thakor, A. V., & Boot, A. W. (2019). *Contemporary financial intermediation.* Academic Press.

Haroon, M., & Hayyat, M. (2025). Assessing the dual impact of gold mining on local communities: Socio-economic benefits and environmental challenges. *Resources Policy, 103,* Article 105559.

Humpe, A., McMillan, D. G., & Schöttl, A. (2025). Macroeconomic determinants of the stock market: A comparative study of Anglosphere and BRICS. *Finance Research Letters, 75,* Article 106869.

Iorngurum, T. D. (2025). The exchange rate pass-through to domestic prices: A meta-analysis. *Journal of Economic Surveys, 39*(3), 1092–1124.

Iqbal, J., Mahmood, F., Nosheen, M., & Wohar, M. (2023). The asymmetric impact of exchange rate misalignment on economic growth of India: An application of Hodrick-Prescott filter technique. *Economic Analysis and Policy, 77,* 809–823.

Ivanovski, K., & Hailemariam, A. (2023). Forecasting the stock-cryptocurrency relationship: Evidence from a dynamic GAS model. *International Review of Economics & Finance, 86,* 97–111.

Kamal, E., Jalkh, N., & Bouri, E. (2025). Inflation expectations and the stock-bond nexus in the US: Hedging implications. *The European Journal of Finance, 31*(6), 671–695.

Laker, M. C. (2023). Environmental impacts of gold mining—with special reference to South Africa. *Mining, 3*(2), 205–220.

Lama, A., Budha, B. B., Prabhesh, K. P., & Rana, S. (2025). Exchange rate pass-through in Nepal. *Journal of Asian Economics, 97,* Article 101897.

Lee, C. C., Yu, C. H., & Zhang, J. (2023). Heterogeneous dependence among cryptocurrency, green bonds, and sustainable equity: New insights from Granger-causality in quantiles analysis. *International Review of Economics & Finance, 87,* 99–109.

Levine, R. (1992). Financial intermediary services and growth. *Journal of the Japanese and International Economies, 6*(4), 383–405.

Levine, R. (1997). Financial development and economic growth: Views and agenda. *Journal of Economic Literature, 35*(2), 688–726.

Lichtenberger, A., Braga, J. P., & Semmler, W. (2022). Green bonds for the transition to a low-carbon economy. *Econometrics, 10*(1), 11.

Liu, P., & Yuan, Y. (2024). Is Bitcoin a hedge or safe-haven asset during the period of turmoil? Evidence from the currency, bond and stock markets. *International Review of Financial Analysis, 96,* Article 103663.

Liu, Z., Zhang, J., Gu, R., Hu, Q., & He, S. (2025). Driving effects of US monetary policy and geopolitical risks on gold reserve share. *International Review of Financial Analysis,* 104391.

Majumder, S. B. (2025). Is cryptocurrency a new digital gold? Evidence from the macroeconomic shocks in selected emerging economies. *Journal of Economic Studies, 52*(1), 88–103.

Matsvai, S. (2025). Exchange Rates and Inflation Dynamics in multicurrency regimes: The case of Zimbabwe (2014 to 2024). *International Journal of Financial Studies, 13*(2), 93.

McKinnon, R. I. (2010). *Money and capital in economic development.* Brookings Institution Press.

Meng, J., Ye, Z., & Wang, Y. (2024). Financing and investing in sustainable infrastructure: A review and research agenda. *Sustainable Futures,* 100312.

Meniago, C., Mazorodze, B. T., & Mah, G. (2025). Linking financial development and economic growth: Do we have new evidence of the role of institutions in CFA countries? *Cogent Economics & Finance, 13*(1), 2460067.

Mensah, J., Amoah, J. O., & Nketsiah-Essoun, A. (2025, May). Effects of artisanal gold mining and routes towards sustainable development for a low-profile mining community in Ghana. In *Natural Resources Forum* (Vol. 49, No. 2, pp. 1584–1601). Blackwell Publishing Ltd.

Meutia, A. A., Bachriadi, D., & Gafur, N. A. (2023). Environment degradation, health threats, and legality at the artisanal small-scale gold mining sites in Indonesia. *International Journal of Environmental Research and Public Health, 20*(18), 6774.

Ngene, G. M., Mungai, A. N., & Hassan, M. K. (2025). Hedging with gold, correlation cycles and risk aversion: Evidence from global economic sectors. *International Journal of Finance & Economics.*

Nguyen, H. C., & Duong, H. K. (2025). An international empirical study of the impact of green bonds on sustainable development goals. *Review of Behavioral Finance, 17*(3), 499–523.

Nneka, U. J., Ngong, C. A., Ugoada, O. A., & Onwumere, J. U. J. (2025). Effect of bond market development on economic growth of selected developing countries. *Journal of Economic and Administrative Sciences, 41*(1), 132–148.

Nuta, A. C., Abban, O. J., Ayad, H., & Nuta, F. M. (2025). Role of financial development and inclusivity in moderating the environmental effects of human development. *Research in International Business and Finance, 73,* Article 102623.

Olamide, E., Ogujiuba, K., & Maredza, A. (2022). Exchange rate volatility, inflation and economic growth in developing countries: Panel data approach for SADC. *Economies, 10*(3), 67.

Oosterlinck, K., Reyns, A., & Szafarz, A. (2023). Gold, bitcoin, and portfolio diversification: Lessons from the Ukrainian war. *Resources Policy, 83,* Article 103710.

Ouoba, Y. (2023). Gold companies and local economic sustainability: The case of Kalsaka Mining SA in Burkina Faso. *Journal of Environmental Economics and Policy, 12*(1), 79–95.

Pastpipatkul, P., & Ko, H. (2025). Is Bitcoin a safe-haven asset during US presidential transitions? A time-varying analysis of asset correlations. *International Journal of Financial Studies, 13*(3), 134.

Petlele, O., & Buthelezi, E. M. (2025). Shocks of government bonds and yield impact economic growth in South Africa. *Cogent Economics & Finance, 13*(1), 2448219.

Prescott, E. C. (2016). RBC methodology and the development of aggregate economic theory. *Handbook of Macroeconomics, 2,* 1759–1787.

Ramsey, F. P. (1928). A mathematical theory of saving. *The Economic Journal, 38*(152), 543–559.

Ridhwan, M. M., Ismail, A., & Nijkamp, P. (2024). The real exchange rate and economic growth: A meta-analysis. *Journal of Economic Studies, 51*(2), 287–318.

Romer, P. M. (1990). Endogenous technological change. *Journal of Political Economy, 98*(5), S71–S102.

Sadeghi, A., Marzban, H., Samadi, A. H., Azarbaiejani, K., & Rostamzadeh, P. (2022). Financial intermediaries and speculation in the foreign exchange market: The role of monetary policy in Iran's economy. *Journal of Economic Structures, 11*(1), 13.

Sadeghi, A., Marzban, H., Samadi, A. H., Azarbaiejani, K., & Rostamzadeh, P. (2024). Inflationary effects of the foreign currency shocks with different sources: The response of monetary policy in a developing economy. *Iranian Economic Review, 28*(3), 695–729.

Sadeghi, A., Roudari, S., & Nammouri, H. (2025). Green finance, fossil energy, and institutional factors in the context of sustainable development. *Social Sciences & Humanities Open, 12,* Article 101939.

Sadeghi, A., Tayebi, S. K., & Roudari, S. (2023). Financial markets, inflation and growth: The impact of monetary policy under different political structures. *Journal of Policy Modeling, 45*(5), 935–956.

Schumpeter, J. (1954). *History of Economic Analysis.* Oxford University Press.

Sheykhi, A., Taleblou, R., & Mohajeri, P. (2025). The impact of exchange rate volatility on economic growth: A meta-analysis approach. *Journal of Economic Studies.*

Singleton, K. (1987, March). Speculation and the volatility of foreign currency exchange rates. In *Carnegie-Rochester Conference Series on Public Policy* (Vol. 26, pp. 9–56). North-Holland.
Solow, R. M. (1956). A contribution to the theory of economic growth. *The Quarterly Journal of Economics, 70*(1), 65–94.
Soltani, H., & Abbes, M. B. (2025). Regime-specific spillover effects between financial stress, GCC stock markets, Brent crude oil, and the gold market. *Journal of the Knowledge Economy, 16*(2), 8840–8866.
Thorbecke, W. (2025). The impact of inflation on the US stock market after the COVID-19 pandemic. *International Journal of Financial Studies, 13*(1), 9.
Valadkhani, A., & O'Mahony, B. (2024). Dynamic hedging responses of gold and silver to inflation: A Markov regime-switching VAR analysis. *International Review of Economics & Finance, 96,* Article 103741.
Valadkhani, A., Nguyen, J., & Chiah, M. (2022). When is gold an effective hedge against inflation? *Resources Policy, 79,* Article 103009.
Walsh, C. E. (2010). *Monetary theory and policy.* MIT press.
Wang, G., Liu, C., Sbai, E., Sheng, M. S., Hu, J., & Tao, M. (2024). Interrelations between bitcoin market sentiment, crude oil, gold, and the stock market with bitcoin prices: Vision from the hedging market. *Studies in Economics and Finance, 41*(5), 1166–1190.
Xiao, Z., Cui, S., Xiang, L., Liu, P. J., & Zhang, H. (2023). The environmental cost of cryptocurrency: Assessing carbon emissions from bitcoin mining in China. *Journal of Digital Economy, 2,* 119–136.
Yuan, X., Su, C. W., & Peculea, A. D. (2022). Dynamic linkage of the bitcoin market and energy consumption: An analysis across time. *Energy Strategy Reviews, 44,* Article 100976.
Zhang, F., Ma, Y., Liu, X., & Zhou, X. (2025). Revisiting the hedging and safe haven roles of gold: Evidence from quantile-on-quantile approach. *The North American Journal of Economics and Finance,* 102516.
Zhang, Y. (2024). Role of green finance, green bonds, public private partnership, and technology innovation in carbon neutrality and sustainable development. *Heliyon, 10*(18).
Zribi, W., Boufateh, T., & Guesmi, K. (2023). Climate uncertainty effects on bitcoin ecological footprint through cryptocurrency environmental attention. *Finance Research Letters, 58,* Article 104584.

Chapter 3
Monetary Policy and Financial Markets

3.1 Introduction

Based on the literature discussed in Chap. 1, national and major global currencies, gold, stocks, bank deposits, bonds, and cryptocurrencies can all serve as channels for absorbing liquidity. Given the advantages and risks associated with each of these markets, which differentiate them from one another, these markets can act as either substitutes or complements in attracting the flow of money.

According to the theoretical and empirical literature reviewed in Chap. 2, there may be a significant relationship between each of these markets and economic development. These relationships influence the flow of money between them, a process referred to in the financial development literature as financial resource mobility. This mobility plays a key role in enabling the essential prerequisite for economic development, namely continuous and adequate access to financial resources.

Beyond the unique attractions and risks of each market, another important factor influencing investor decisions regarding target markets, and thus the flow of money between them, is monetary policy. Central banks, through the monetary instruments at their disposal, can enhance or reduce the attractiveness and risks associated with each of these markets, thereby influencing money flows across markets.

Accordingly, this chapter separately examines the theoretical literature on the potential of interest rate-related monetary policies to influence the attractiveness and risks of the target markets previously discussed in Chap. 1. Particular attention is paid to the cryptocurrency market, given that these emerging markets are relatively new. As mentioned earlier, their potential began to attract significant global attention after 2015, and especially following 2020. Therefore, this chapter, like the previous ones, places relatively greater emphasis on these markets.

The comparative approach followed throughout the earlier chapters is also continued in this chapter. This is intended to provide readers with a clear and differentiated understanding of how each of these markets responds to monetary policy, thereby helping reduce potential miscalculations in selecting target markets

A. Sadeghi et al., *Financial Markets, Speculation, and Development*,
https://doi.org/10.1007/978-981-95-5895-7_3

for investment. As a complement to the theoretical discussion, a brief review of empirical studies examining the relationship between monetary policy and these markets is also provided. This review aims to enrich and clarify the theoretical content, consistent with the approach adopted in the preceding chapters.

3.2 Interest Rate Policy and Economic Development

In this section, we explore central banks' interest rate policies and their connection to economic development, placing significant emphasis on classical literature within this context. The main goal of this section is to make these topics understandable and to simplify their complexities, thereby facilitating the easy communication of concepts.

As discussed in Chap. 1, investment decisions form the core of economic growth theories. Moreover, financial development highlights the importance of mobilizing financial resources—a fundamental prerequisite for investment—as well as the influence of interest rate policies and financial markets in shaping this process. When it comes to investment decisions, motivations play a key role in these decisions and, subsequently, in the selection of the target market. Motives for lending and borrowing—key factors influencing household decisions on saving and investment—are closely tied to interest rates. Changes in these motives can redirect funds across different financial markets, thereby channeling money into various sectors of the economy. Financial resources mainly flow through bank loans and stock purchases, with interest rates impacting the attractiveness of the stock market and the housing sector. These dynamics will be explored in greater detail in the following sections of this chapter.

Interest rates have historically shaped lending and borrowing behavior, dating back to the medieval period. Several studies examining this extended historical context provide evidence for the importance of interest rates as an institutional monetary instrument, revealing a persistent historical trend. As Bell et al., (2009, 2017) note, political and religious restrictions on usury in early European societies constrained lending, investment, and economic growth. Prior to the academic formalization of monetary policy, interest rates were largely regulated by institutional and religious norms. Drawing on Weber's analysis, the removal of these prohibitions during the Renaissance is seen as a catalyst for Western economic development. Furthermore, other economies shaped by Jewish, Christian, or Islamic teachings were also subject to similar constraints, as discussed by Kaye (2024). Botticini (2000) further illustrates how Catholic doctrine restricted Christian communities' access to finance through bans on interest-based lending.

When we enter the realm of monetary policy, it functions within a framework of well-defined rules. These rules typically require central banks to set explicit inflation targets and use interest rates to keep inflation close to those targets. Such targets can be specified as an inflation range or as an average inflation rate over a given period. The Taylor Rule (Taylor, 1993) suggests that interest rates should respond to both inflation and real output, while later research (Taylor, 1999) emphasizes that the main challenge within this framework is determining the appropriate responses of interest rates to changes in inflation. Some perspectives argue that interest rates should respond more than one-for-one to inflation (i.e., $IRt = b\, INFt, b > 1$) to promote price stability and investment. Simple, rule-based approaches are often considered more effective (Taylor & Williams, 2010), with Wright (2002) and Clarida et al. (1998) advocating for an active central bank response to inflation.

Interest rate responses to inflation play a critical role in shaping lending and borrowing incentives, thereby influencing the provision of financial resources. Mishkin (1981) highlights interest rates as a central channel through which monetary policy impacts investment and broader macroeconomic outcomes, noting that persistently high real interest rates contributed to the Great Depression. When we shed light on how interest rates respond to inflation changes, we uncover a crucial monetary phenomenon that significantly affects investment decisions and the rationale behind target market selection—known in economic literature as monetary illusion. This occurs when individuals fail to fully account for inflation, resulting in a misperception between nominal and real interest rates.

In brief, monetary illusion can influence financing and the mobilization of financial resources through the following channels:

- Borrowing and lending motivations
- Household consumption behavior and decisions related to saving
- Miscalculation of the real value of assets and, consequently, the target market for investment

Money illusion is typically shaped by institutional structures, policymakers, governments, and how economic agents perceive the relationship between nominal interest rates and inflation. Individuals often focus on nominal rates without adequately accounting for inflation, a problem that becomes especially pronounced in high-inflation environments. To simplify this concept, let us provide some real-world examples—based on time series data from the central banks of Turkey and Argentina. Turkey's 47% nominal interest rate in 2000 seemed appealing, but with 55% inflation, the real rate was actually −8%. Let's consider Argentina, which experienced nominal interest rates as high as 1520%, while its inflation rate was close to 2300%. In such conditions, although nominal interest rates are high and seemingly attractive, real interest rates are annoyingly high negative, causing some grounds for miscalculation and thus for money illusion.

Besides financial literacy, factors like monetary policy credibility, interest rate stickiness—particularly upward, known in financial literature as interest rate repression—and price rigidity—often downward, aligning with government interests—also play important roles in creating money illusion. When central banks lack independence, governments can exploit money illusion by repressing nominal interest rates during inflation, aided by downward price rigidity. This enables short-term budget deficit financing through increased liquidity, inflation taxation, and reduced real debt burdens.

This is a phenomenon that has occurred and continues to occur in the real world. To better understand this issue, let us provide an example from the real world. Consider the economy of Iran, where a political structure sensitive to religious rules and dominant over the central bank has repressed nominal interest rates from rising, while at the same time, the general price level exhibits strong downward rigidity, resulting in a persistently upward inflation trend. For 2000–2023, the average nominal bank interest rate, at 16.1%, appears quite attractive in this developing country. However, when we take into account an average inflation rate close to 21.4%, the real interest rates become significantly negative, around −5.3% on average, which can lead to miscalculations in household decisions and economic behavior. These negative real interest rates help offset a significant portion of the government's budget deficit, effectively reducing the real value of debt, increasing money supply growth, inflation, and consequently, inflationary taxes.

However, governments' use of non-independent central banks undermines the credibility and reputation of monetary policy. In contrast, independent central banks implementing consistent inflation-targeting policies foster trust, enhancing the effectiveness of interest rates in influencing economic behavior. When a central bank actively and consistently addresses inflation through interest rate policies, it builds confidence, encouraging economic agents to base their decisions on the central bank's announced nominal rates.

3.3 Interest Rate Policy and National Currency

The importance of the foreign currency market in economic development and its strengths and weaknesses in attracting the flow of money were discussed in Chaps. 2 and 1, respectively. In this section, we focus on its relationship with central bank interest rate policies.

The monetary policy instrument of the interest rate can influence the foreign exchange market through various channels:

- Supply of and demand for national and foreign currencies, influenced by the domestic economy's appeal to foreign investors.
- Sensitivity of investment and economic growth as the backing of the national currency's value, mediated by the influence of interest rates on financial provision and borrowing cost.
- Motives for lending and borrowing, and thus the volume of liquidity, which affect the supply of and demand for money.
- Appeal of alternative markets to investors.
- Opportunity costs of holding cash.
- Consumer purchasing power, influenced by the volume of liquidity and inflation, affects the demand for cash.
- Sensitivity of net exports to monetary policy conditions, originating from liquidity conditions in the consumption, production, and service sectors.

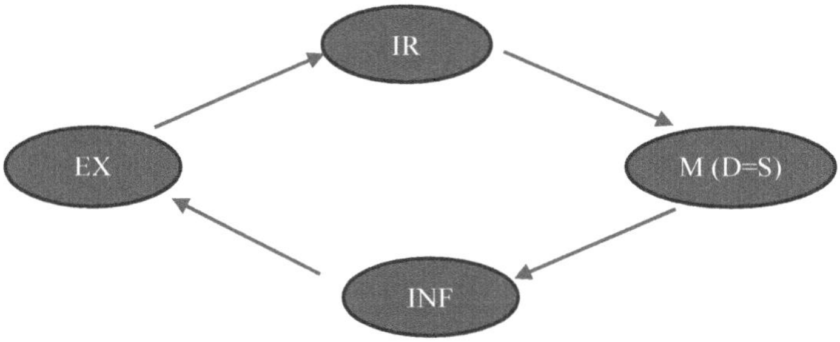

Fig. 3.1 Cyclic interactions among interest rates, liquidity volume, inflation, and exchange rates. (*Note*: IR, M, D, S, INF, and EX represent interest rates, liquidity volume, money demand, money supply, inflation, and foreign exchange rates, respectively. Interest rate policies influence borrowing and lending motivations, as well as money supply and demand, thereby affecting liquidity volume. Changes in liquidity volume subsequently impact inflation and exchange rates. Fluctuations in inflation and the value of national currencies trigger reactions from central banks, leading to adjustments in interest rates. As a result, changes in interest rates set off a chain reaction and cyclical interactions described above, ultimately forming a vicious cycle)

Given the above, interest rates have significant potential to influence the foreign exchange market and its fluctuations. For example, if central banks implement an expansionary monetary policy, i.e., interest rate cuts, the tendency of economic agents to get bank loans increases. This can lead to a larger injection of money into the economy, resulting in liquidity growth. Increased liquidity, in turn, drives higher inflation rates. Consequently, the value of the national currency decreases, causing the exchange rate to rise. Furthermore, lower interest rates combined with higher inflation can reduce investment returns in the domestic economy, making it less attractive to foreign investors. This decline in attractiveness reduces demand for the national currency, further depreciating its value. Therefore, as shown in Fig. 3.1, the interactions between interest rates, liquidity volume, inflation, and exchange rates can create a vicious cycle, potentially leading to economic instability and volatility in the foreign exchange market (Fig. 3.1).

On the other hand, the supply of and demand for national currencies are also influenced by changes in the condition of parallel markets after interest rate cuts or hikes. For example, an increase in liquidity and inflation rates resulting from a cut in interest rates may increase the attractiveness of investing in parallel markets such as gold, stock, crypto, and major currencies. This could reduce the motivation to hold the national currency and lead to an increase in the exchange rate due to the money supply growth. Let us consider a real-world example. After the outbreak of COVID-19 and the sudden shutdown of economic activities in 2020, accompanied by interest rate cuts to near-zero levels to support domestic economies, capital flows shifted away from stock markets, cryptocurrencies, and national currencies toward gold and major safe-haven currencies like the U.S. dollar. This shift in capital led to a significant decline in the value of national currencies across much of the globe.

Therefore, changes in interest rates can influence the appeal of holding both national currencies and major global currencies to be considered in investors' portfolios. Additionally, such interest rate changes may intensify the motivation to seek short-term gains through speculation in the foreign exchange market, potentially increasing volatility in this market.

As discussed, the interest rate plays a key role in enhancing the attractiveness of the domestic economy for foreign investors and, consequently, in increasing the demand for the national currency. Under the uncovered interest rate parity (UIP), the expected depreciation of a national currency is equal to the interest rate differential between two countries:

$$EX_{t+1} - EX_t = IRD_t - IRF_t \tag{3.1}$$

where EX is the logarithm of nominal exchange rates (domestic currency per unit of foreign currency), IRD is the domestic interest rate, and IRF is the foreign interest rate.

This relationship implies that interest rate hikes should appreciate the national currency, as higher rates attract foreign capital, increasing demand for the national currency. Conversely, lower interest rates may lead to capital outflows and currency depreciation.

3.4 Interest Rate Policy and Gold

Considering the literature in the first and second chapters, which respectively focused on the potentials and weaknesses of the gold market and its relationship with economic development, this section examines the impact of central bank interest rate policies on the gold market. This impact is analyzed through the following channels, presented in a case-by-case manner:

- Money supply and inflation
- Opportunity cost of holding gold
- Conditions of other markets

The appeal of gold, which arises from its immunity to rising inflation and political and economic instability, makes it highly sensitive to monetary policies that lead to changes in the money supply and, consequently, inflation rates. In other words, monetary policies target the money supply and inflation—the very factors that contribute to gold's attractiveness—resulting in gold being significantly impacted by these policies. Expansionary monetary policies, i.e., interest rate cuts, strengthen borrowing incentives while reducing lending incentives, which increases the money supply in the economy. The growth of the money supply leads to an increase in the general price level. In inflationary conditions, the appeal of gold increases due to its value-storing advantage, while the risk of holding national currencies and major currencies also rises, leading to a higher demand for gold.

Gold has always been recognized as a powerful and attractive alternative to major global currencies, particularly when central banks of major global economies such as the United States, the United Kingdom, and the European Union adopt expansionary monetary policies. In global financial markets, after the adoption of contractionary monetary policies, i.e., interest rate hikes, by the U.S. Federal Reserve or central banks of the United Kingdom and the EU, the demand for major global currencies such as the U.S. dollar, British pound, and euro grows significantly, while demand for gold sharply decreases. Therefore, in inflationary environments with high-inflation expectations, if central banks follow low interest rates, it can increase gold's appeal as an inflation hedge and a substitute for these major currencies.

To better understand this, let's consider a real-world example. After the severe contractionary monetary policies followed by the Eurozone, the United Kingdom, and the United States to manage high-inflation rates, which were caused by the liquidity injections into these economies during the COVID-19 recession in 2023, interest rates rose to 4%, 5.25%, and 5.5%, respectively. Expectations for expansionary monetary policies and interest rate cuts have been strengthened, and these expectations for lower interest rates from mid-2024 to the present have led to unprecedented demand for gold. As a result, its market value has approached a historic peak of $25 trillion in September 2025, while its market value in 2023 was around $15 trillion. Therefore, such clear real-world evidence shows that these theoretical discussions are not limited to academic literature but are experienced in the real world, aligning with the expectations formed from this theoretical literature.

Another point to consider regarding the impact of central bank interest rate policies on the gold market is the opportunity costs of holding gold and the effects that rival markets experience due to these policies. One weakness of gold, which reduces its attractiveness, especially in economies with high interest rates, is the lack of interest payments for gold holders, which raises the opportunity costs of holding gold in high interest environments compared to markets like bonds or bank deposits that offer interest. Furthermore, the influence that competing markets with strong potential, such as cryptocurrency, as discussed in the first chapter, which offer stronger capabilities in terms of payment methods, smart networks, and value storage compared to gold, experience from interest rate policies can affect the flow of money into the gold market and, consequently, influence the degree to which gold is impacted by these interest rate policies.

Another point to consider is that part of the demand for gold is not related to investment and its associated risks, but rather to ornamental and luxury consumption. Central bank interest rate policies can make these uses more costly for households or reduce their costs. Therefore, interest rate policies can also potentially affect this segment of the demand for gold.

3.5 Interest Rate Policy and Banking Sectors

The banking network is a part of the economy that is inherently most closely tied to the interest rate policies of central banks. As discussed in Chap. 2, due to its pivotal role in financing and the mobilization of financial resources, it can play a key role in economic development. The attractiveness of the banking network for investors relates to the conditions of deposits and loans, both of which are dependent on interest rates.

The appeal of depositing funds in the banking system largely depends on the interest rates applied to deposits. This becomes especially crucial during periods of inflation, as the real interest rates—adjusted for the effects of inflation on nominal rates—play a pivotal role in either attracting or deterring the flow of money into bank deposits. In essence, the relationship between nominal deposit interest rates and inflation rates dictates the real returns on deposits over time. As discussed earlier in this chapter, monetary policymakers in many economies aim to maintain a balance between nominal interest rates and inflation rates, ensuring that the gap between them remains narrow to align the motives for borrowing and lending. More specifically, nominal interest rates should rise greater than a one-to-one ratio with inflation rates, resulting in positive real interest rates on deposits.

However, in economies experiencing financial repression, where nominal interest rates cannot adjust proportionally to inflation, this balance is not achievable. This situation raises the investment risk in bank deposits for depositors, most of whom are risk-averse investors. Negative interest rates on deposits essentially act as an inflation tax on depositors, which reduces the appeal of bank deposits.

To make the discussion clearer and more understandable, let us consider a real-world example. One such example is the developing economy of Iran, where nominal interest rates have consistently been subject to repression, and there is no alignment between nominal interest rates and inflation rates. As a result, Iran's economy offers significant insight for researchers interested in examining the consequences of such an approach. The high volatility of inflation further enhances the appeal of studying the potential impacts of interest rate repression in Iran.

The Consumer Price Index (CPI) in Iran shows a consistently steep upward trend, with no year experiencing a decrease compared to the previous one, as shown in Table 3.1. Moreover, there is no clear alignment between inflation rates and the nominal interest rates on bank deposits and loans allocated to various sectors of the economy, indicating the passive stance of Iran's central bank interest rate policies in response to inflation fluctuations. Therefore, the inflationary environment in Iran, coupled with the repressive approach leading to passive interest rate policies, has led to negative real interest rates. This, in turn, has diminished the appeal of bank deposits for investors. While removing financial repression and liberalizing interest rates could foster greater competition among banks to attract deposits, bringing more stability to the banking sector.

The years 2020 and 1995 mark key turning points in this interest rate repression. The highest inflation rates were recorded in 1995 and 2020, at 49% and 47%,

Table 3.1 Inflation rates and interest rates on banking loans and deposits in Iran

Year	IF	SH	LONG	BS	H	IN	AG
1992	20.7	6.5	9	18	16–12	13–11	9–6
1993	24.4	7.5	10	18	16–12	13	9
1994	22.9	8	11.5	24–18	16–12	18–16	16–12
1995	35.2	8	11.5	24–18	15	18–16	16–12
1996	49.4	8	14	25–22	16–15	19–17	16–13
1997	23.2	8	14	25–22	16–15	19–17	16–13
1998	17.3	8	14	25–22	16–15	19–17	16–13
1999	18.1	8	14	25–22	16–15	19–17	16–13
2000	20.1	8	14	25–22	16–15	19–17	16–13
2001	12.6	8	14	25–22	16–15	19–17	16–13
2002	11.4	7	13	23	16–15	18–16	15–14
2003	15.8	7	13	22	15–14	17–15	14–13
2004	15.6	7	13	21	15	16	5/13
2005	15.2	7	13	21	15	15	5/13
2006	10.4	7	13	16	15	16	16
2007	11.9	7	16–7	14	13	14	14
2008	18.4	7	16–7	12	11	12	12
2009	25.4	9	15	12	11	12	12
2010	10.8	9	5/14	12	11	12	12
2011	12.4	6	14	12–14	11–14	12–14	12–14
2012	21.5	15–7	17	14–15	11–15	14–15	14–15
2013	30.5	15–7	17	14–15	11–15	14–15	14–15
2014	34.7	20–7	-1721.5	14–15	11–15	14–15	14–15
2015	15.6	10–22	24–22	22	14–16	22	22
2016	11.9	18–10	20–18	20–21	14–16	20–21	20–21
2017	9	10	-1515.5	18	8–17.5	18	15–18
2018	9.6	10	15	18	8.17.5	18	15–18
2019	31.2	10	15	18	18–6	18	15–18
2020	41.2	10	15	18	18–6	18	15–18
2021	47.1	10	16	18	18–6	18	15–18
2022	21.3	10	16	18	18–6	18	15–18

Note: All data is presented in percentages and extracted from Iran's Central Bank. The abbreviations IF, SH, LONG, BS, H, IN, and AG represent, in order: inflation rate, interest rates on short-term and long-term deposits, interest rates on banking loans allocated to the sectors of services and trade, construction and residential housing, industry and mining, and agriculture.

respectively. While the inflation rate in 1995 saw a 100% increase compared to the previous two years, the nominal interest rates on short-term bank deposits remained unchanged, and the nominal interest rates on long-term deposits only increased by 2.5%. Between 2016 and 2020, inflation surged by nearly 400%, yet nominal interest rates on deposits did not change. This strange passivity of the central bank reflects the intensity of nominal interest rate repression in Iran's economy. As mentioned earlier, depositing funds in the banking sector has not been an attractive option for investors seeking to hedge against inflation and the risk of currency depreciation over time. According to Table 3.1, a similar situation has also been observed regarding bank loans allocated to various sectors of the Iranian economy.

If we consider the phenomenon of monetary illusion, which was discussed at the beginning of this chapter, we can see that the conditions for its emergence have been present in Iran's economy: nominal interest rates on bank deposits that appear attractive, but negative real interest rates that are discouraging, potentially leading to miscalculations by investors in such economic environments. Therefore, when discussing interest rates, it is important to give proper attention to the possibility of monetary illusion occurring. The interest rates announced by monetary policymakers are nominal rates, but what actually governs real economic transactions—deposits and loans—are real interest rates, which reflect the impact of inflation.

To further clarify this concept, let's consider the economies of Turkey and Norway, both developing and developed, where their central banks have pursued active interest rate policies in response to inflation. In fact, we aim to conduct a comparative analysis of these three economies to make the understanding of this concept clearer. Both Norway and Turkey have maintained interest rate policies where nominal rates exceed inflation by a considerable margin, reflecting more than a one-to-one ratio.

According to Fig. 3.2, the Norwegian Central Bank has generally favored positive real interest rates, demonstrating considerable activity in managing inflation. As shown in Fig. 3.2, nominal interest rates have been higher than inflation for most of the period under review, indicating the Central Bank's sensitivity to inflation and its efforts to maintain inflation within a restricted range of 1% to 4%. Norway has maintained relatively high nominal and real interest rates, averaging 2.8% and 2.2%, respectively, alongside a low average inflation rate of 0.6%. This level of responsiveness suggests a conservative stance by the Norwegian Central Bank toward inflation management.

Turning to Fig. 3.3, nominal interest rates in Iran have shown little to no response to inflation increases over this extended period—a phenomenon known in financial literature as interest rate repression. Iran has faced significantly negative real interest rates, averaging −5.3%, driven by a high average inflation rate of 21.4% and a lower nominal interest rate of 16.1%. Unlike Iran, the Turkish Central Bank has been relatively proactive in responding to inflation. According to Fig. 3.4, the Central Bank of Turkey has attempted to adjust nominal interest rates proportionally to changes in inflation. Consequently, the changes in inflation and nominal interest rates have remained closely aligned. Turkey's central bank has pursued high nominal (15.1%) and real (10.3%) interest rates, with an average inflation rate of 4.7%.

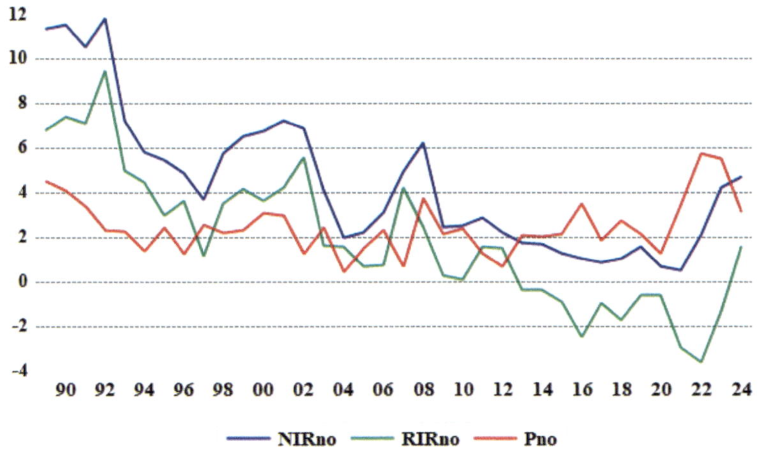

Fig. 3.2 Norway's inflation (Pno), nominal interest rates (NIRno), and real interest rates (RIRno) for 1989–2024. (*Note*: Inflation, nominal interest rates, and real interest rates are shown in red, blue, and green, respectively. Black horizontal lines mark distinct ranges of variation. The x-axis represents the time period, and the y-axis shows the rates as percentages)

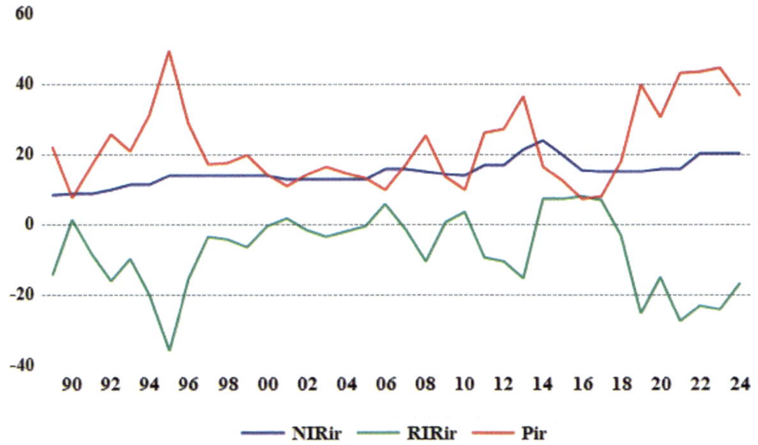

Fig. 3.3 Iran's inflation (Pir), nominal interest rates (NIRir), and real interest rates (RIRir) for 1989–2024. (*Note*: Inflation, nominal interest rates, and real interest rates are shown in red, blue, and green, respectively. Black horizontal lines mark distinct ranges of variation. The x-axis represents the time period, and the y-axis shows the rates as percentages)

It should be noted that since the flow of money toward bank deposits and the costs associated with accessing these funds are also influenced by the mismatch between nominal interest rates and inflation, stock markets and cryptocurrencies, both of which require continuous financial resources for activity development, will

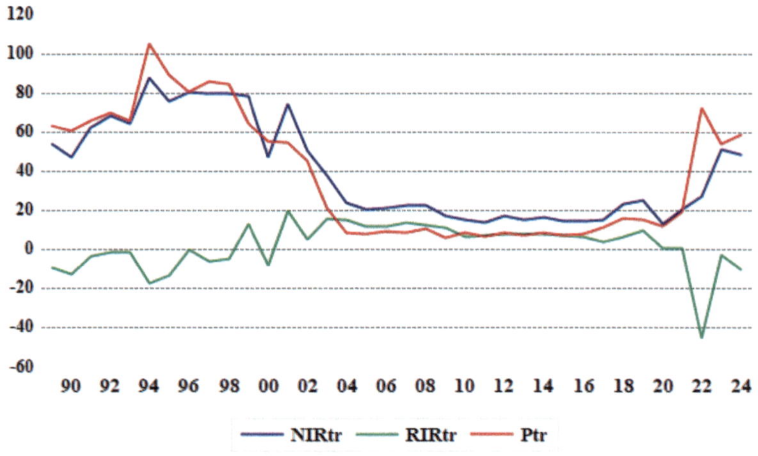

Fig. 3.4 Turkey's inflation (Ptr), nominal interest rates (NIRtr), and real interest rates (RIRtr) for 1989–2024. (*Note*: Inflation, nominal interest rates, and real interest rates are shown in red, blue, and green, respectively. Black horizontal lines mark distinct ranges of variation. The x-axis represents the time period, and the y-axis shows the rates as percentages)

also be affected. On the other hand, negative real interest rates, which result from the repression of nominal interest rates, reduce the incentives for lending and increase the incentives for borrowing. This can impact the liquidity volume and, in turn, affect national currency and gold markets. Additionally, the upward trend in inflation rates and the repression of nominal interest rates also diminish the attractiveness of bond yields.

The shorter time frame for Turkey is due to the limited availability of housing sector data. For Norway and Turkey, time series data were sourced from the European Commission (https://ec.europa.eu/eurostat), the Federal Reserve Bank of St. Louis (https://fred.stlouisfed.org), and the Organization for Economic Co-operation and Development (https://data.oecd.org, [OECD]). An exception is the housing sector in Turkey, for which data were obtained from the Central Bank of Turkey (https://tcmb.gov.tr). For Iran, we used time series data from the Iranian Central Bank (https://cbi.ir).

Furthermore, it is important to recognize that, like any other economic institution, the banking network aims to maximize profit. Therefore, the interest rate offered on investors' deposits should maintain a reasonable gap compared to the interest rate charged on loans to borrowers. In a conventional economy, the interest rates applied to bank loans are typically higher than those for deposits, often exceeding a one-to-one ratio, in order to generate profit margins for the banking network.

3.6 Interest Rate Policy and Stock Markets

The stock market, like the banking network, is another financial intermediary inherently linked to central bank interest rate policies, and the flow of money toward it can help maintain continuous access to the financial resources needed for development projects. This is because access to bank loans and the costs associated with this access play a decisive role in the liquidity conditions of companies and the realization of their investment plans. Therefore, the monetary policy instrument of interest rates, with the capacity to influence the performance of companies listed in the stock market and their profit outlook through financing and borrowing costs, can turn the central bank into a key player in driving the flow of money toward this market.

Interest rate changes affect investors' decisions regarding the allocation of risky assets and bank deposits in their asset portfolios. As interest rates rise, the attractiveness of depositing in the banking network increases for investors, and they may prefer bank deposits over risky assets, which strengthens the lending capacity of the banking network. Consequently, this leads to greater access for companies listed in the stock market to financial resources through bank loans, which could have a positive effect on the outlook of the stock market. However, interest rates can also have a dual effect on the growth of the stock market. Interest rate hikes raise the cost of financing for companies via bank loans, which negatively affects their performance and profit outlook. Therefore, the final impact of an interest rate hike on the stock market depends on whether the positive effects of greater access to bank loans outweigh the negative effects of higher borrowing costs.

Additionally, interest rate changes may impact investor preferences for bank deposits and shares of companies listed in the stock market, which in turn affects the real economy. For example, if the central bank cuts interest rates and the attractiveness of bank deposits declines for investors, while the appeal of investing in the stock market increases due to lower financing costs from bank loans, money flow probably shifts from bank deposits to stock markets. The impact of this shift in the flow of money from the banking network to the stock market on the real economy and the development process depends on whether the stock market can compensate for the reduced access to financing caused by the reduced lending capacity of banks due stemming from lower deposits.

Let's consider a real-world example for easier understanding. In 2020, as the global economies were widely affected by the COVID-19 pandemic, due to uncertainty in economic conditions, both the banking network and especially the stock market were significantly impacted. Stock market indices in the United States, the United Kingdom, the Eurozone, and the Pacific region faced declines of 30% to 50% on average. The Federal Reserve, the Bank of England, the European Central Bank, and the central banks of Australia and New Zealand followed strong expansionary monetary policies to support the economy and companies active in the stock market, which play a crucial role in boosting the real economy. These policies led to a significant reduction in nominal interest rates close to zero. It should be noted that the interest rate policies of these major economies also impact other global

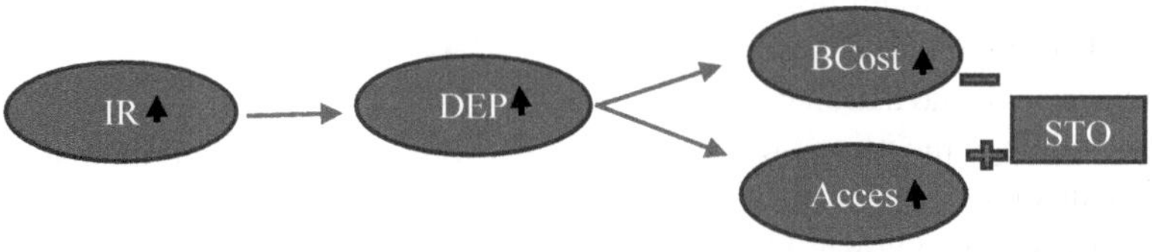

Fig. 3.5 Potential diverse impacts of interest rates on the stock market. (*Note*: IR, DEP, BCost, Access, and STO respectively represent the interest rate, funds attracted to bank deposits, borrowing costs from bank resources, access to bank loans, and the stock market. With a hike in interest rates, more funds are drawn into bank deposits. As a result, the level of access for companies listed in the stock market to bank financing increases, which has a positive effect on the stock market. On the other hand, borrowing costs from the banking system also rise, which imposes additional financial burdens on companies, leading to a negative impact on the stock market. Therefore, the net effect of hiking interest rates on the stock market is uncertain in advance; it depends on the balance between the positive effect of increased access to bank financing and the negative effect of higher borrowing costs)

economies due to the interconnectedness of the global economy. This drastic reduction in interest rates caused a significant flow of money into the stock market, which not only reversed the heavy downturns but also helped improve conditions in stock markets and sparked remarkable growth.

The realization of many productive projects pursued by companies in the stock market depends on continuous and steady access to financial resources. Therefore, as shown in Fig. 3.5, it is not possible to definitively determine the final impact of an interest rate hike on the stock market. The answer to the question of whether the level of access to financial resources is more important than the cost of accessing these resources can shed more light on how the performance and profitability of companies listed in the stock market are affected by hiking interest rates. However, it can be said that, initially, access to financial resources is what makes the realization of productive projects possible. In other words, as long as financial resources are not sufficiently accessible, the issue of the cost of accessing these resources will not arise.

Hence, low interest rates—particularly in economies experiencing inflationary environments—may not guarantee improved profitability prospects for companies. This is due to the potential decline in lending incentives and, consequently, insufficient deposit accumulation in the banking system, which reduces the banks' lending capacity. As such, interest rate cuts can only lead to a positive outlook for the stock market due to lower borrowing costs if companies maintain favorable and stable liquidity conditions.

3.7 Interest Rate Policy and Bond Markets

The bond market, as discussed in Chaps. 1 and 2, like the stock market and the banking network, is supported by governments and central banks due to its key role in financing productive investments and development projects. Similar to the stock market and the banking network, this market is inherently influenced by the interest rate policies of central banks.

The sensitivity of the bond market to central banks' interest rate policies occurs through the following channels, presented in a case-by-case manner:

- Inflation expectations and liquidity volume
- Economic outlook
- Proportion between inflation and interest rates—bond yields
- Competing markets
- Opportunity costs of holding assets that do not earn interest

The factor that attracts investors to this market is the real interest rate—i.e., the yield on bonds. Therefore, fluctuations in inflation rates and changes in interest rates play a decisive role in investors' decisions to purchase bonds. In other words, bonds are among the few markets where holders actually receive interest. Consequently, in economies with high interest rates and low inflation, where the opportunity costs of not holding bonds in the asset portfolio increase, bonds become significantly attractive.

Conversely, in economies where inflation rates are high and nominal interest rates tend to stick upward, investing in the bond market is not attractive to investors. To better illustrate this concept, let's consider an example from the real world. After the widespread outbreak of the COVID-19 virus and the negative shock to the global economy, as discussed, central banks in global economies adopted strong expansionary monetary policies to support their domestic economies and inject liquidity. This resulted in low interest rates and rising inflation rates. Subsequently, bond yields, i.e., the real interest rates on bonds, in major global economies fell, leading to a decrease in demand for bonds and a shift of money flow toward competing markets that are more attractive in inflationary environments with low interest rates, such as gold and cryptocurrencies.

However, when the economy is in a favorable state and close to full employment, central banks usually do not see a need to use expansionary monetary policies and instead use contractionary monetary policies to manage inflation. As a result, nominal interest rates rise and inflation declines, which increases bond yields. Therefore, under such conditions, the bond market becomes more attractive, leading investors to favor it more. Conversely, if the economic outlook is negative and a recession is expected, then expectations for expansionary monetary policies and lower interest rates increase, which reduces the attractiveness of buying bonds.

Next, let's look at this market from the perspective of governments. Selling bonds is one of the most important tools that governments use to finance themselves and cover budget deficits. According to the literature in Chap. 1, government financing through bonds entails a debt burden. Central banks' interest rate policies, along with the inflationary conditions of economies, can either decrease or increase the real value of these debts. If economic agents lead to expectations of expansionary monetary policies—lower interest rates—from the central bank, creating a positive trend in inflation expectations, the anticipated future reduction in the real value of the principal and interest on bonds can increase the motivation for governments to finance themselves by issuing bonds.

As discussed in Chap. 2, given the role of green bonds in sustainable development through supporting clean and renewable energies, which is one of the key pillars in the global community's macro-planning to prevent environmental and climate issues, the bond market has seen significant growth globally. In this context, the interest rates assigned to these bonds, along with the importance of environmental and climate issues for various societies and the quality of life for future generations, can further boost demand for this type of bond. However, some viewpoints believe that the development of green bonds can be accelerated by offering preferential interest rates that increase the appeal of these bonds.

3.8 Interest Rate Policy and Crypto Markets

To begin this section, let's get back shortly to the literature discussed in Chap. 1, where Bitcoin, with the highest market value among all cryptocurrencies and a limited and predefined supply ceiling, and Ethereum, the second-largest cryptocurrency by market value with its coin-burning mechanism, are both shown to exhibit low vulnerability in inflationary environments. In other words, similar to the gold market, Ethereum, and especially Bitcoin, can serve as effective stores of value for investors in times of inflation.

Therefore, considering that interest rate policies influence both liquidity volume and inflation, they also affect how attractive the cryptocurrency market appears to investors. Just like with gold, it is expected that liquidity growth and inflation, resulting from expansionary monetary policies (i.e., interest rate cuts) by central banks of major global economies, increase demand for Bitcoin and Ethereum, leading to price growth in these assets.

With this introduction, the channels that drive the cryptocurrency market's sensitivity can be listed in a case-by-case manner as follows:

- Inflation expectations and liquidity volume
- Opportunity costs of holding cryptocurrencies
- Conditions of competing markets
- Financing and borrowing costs

The crypto market is one of the markets where investors do not earn interest on their holdings. As a result, in economic environments characterized by low-inflation and high interest rates, the opportunity cost of holding cryptocurrencies rises, which in turn reduces the attractiveness of the market for investors.

In addition, high interest rates and low inflation increase the appeal of major global currencies, due to reduced liquidity, while diminishing the attractiveness of the crypto market. This could cause a shift in money flows from crypto assets to major currencies. As discussed earlier, unlike national currencies, which can be printed without limit and therefore become vulnerable in inflationary environments, Bitcoin's limited and predefined supply makes it more attractive in inflationary environments. Thus, since liquidity and inflation are influenced by central bank interest rate policies, the crypto market's sensitivity to these policies is inevitable.

To make this concept more concrete, consider the interest rate policies of central banks before and after the outbreak of the COVID-19 pandemic. The liquidity growth and inflation, triggered by the expansionary monetary policies adopted by central banks to combat the recession prior to 2022, strengthened expectations for contractionary policies—i.e., interest rate hikes—in 2022. This outlook, tied to lower inflation expectations, drove money flows away from markets whose appeal stems from their store-of-value function in inflationary conditions, namely gold and cryptocurrencies. This expectation of contractionary policies had an even stronger effect on the crypto industry, which relies heavily on liquidity for its growth. As a result, Bitcoin's price index declined by nearly 80% in 2022.

Interest rate changes also influence financing conditions and borrowing costs. This is particularly important for the cryptocurrency market compared to other markets, because being an emerging and relatively new industry, its development is highly dependent on financing for projects, innovations, and upgrades, especially given the intense intra-industry competition. Beyond financing, the costs of this financing also affect the performance outlook and returns of this emerging market.

Just like the stock market, the exact way in which the crypto market responds to interest rate policies cannot be stated with certainty. However, due to its emerging nature, the further development of this market critically depends on access to financial resources, as it faces significant costs, primarily in technology and skilled labor. Therefore, with rising interest rates and increased bank deposits, this access to resources may become possible, enabling the realization of many productive investments and development projects currently underway in the industry. At this point, improved access to financial resources may be more important to industry participants than the costs of that access.

3.9 A Concise Distillation of the Discussions

National and major global currencies, gold, stocks, bank deposits, bonds, and cryptocurrencies each possess certain advantages while also facing specific weaknesses. These strengths and weaknesses influence their attractiveness to investors and, consequently, affect the flow of money into or out of them.

These strengths and weaknesses are directly related to each market's sensitivity to inflation, lending and borrowing motivations, the degree of access to financial resources, as well as borrowing costs. Based on this, interest rate policies influence investor decisions about entering or exiting markets and therefore shape money flows between them by potentially affecting these strengths and weaknesses.

To sum up, central banks and their interest rate policy can impact the flow of money between different markets through the following channels:

- Inflation expectations and liquidity volume
- Opportunity costs of holding different assets
- Conditions of competing markets
- Financing and borrowing costs
- Real interest rates on bonds and bank deposits
- Labor costs and household purchasing power
- Financing and borrowing costs
- Lending and borrowing motivations

In light of the above channels, the relationship between interest rates and inflation becomes critically important, an emphasis found throughout monetary policy frameworks. Put differently, whether interest rate policies respond actively or passively to inflation fluctuations can significantly influence money flows between markets, which play a key role in driving economic development. Moreover, such dynamics can give rise to monetary illusion concerning interest rates, potentially distorting investor perceptions and affecting their choice of investment markets.

3.10 A Brief Review of Empirical Studies

This section offers a concise review of recent empirical studies examining money illusion and the relationships between interest rate policies and the target markets outlined in this chapter. By combining this empirical literature with the book's theoretical foundation, it provides a valuable complement to the theoretical discussion, enhancing the overall body of knowledge. Additionally, it helps readers grasp the underlying philosophy of how money flows between markets in response to interest rate policies, making these dynamics easier to understand.

Money illusion, i.e., decision-making based on nominal rather than real interest rates: This monetary phenomenon has been confirmed by several empirical studies, including those by Cochrane (2024), Sadeghi et al. (2023), Felici et al. (2023), and Tsai (2020).

Bonds and interest rates: Investors are drawn to this market primarily by the real interest rate, which reflects the yield on bonds. As a result, changes in inflation and interest rates potentially influence their decisions to buy bonds. Thus, it is expected that there is a significant relationship between interest rate policies and bonds. In some empirical studies, such as Akram and Uddin (2025), Ceballos et al. (2025), Granziera and Sihvonen (2024), and Hasan et al. (2024), this relationship was confirmed.

Stock markets and interest rates: The performance of companies listed in the stock market and their profit outlook potentially depends on financing and borrowing costs. Therefore, a connection between stock markets and interest rate policies is not unexpected. In some empirical studies, such as Parrondo and Sala (2025), Gordon and Lunsford (2024), Ballestra et al. (2024), and Lyu and Hu (2024), this connection was obtained.

Banking sectors and interest rates: The appeal of banking sectors considerably relies on the conditions of deposits and loans, both of which are tied to interest rates. Hence, we can expect a significant relationship between the banking sector and interest rate policies, as observed in some empirical studies such as Wang (2025), Chen et al. (2025), Ngaruiya et al. (2025), Kang et al. (2024), and Gunji (2024).

National currency markets and interest rates: Considering the dependence of the national currency's value on the volume of liquidity, inflation, macroeconomic conditions influenced by financing, as well as the attractiveness of the domestic economy for foreign investors, all of which have the potential to be affected by interest rates, a relationship between national currency markets and interest rate policies is not unexpected, as found in some empirical studies such as Ozgur and Aslan (2025), Rastogi et al. (2024), Ishii (2023), and Cepoi et al. (2023).

Gold and interest rates: Gold's appeal derives from its resilience to inflation. This makes it particularly sensitive to interest rate policies that affect money supply and inflation rates. Therefore, a significant relationship between gold and interest rate policies is not surprising, as supported by empirical studies such as Liu et al. (2025), Wang et al. (2024), Shaikh and Vallabh (2024), and Gu et al. (2023).

Cryptocurrencies and interest rates: Since the development of the emerging crypto market depends on financing, and both the opportunity costs of holding crypto assets and their value-storing advantage in inflationary environments with high liquidity are potentially influenced by interest rates, a relationship between this market and interest rate policies is therefore not unexpected, as evidenced by empirical studies such as Tian et al. (2025), Alam et al. (2024), Bhuiyan et al. (2025), Auzairy and Ibrahimy (2024), and Manickavasagam et al. (2025).

References

Akram, T., & Uddin, S. A. H. (2025). Chilean government bond yields: An econometric analysis. *Journal of Applied Economics, 28*(1), 2434918.

Alam, M. S., Amendola, A., Candila, V., & Jabarabadi, S. D. (2024). Is monetary policy a driver of cryptocurrencies? Evidence from a structural break GARCH-MIDAS approach. *Econometrics, 12*(1), 2.

Auzairy, N. A., & Ibrahimy, A. I. (2024). Monetary policy, COVID-19 and Bitcoin: The tales of 3 countries. *Springer Nature Singapore,* 105–115.

Ballestra, L. V., D'Innocenzo, E., & Guizzardi, A. (2024). A new bivariate approach for modeling the interaction between stock volatility and interest rate: An application to S&P500 returns and options. *European Journal of Operational Research, 314*(3), 1185–1194.

Bell, A. R., Brooks, C., & Moore, T. K. (2009). Interest in medieval accounts: Examples from England, 1272–1340. *History, 94*(316), 411–433.

Bell, A. R., Brooks, C., & Moore, T. K. (2017). Cambium non est mutuum: Exchange and interest rates in medieval Europe. *The Economic History Review, 70*(2), 373–396.

Bhuiyan, R. A., Chin, T. C., & Mukherjee, T. C. (2025). The Influence of Macro Policy Uncertainty on Blockchain Adoption, Crypto Economy, and Digital Asset Infrastructure. *Journal of the Knowledge Economy,* 1–41.

Botticini, M. (2000). A tale of "benevolent" governments: Private credit markets, public finance, and the role of Jewish lenders in Medieval and Renaissance Italy. *The Journal of Economic History, 60*(1), 164–189.

Ceballos, L., Christensen, J. H., & Romero, D. (2025). A post-pandemic new normal for interest rates in emerging bond markets? Evidence from Chile. *Journal of International Money and Finance, 150,* Article 103234.

Cepoi, C. O., Dumitrescu, B. A., Georgescu, G. C., Gherghina, R., & Iacob, M. (2023). Investigating the impact of monetary policy on foreign exchange market in Europe during COVID-19 pandemic. *Applied Economics Letters, 30*(8), 1139–1144.

Chen, W., Li, G., & Liu, J. (2025). The impact of interest rate liberalization on loan pricing efficiency: Theory and evidence. *International Review of Financial Analysis, 103,* Article 104207.

Clarida, R., Galı, J., & Gertler, M. (1998). Monetary policy rules in practice: Some international evidence. *European Economic Review, 42*(6), 1033–1067.

Cochrane, J. H. (2024). Expectations and the neutrality of interest rates. *Review of Economic Dynamics, 53,* 194–223.

Felici, M., Kenny, G., & Friz, R. (2023). Consumer savings behaviour at low and negative interest rates. *European Economic Review, 157,* Article 104503.

Gordon, M. V., & Lunsford, K. G. (2024). The effects of the Federal Reserve Chair's testimony on interest rates and stock prices. *Economics Letters, 235,* Article 111537.

Granziera, E., & Sihvonen, M. (2024). Bonds, currencies and expectational errors. *Journal of Economic Dynamics and Control, 158,* Article 104790.

Gu, C., Kurov, A., & Stan, R. (2023). Monetary policy and uncertainty resolution in commodity markets. *Finance Research Letters, 55,* Article 103907.

Gunji, H. (2024). Did the BOJ's negative interest rate policy increase bank lending? *The Japanese Economic Review,* 1–30.

Hasan, M. B., Rashid, M. M., Sarker, T., & Shafiullah, M. (2024). Exploring the determinants of green bond market development in Bangladesh. *Eurasian Economic Review,* 1–21.

Ishii, H. (2023). Yield curve shapes and foreign exchange rates: The term structure of interest rates model approach. *Applied Economics, 55*(38), 4402–4414.

Kang, K., Ashhari, Z. M., Yahya, M. H. D. H., Ni, S. W., & Li, Y. (2024). Interest rate liberalization and the stability of the Chinese banking system: Exploring chained mediation effects of deposit competitiveness and wealth management products. *Finance Research Letters,* 105222.

Kaye, J. (2024). Introduction to the Medieval and Renaissance Period. *In the Palgrave Handbook of Philosophy and Money: Ancient and Medieval Thought, 1,* 523–531.

Liu, Z., Zhang, J., Gu, R., Hu, Q., & He, S. (2025). Driving effects of US monetary policy and geopolitical risks on gold reserve share. *International Review of Financial Analysis,* 104391.

Lyu, X., & Hu, H. (2024). The dynamic impact of monetary policy on stock market liquidity. *Economic Analysis and Policy, 81,* 388–405.

Manickavasagam, J., Ayyalusamy, K., Bhaiyat, F., Jha, S., Jain, T., & Poddar, S. (2025). Bitcoin prices: Configurational effects of technological drivers, macroeconomic fundamentals and economic agents' expectation. *International Journal of Finance & Economics.*

Mishkin, F. S. (1981). The real interest rate: An empirical investigation. *In Carnegie-Rochester Conference Series on Public Policy, 15,* 151–200.

Ngaruiya, J., Obi, P., & Mathuva, D. (2025). Interest rate regulation and bank lending behaviour: Evidence from Kenya. *Journal of Financial Regulation and Compliance, 33*(3), 326–346.

Ozgur, O., & Aslan, M. (2025). Monetary policy stance and foreign currency lending: Evidence from a persistently dollarized emerging market. *Economic Change and Restructuring, 58*(4), 52.

Parrondo, L., & Sala, C. (2025). Connectedness between traditional finance, cryptocurrencies and DeFi in the post COVID period. *Finance Research Letters,* 106897.

Rastogi, S., Kanoujiya, J., & Doifode, A. (2024). Volatility integration of crude oil, gold, and interest rates on the exchange rate: DCC GARCH and BEKK GARCH applications. *Cogent Business & Management, 11*(1), 2289700.

Sadeghi, A., Tayebi, S. K., & Roudari, S. (2023). Financial markets, inflation and growth: The impact of monetary policy under different political structures. *Journal of Policy Modeling, 45*(5), 935–956.

Shaikh, I., & Vallabh, P. (2024). Impact of policy uncertainty on gold price in India: Evidence from multi commodity exchange (MCX) India and World Gold Council prices. *Applied Economics, 56*(32), 3837–3855.

Taylor, J. B. (1993). *Macroeconomic policy in a world economy: From econometric design to practical operation.* W.W. Norton.

Taylor, J. B. (1999). The robustness and efficiency of monetary policy rules as guidelines for interest rate setting by the European Central Bank. *Journal of Monetary Economics, 43*(3), 655–679.

Taylor, J. B., & Williams, J. C. (2010). Simple and robust rules for monetary policy. *In Handbook of Monetary Economics, 3,* 829–859.

Tian, L., Wu, H., & Xie, Q. (2025). The impact of FOMC announcements on cryptocurrency risk spillover across different market conditions. *Review of World Economics,* 1–35.

Tsai, I. C. (2020). Alternative explanation of the money illusion: The effect of unexpected low inflation. *International Review of Economics & Finance, 69,* 110–123.

Wang, M. C., Chang, T., Mikhaylov, A., & Linyu, J. (2024). A measure of quantile-on-quantile connectedness for the US treasury yield curve spread, the US Dollar, and gold price. *The North American Journal of Economics and Finance, 74,* Article 102232.

Wang, O. (2025). Banks, low interest rates, and monetary policy transmission. *The Journal of Finance, 80*(3), 1379–1416.

Wright, S. (2002). Monetary Policy, Nominal Interest Rates, and Long-Horizon Inflation Uncertainty. *Scottish Journal of Political Economy, 49*(1), 61–90.

Chapter 4
Empirical Appendix

4.1 Introduction

In this chapter, empirical appendices for each of Chaps. 1, 2, and 3 are provided using appropriate and distinct methods. Relying solely on theoretical literature without bringing it into the real world and providing appendices for empirical investigations, which makes understanding complex and multifaceted topics easier and more accessible, can lead to a lack of proper connection between readers and the presented concepts, sometimes even discouraging them from delving deeper into the topics. Therefore, an effort has been made to include supplements such as real-world examples and the empirical appendices provided in this chapter for the literature in Chaps. 1, 2, and 3.

In Chap. 1, we discussed that, given the attractions and risks of each financial market, the flow of money can be attracted to any of them. In this context, due to the importance of bonds and financial intermediaries—the stock market and the banking network—as they play a key role in providing the financial resources required by the real sectors of the economy, which are essential for economic growth and productive investment, the stability of these markets is reflected in the monetary policies of central banks and the supportive policies of governments. This can reduce investment risks in these markets and increase their attractiveness as target markets for investment.

Additionally, the stability of the foreign exchange market, considering its potential impact on both nominal and real sectors of the economy, holds considerable importance for governments and central banks, which is reflected in the inclusion of its stability in monetary policies. On the other hand, major global currencies, gold, and cryptocurrencies such as Bitcoin and Ethereum, which benefit from features like limited supply caps and coin-burning programs, have the potential to be accepted globally as means for payment and value storage, which increases their attractiveness

A. Sadeghi et al., *Financial Markets, Speculation, and Development*,
https://doi.org/10.1007/978-981-95-5895-7_4

to investors, thereby attracting money flows. Moreover, through comparative analyses, the potential of each of these markets for speculative motivations and short-term profits from price fluctuations was also examined.

Therefore, the first empirical appendix of this chapter is dedicated to the empirical investigation of the literature of Chap. 1—relationships among target markets—which identifies the possible flow of money among them.

In the literature of Chap. 2, we discussed that speculative motivations might attract or repel risk-lover and risk-averse investors from target markets. Limiting these motivations and directing the flow of money toward markets that have the potential to support productive investments has always been a challenging and key issue in economic development literature. To clarify the importance of money flow between markets for sustainable economic development, the relationships between each target market and economic development were examined. In other words, the capacity of target markets to influence economic development was separately discussed through comparative analyses. Therefore, the second empirical appendix of this chapter is dedicated to the empirical investigation of the literature of Chap. 2—links between target markets and indicators representing economic development.

In Chap. 3, we discussed that the flow of money between markets and the possible impact of such flows on the nominal and real sectors of the economy become more significant when central banks use interest rate policies, either actively or passively, to address fluctuations in inflation. In other words, the potential impacts of interest rate policies on the strengths and weaknesses of each target market, which could affect their risk or attractiveness and thus the flow of money between them, were also examined. Therefore, the third empirical appendix of this chapter is dedicated to the empirical investigation of the literature of Chap. 3—relationships between target markets and interest rate policies. Furthermore, this empirical appendix aims to explore the grounds for speculative motivations.

In the final section of this chapter, by aggregating the results from the empirical appendices for Chaps. 1, 2, and 3, an overview of the relationship between financial markets, monetary policies, and economic development is obtained. This makes understanding this relationship easier and clearer for readers, taking into account both the theoretical literature of Chaps. 1, 2, and 3, which was accompanied by real-world examples, and the empirical appendices created separately for each of them in this chapter. Therefore, in the final section of this chapter, by summarizing the results from the first to the third empirical appendices and establishing connections between them, the potential capacities of central banks and their interest rate policies in influencing the process of economic development through the channel of money flow between target markets are made comprehensively understandable.

We aim to briefly and concisely outline the framework and advantages of the models used, providing the necessary information to readers while staying focused on the empirical outcomes relevant to our discussions, without deviating from them.

Regarding the selection of target economies for the empirical investigations, an effort has been made to consider major global geographical regions, ensuring the generalizability of the results. Additionally, since the main strengths and weaknesses of gold and Bitcoin, stemming from their potentials as payment means and stores of value, may also be relevant to the currencies with the largest share in the global economy—the U.S. dollar, euro, pound, and yen—each of their conditions can influence the demand for the others. This has led us to select the economies of the United States, the United Kingdom, Japan, and Germany, which is the largest economy within the Eurozone, as case studies. Furthermore, the monetary policies and market conditions of these major global economies, considering the current open global economy, have the greatest impact on markets in other geographical regions. Their approach to emerging markets, particularly the crypto market under study, will play a significant role in the future of these markets.

4.2 Connections Between Financial Markets

As discussed in the literature of previous chapters, considering the advantages and weaknesses of target markets, including national and major global currencies, bonds, gold, stocks, bank deposits, and cryptocurrencies, the flow of money directed toward each of them can be influenced by the prevailing conditions in these markets. Therefore, it is essential to first examine the potential spillover effects between these markets and the degree of sensitivity each market has to the others. For this purpose, we employ Vector Autoregression models with time-varying parameters (TVP-VAR) and weekly time series data from March 2012 to December 2023. As previously mentioned, Bitcoin was introduced to global markets in 2009, but its price volatility began to intensify from 2012 onwards. Thus, the end of the first quarter of 2012 is selected as the starting point for the time period.

One of the key advantages of TVP-VAR models in relation to our objectives is their ability to effectively capture the sensitivity between markets. These models account for potential structural changes by allowing the coefficients of the vector autoregressive models to vary over time. Additionally, they enable the identification of how volatility is transmitted across markets over time. To achieve this, we employ the models developed by Antonakakis et al. (2020), which extend the frameworks of Diebold and Yilmaz (2012, 2014). As noted by Dai and Zhu (2022), these extended models offer the flexibility to adjust window sizes without losing observations. Antonakakis et al. (2020) argue that their model improves the dynamic connections derived from the original Diebold and Yilmaz models and provides a more accurate reflection of potential coefficient changes over time.

A TVP-VAR model is specified as follows:

$$Y_t = B_t Z_{t-1} + \varepsilon_t, \varepsilon_t | \text{INF}_{t-1} \sim N(0, £_t) \quad (4.1)$$

$$vec\,(B_t) = vec\,(B_{t-1}) + \eta_t, \eta_t \mid INF_{t-1} \sim N\,(0, \mathcal{J}_t) \quad (4.2)$$

Access to information up to time $t - 1$ is denoted by INF_{t-1}, while Z_{t-1} represents vectors of dimensions m × 1 and mp × 1. B_t is a matrix of dimension mp × 1, ε_t and η_t are vectors of dimensions m × 1 and $m^2p \times 1$. $£_t$ and $\int_t$ denote time-varying variance–covariance matrices. These matrices, along with time-varying coefficients, are employed to estimate connectedness within a network of variables, following the Diebold and Yilmaz (2014) framework based on Generalized Impulse Response Functions (GIRF) and Generalized Forecast Error Variance Decompositions (GFEVD) (Antonakakis et al., 2020). The application of the TVP-VAR model allows us to assess overall connectedness among network variables, pairwise connectedness between specific variables, and the transmission of effects from one variable to others within the network.

$$PDC_{ij,t}(H) = \frac{\sum_{t=1}^{H-1} \Psi_{ij,t}^2}{\sum_{j=1}^{m} \sum_{t=1}^{H-1} \Psi_{ij,t}^2} \tag{4.3}$$

Equation (4.3) illustrates the effect that variable i receives from variable j in a network, denoted as $\text{PDC}_{\text{ij,t}}$. $\Psi_{\text{ij,t}}^2$ represents the response of variable j to a shock in variable i. According to Eq. (4.4), subtracting the pairwise connectedness between variables reveals whether a variable dominates or is dominated by another:

$$net(PDC_{ij}(H)) = PDC_{ji,t}(H) - PDC_{ij,t}(H) \tag{4.4}$$

If the result of Eq. (4.4) is positive; it indicates that variable i dominates variable j within the network. The sensitivity of the network's variables to one another is further illustrated in Eqs. (4.5) and (4.6), respectively:

$$V_{i \to j,t}(H) = \frac{\sum_{j=1, i \neq j}^{m} PDC_{ji,t}(H)}{\sum_{j=1}^{m} PDC_{ji,t}(H)} * 100 \tag{4.5}$$

$$V_{i \leftarrow j,t}(H) = \frac{\sum_{j=1, i \neq j}^{m} PDC_{ij,t}(H)}{\sum_{i=1}^{m} PDC_{ij,t}(H)} * 100 \tag{4.6}$$

Subtracting Eq. (4.6) from Eq. (4.5) yields the net effect of variable i within the network, as defined by Eq. (4.7):

$$net(V_{i,t}) = V_{i \to j,t}(H) - V_{i \leftarrow j,t}(H) \tag{4.7}$$

According to Eq. (4.7), a positive result indicates that the influence of variable i on the network exceeds its sensitivity to the network.

4.2.1 *Empirical Results—TVP-VAR Models*

Given that weekly time series are used, which represent percentage changes, it is necessary to check for the presence of unit roots before estimating the TVP-VAR models. For this purpose, the Augmented Dickey-Fuller (ADF) test with a minimum t-statistic, which also accounts for potential structural breaks, is employed. According to Table 4.13, the null hypothesis indicating the presence of a unit root is rejected, confirming the stationarity of all the variables used. The results of the unit root test, to maintain coherence and focus more on the outputs related to the theoretical literature, are moved to the end of this chapter.

After making sure of the stationarity of the United States, Britain, the European Union, and Japan's time series, considering initial VAR estimations as well as Schwartz information criterion (SIC), two lags are set to run the TVP-VAR models. In addition, the window sizes are also determined based on the number of observations used for any of our case studies. Considering the information mentioned above, we separately estimate the TVP-VAR models for the United States, Britain, the European Union, and Japan, respectively.

4.2.1.1 The U.S. Financial Network

Initially, the estimation of TVP-VAR models is conducted for the United States network, which includes national currency, gold, bonds, stocks, bank deposits, and Bitcoin. Since the economies under study are developed, and market-based financing predominates over bank-based financing, the focus of the estimations is on the stock market. The only exception considered in this regard is the inclusion of bank deposits in the United States financial markets network.

As shown in Fig. 4.1, and as expected based on the literature of Chap. 1, there is a significant connection between the markets in the U.S. network. According to Fig. 4.2, gold and the U.S. dollar index exhibit the strongest connection within the network, while Bitcoin shows a very weak connection with both gold and the U.S. dollar index. As discussed in Chap. 1, the strengths and weaknesses of the U.S. dollar, gold, and Bitcoin are related, meaning the demand for one can impact the demand for the other. More specifically, the strengths and weaknesses derived from their potential as means of payment and stores of value contribute to the high sensitivity of these three markets to each other. The strong connection between gold and the U.S. dollar index is as expected and aligns with the literature from Chap. 1. However, their weak sensitivity to Bitcoin is not in line with the expectations set in Chap. 1, suggesting that Bitcoin's potential to challenge the demand for the U.S. dollar and gold has not yet materialized in the U.S. financial network. This can be attributed to the emerging nature of the crypto market, which makes it justifiable. As discussed in Chap. 1, serious attention to the crypto market has only occurred since 2020, following the development of Binance, Solana, and Ethereum smart networks, along with intra-industry competition to increase transaction speeds and reduce fees.

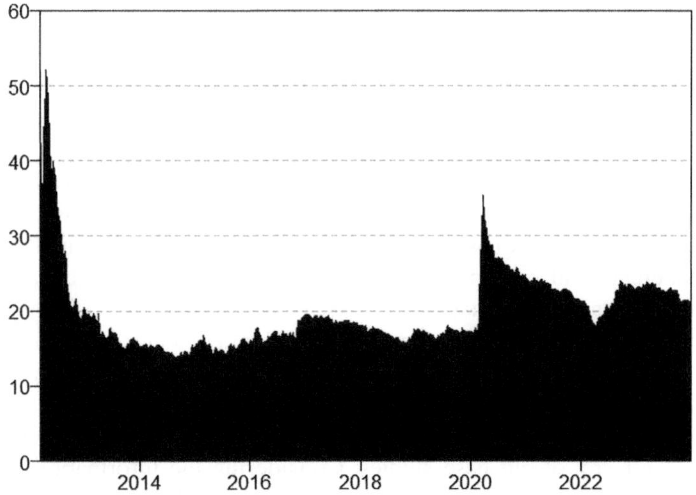

Fig. 4.1 Dynamic total connectedness within a U.S. network of six markets: Bitcoin (BTC), the U.S. dollar index, bank deposits, gold, the Nasdaq index, and U.S. bonds

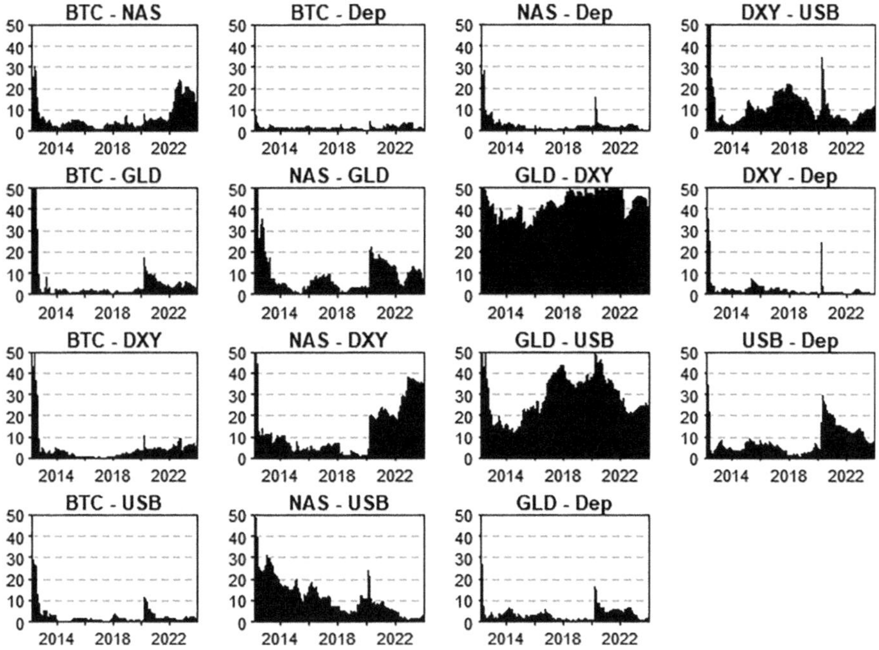

Fig. 4.2 Dynamic pairwise connectedness within a U.S. network of six markets: Bitcoin (BTC), the U.S. dollar index (DXY), bank deposits (Dep), gold, the Nasdaq index (NAS), and U.S. bonds (USB)

Figures 4.3 and 4.4 further clarify this point. As seen in these figures, unlike the U.S. dollar and gold, which exhibit the strongest influence in the U.S. financial network, Bitcoin's influence is much weaker. Another observation is that Bitcoin not only has weak influence within the network but also shows very low sensitivity. The low sensitivity of Bitcoin to gold, the U.S. dollar, and other markets in the network raises the question: where do Bitcoin's high fluctuations stem from? A potential explanation could be the weakness discussed in Chap. 1. As shown in Table 4.1, Bitcoin is most affected by its own fluctuations, with a sensitivity of 94%. The uneven distribution of Bitcoin, where a significant amount is controlled by a few individuals and institutions, leads to the creation of abundant supplies driven by the pursuit of short-term speculative profits, thereby weakening Bitcoin's role as a store of value.

In relation to markets that benefit from government and central bank support due to their role in financing—such as stock markets, bonds, and bank deposits—there are some interesting insights. The stock and bond markets' taking effects from the network is greater than their influence. Given that most of the companies active in the stock market are export-oriented, they are particularly sensitive to fluctuations in the U.S. dollar index. As shown in Fig. 4.5, the stock market shows greater sensitivity to fluctuations in the dollar index, acting more as a receiver of volatility than a transmitter. Gold, being a safe-haven asset, attracts mostly risk-averse investors,

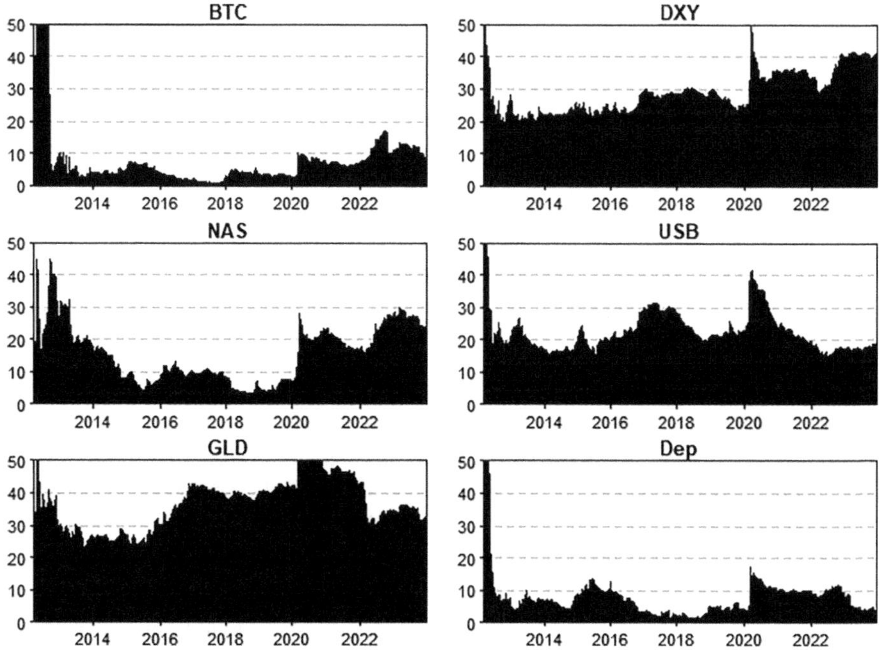

Fig. 4.3 Spillovers transmitted to the U.S. network by Bitcoin (BTC), the U.S. dollar index (DXY), bank deposits (Dep), gold, the Nasdaq index (NAS), and U.S. bonds (USB)

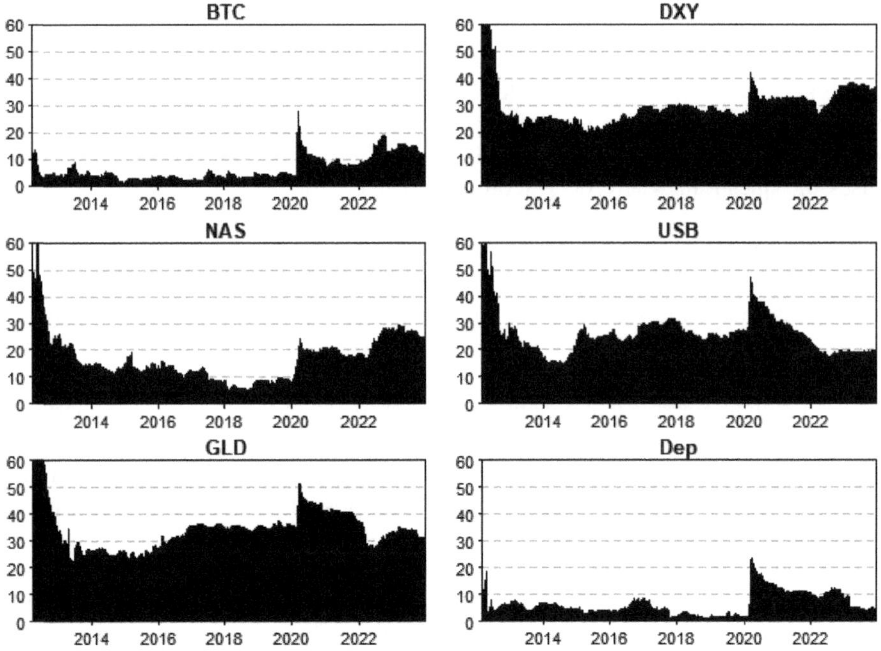

Fig. 4.4 Spillovers received from the U.S. network by Bitcoin (BTC), the U.S. dollar index (DXY), bank deposits (Dep), gold, the Nasdaq index (NAS), and U.S. bonds (USB)

Table 4.1 Spillover measures in a U.S. network of six markets

	BTC	NAS	GLD	DXY	USB	DEP	From
BTC	93.77	2.30	1.42	1.24	0.59	0.68	6.23
NAS	3.09	83.29	2.81	5.15	4.45	1.21	16.71
GLD	2.04	3.19	65.62	17.74	10.39	1.02	34.38
DXY	1.78	4.60	18.56	70.45	3.56	1.04	29.55
USB	1.17	4.67	12.25	4.24	74.33	3.34	25.67
DEP	0.61	0.60	1.36	0.55	3.17	93.70	6.30
TO	8.69	15.36	36.40	28.92	22.16	7.29	118.83
NET	2.46	−1.34	2.02	−0.62	−3.51	0.99	19.81

Note: Spillovers among the six markets, including BTC, the U.S. dollar index (DXY), bank deposits (DEP), gold, Nasdaq index (NAS), and the U.S. bonds (USB). Spillovers that each of these six markets receives from (columns) and transmits to (rows) one another

while, in contrast, the stock market is a riskier environment that tends to attract risk-tolerant investors. However, as shown in Fig. 4.2, the results do not indicate a strong connection between these two markets within the U.S. financial network. On the other hand, the relationship between the bond market and gold is quite notable. Bank

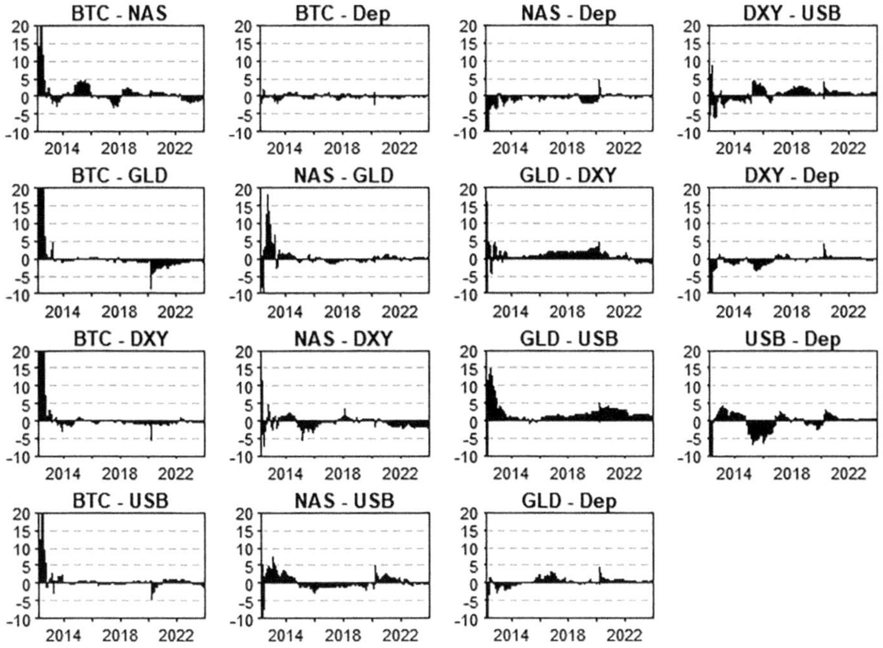

Fig. 4.5 Dynamic net pairwise connectedness within a U.S. network of six markets: Bitcoin (BTC), the U.S. dollar index (DXY), bank deposits (Dep), gold, the Nasdaq index (NAS), and U.S. bonds (USB)

deposits show a very weak connection with other markets in the financial network and are mostly influenced by their own fluctuations. Since financing in the United States is predominantly reliant on the market, as discussed in Chap. 2, the low sensitivity of bank deposits to other markets is not surprising. Another interesting finding is that Bitcoin is most sensitive to fluctuations in the stock market, while it shows the least sensitivity to the bond market.

In conclusion, we observed that strong relationships exist between markets in the U.S. financial network, which aligns with the literature from Chap. 1 and provides evidence supporting the flow of money between them.

4.2.1.2 The U.K. Financial Network

At this stage, similar to the U.S. financial network, we examine the connections between target markets in the U.K. financial network and compare the results with those of the U.S. financial network. As shown in Fig. 4.6, the connections between markets in the U.K. financial network are noteworthy.

There are strong similarities between the U.S. and U.K. financial networks. According to Fig. 4.8 and Table 4.2, similar to the U.S., the most influential markets in the U.K. financial network are gold and the national currency, the pound, while,

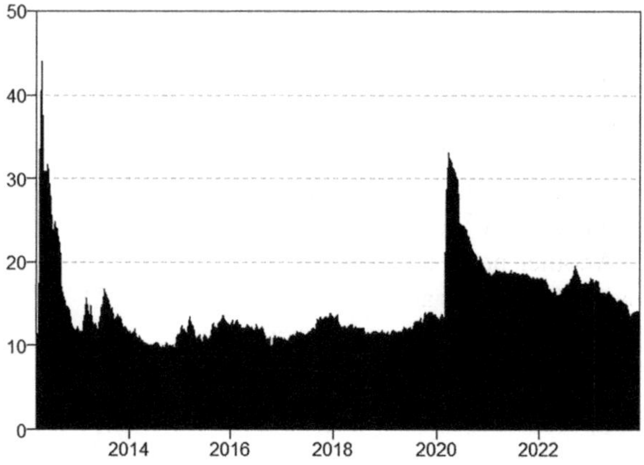

Fig. 4.6 Dynamic total connectedness within a British network of five markets: Bitcoin (BTC), the British pound, gold, the FTSE index, and U.K. bonds

as shown in Fig. 4.9, the network shows minimal sensitivity to Bitcoin fluctuations. Additionally, as seen in Fig. 4.7, the highest mutual sensitivity in the U.K. financial network is between the pound and gold, similar to the U.S. financial network, where the highest mutual sensitivity was observed between gold and the national currency, the U.S. dollar. Since the British pound, like the U.S. dollar, holds a significant share in global markets, the high sensitivity between the pound and gold was expected and in line with the literature from Chap. 1 and the competitive advantages of major global currencies and gold.

However, as shown clearly in Figs. 4.7 and 4.10, the weak connections between Bitcoin and gold, as well as between Bitcoin and the pound, are surprising—especially considering the similar weak correlations observed in the U.S. financial network between Bitcoin and the U.S. dollar, and between Bitcoin and gold. While such a result was unexpected, given the shared and differing competitive strengths and weaknesses of Bitcoin compared to gold and major currencies like the U.S. dollar

Table 4.2 Spillover measures in a U.K. network of five markets

	BTC	FTSE	GLD	GBP	UKB	From
BTC	94.31	2.38	1.10	1.17	1.04	5.69
FTSE	2.11	87.97	2.52	4.19	3.21	12.03
GLD	1.36	3.04	76.36	11.89	7.34	23.64
GBP	1.32	3.33	11.31	81.24	2.81	18.76
UKB	0.57	1.71	8.06	3.74	85.92	14.08
TO	5.37	10.45	22.99	20.99	14.41	74.20
NET	−0.32	−1.58	−0.65	2.22	0.32	14.84

Note: Spillovers among the five markets, including Bitcoin (BTC), the British pound (GBP), gold, the FTSE index, and U.K. bonds (UKB). Spillovers that each of these five markets receives from (columns) and transmits to (rows) one another

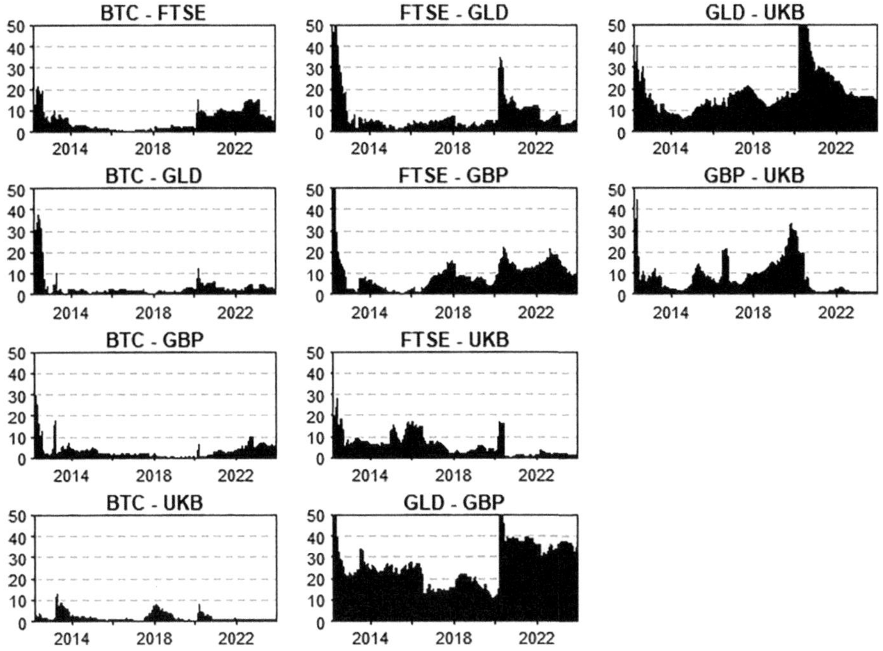

Fig. 4.7 Dynamic pairwise connectedness within a British network of five markets: Bitcoin (BTC), the British pound (GBP), gold, the FTSE index, and U.K. bonds (GBP)

and the British pound—stemming from their roles as means of payment and stores of value—the conditions of each can influence the demand for the others.

According to Table 4.2, another interesting similarity between the financial networks of the United Kingdom and the United States is that, contrary to expectations, Bitcoin shows the highest sensitivity to the stock market rather than to gold or national currencies in both networks. Additionally, Bitcoin shows the lowest sensitivity in both networks to fluctuations in the bond market. Another similarity observed in both financial networks is that Bitcoin shows the least sensitivity to the financial networks, being more influenced by its own fluctuations—about 94% in the U.S. financial network and 94.33% in the U.K. financial network. On the other hand, the greatest sensitivities of stock markets in both financial networks have been to fluctuations in the national currencies, the dollar and the pound. Given that the majority of companies active in the U.S. and U.K. stock markets are export-oriented, this was expected.

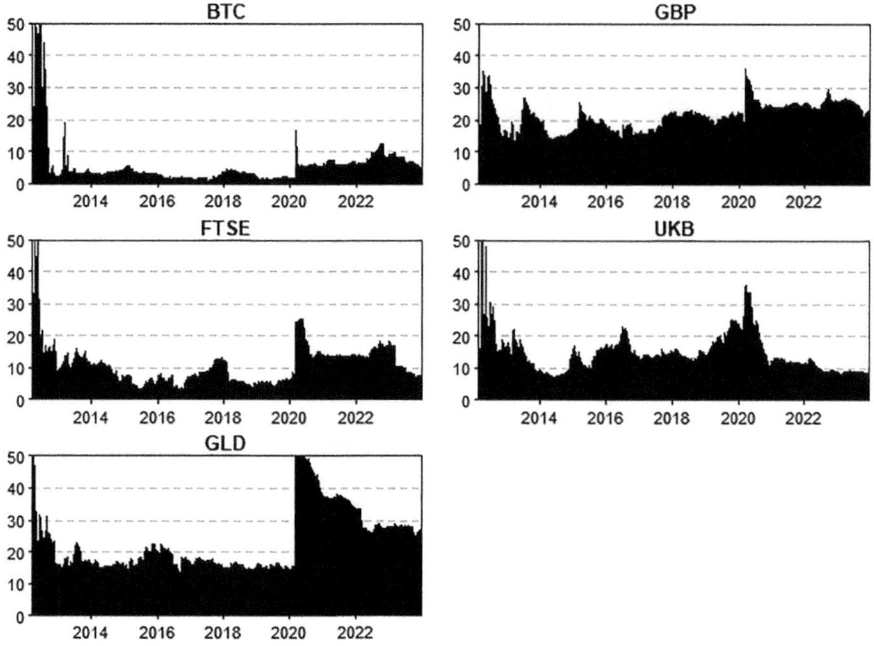

Fig. 4.8 Spillovers transmitted to the British network by Bitcoin (BTC), the British pound (GBP), gold, the FTSE index, and U.K. bonds (UKB)

4.2.1.3 The German Financial Network

Here, we turn to the German financial network as the representative of the European Union, which is its largest economy. This raises the question: Do strong connections between markets exist within Germany's financial network, similar to those observed in the financial networks of the United States and the United Kingdom? Is there a strong connection between the European currency and gold, and a weak connection between them and Bitcoin in the German financial network as well? Is the low sensitivity of the U.S. and U.K. financial networks to Bitcoin fluctuations and the limited influence of Bitcoin on those networks also confirmed in the German financial network? What about Bitcoin's high sensitivity to the stock market and its low sensitivity to the bond market?

In addition, we are interested in determining whether the highest sensitivity of the stock market within Germany's financial network, similar to that of the U.S. and U.K. financial networks, where it was most sensitive to the U.S. dollar and the British pound—will also be toward the euro.

According to Table 4.3 and Figs. 4.11, 4.12, 4.13, and 4.14, the answer to all the above questions regarding the German financial network is affirmative. In other words, all the similarities raised in the form of the above questions, which were observed in the financial networks of the U.S. and the U.K., are also evident in the

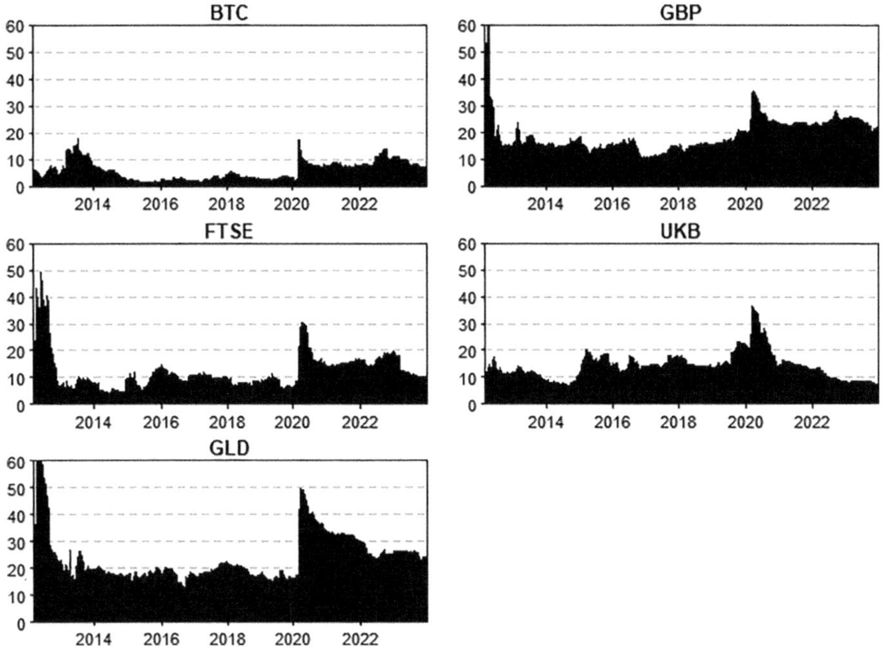

Fig. 4.9 Spillover received from the U.K. network by Bitcoin (BTC), the British pound (GBP), gold, the FTSE index, and U.K. bonds (UKB)

German financial network. Notably, Fig. 4.11 illustrates strong connections between markets within the German financial network, which aligns with the literature discussed in Chap. 1.

On the other hand, unlike the U.S. and U.K. financial networks, where after gold and their respective currencies, the U.S. dollar and British pound, the bond market had the highest sensitivity, the bond market plays a more prominent role in the German financial network. Specifically, the sensitivity of the financial network to the bond market is higher than that to gold and the euro, as indicated in Table 4.3 and Fig. 4.15. According to Fig. 4.15, the bond market has acted more as a transmitter of fluctuations to other markets rather than a receiver of fluctuations from them.

4.2.1.4 The Japanese Financial Network

The Japanese financial network is the last case study we examine at this stage. As mentioned at the beginning of this chapter, an effort has been made to consider the major global geographical regions in the empirical study. Moreover, since the strengths and weaknesses of gold and Bitcoin, stemming from their potential as payment means and stores of value, can also be relevant to the currencies with the largest shares in the global economy, the U.S. dollar, euro, pound, and yen, and since

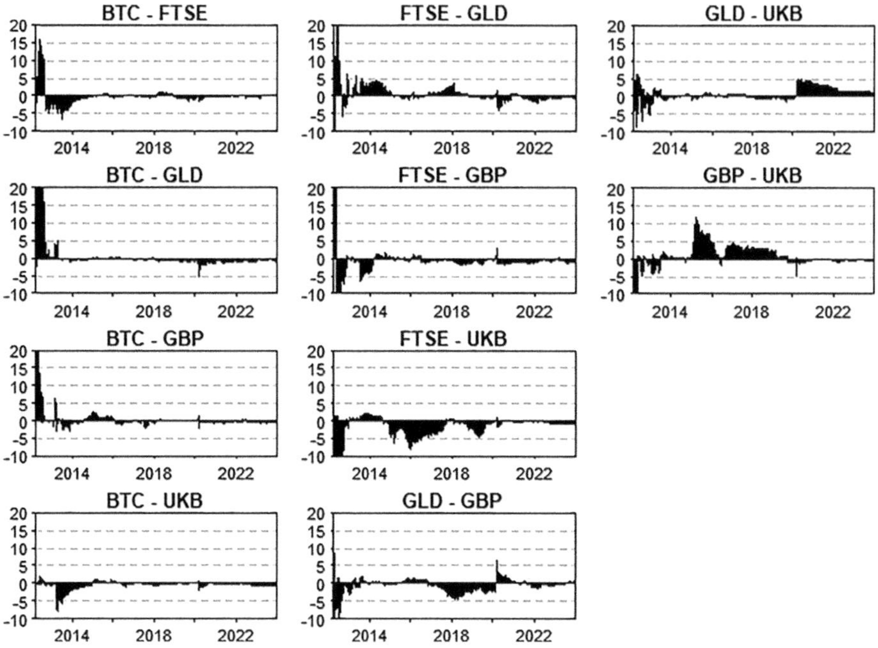

Fig. 4.10 Dynamic net pairwise connectedness within a British network of five markets: Bitcoin (BTC), the British pound (GBP), gold, the FTSE index, and U.K. bonds (UKB)

Table 4.3 Spillover measures in a German network of five markets

	BTC	DAX	GLD	EUR	GRB	From
BTC	95.13	2.36	1.20	0.86	0.46	4.87
DAX	2.61	84.19	2.98	6.21	4.01	15.81
GLD	1.09	2.87	78.53	13.68	3.83	21.47
EUR	1.08	4.95	11.96	68.24	13.77	31.76
GRB	0.12	0.38	0.15	0.55	98.80	1.20
TO	4.90	10.55	16.28	21.30	22.07	75.10
NET	0.03	−5.26	−5.19	−10.46	20.88	15.02

Note: Spillovers among the five markets, including Bitcoin (BTC), the Euro, gold, the DAX index, and German bonds (GRB). Spillovers that each of these five markets receives from (columns) and transmits to (rows) one another

the conditions of each can affect the demand for the others, we decided to analyze the financial networks of the United States, the United Kingdom, Japan, and Germany.

The questions raised and answered regarding Germany's financial network are also relevant to Japan's financial network. We seek to determine whether the similarities found in the financial networks of the United States, the United Kingdom, and Germany also appear in Japan's financial network. Considering Figs. 4.16, 4.17, 4.18,

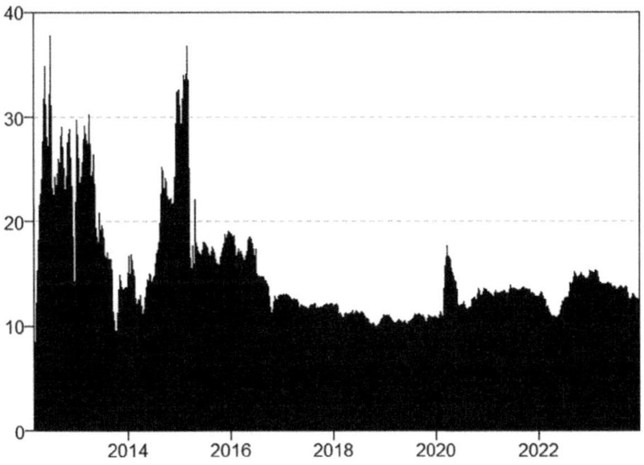

Fig. 4.11 Dynamic total connectedness within a German network of five markets: Bitcoin (BTC), the euro, gold, the DAX index, and German bonds

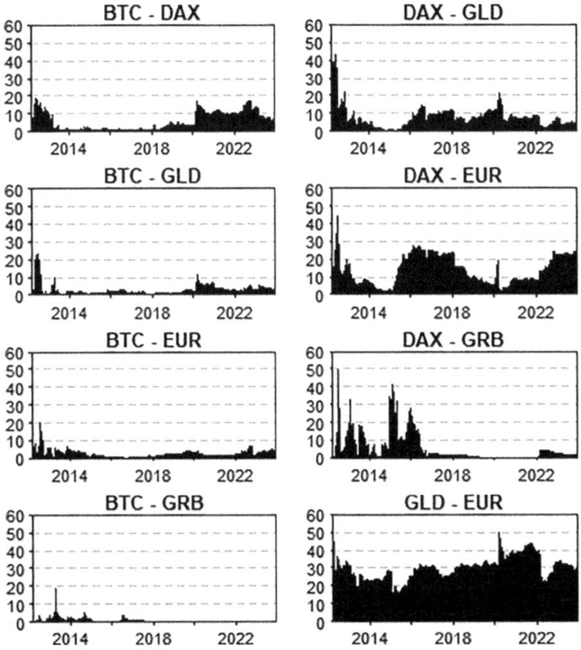

Fig. 4.12 Dynamic pairwise connectedness within a German network of five markets: Bitcoin (BTC), the euro, gold, the DAX index, and German bonds (GRB)

4.19, and 4.20 and Table 4.4, the answer is affirmative. According to Fig. 4.16, strong connections between markets persist over time within Japan's financial network, similar to those observed in the financial networks of the United States, the United Kingdom, and Germany.

Referring to Fig. 4.17, as with the financial networks of the United States, United Kingdom, and Germany, the greatest mutual sensitivity in Japan's financial network is

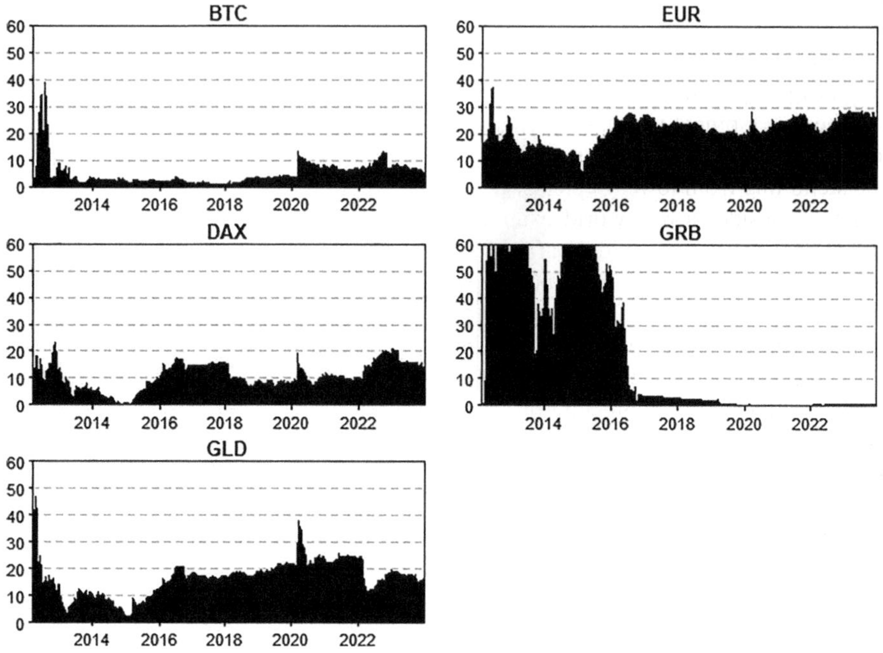

Fig. 4.13 Spillovers transmitted to the German network by Bitcoin (BTC), the euro, gold, the DAX index, and German bonds (GRB)

observed between the yen and gold, while their connection with Bitcoin remains very weak. One similarity between gold and the Japanese yen is that both are recognized as safe-haven assets in financial markets, and there are co-movements between them during times of global tension and instability.

According to Figs. 4.17 and 4.18 as well as Table 4.4, the Japanese financial network exhibits the lowest sensitivity to Bitcoin, and Bitcoin itself shows the least sensitivity to other markets within the financial network, with its volatility largely driven by its own movements. Similar to the financial networks in the United States, the United Kingdom, and Germany, Japan's stock market is most influenced by the yen. This similarity was not unexpected, as most companies active in the stock markets of these four countries are export-oriented. Like Germany's financial network, the highest sensitivity in Japan's financial network is to the bond market, followed by the yen and gold. Despite the strong influence of the bond market, the stock market in Japan is the greatest receiver of spillovers within the financial network. In other words, compared to the bond market, the yen, and gold, the stock market in Japan tends to receive more effects from these markets than it transmits to them, as shown in Fig. 4.20.

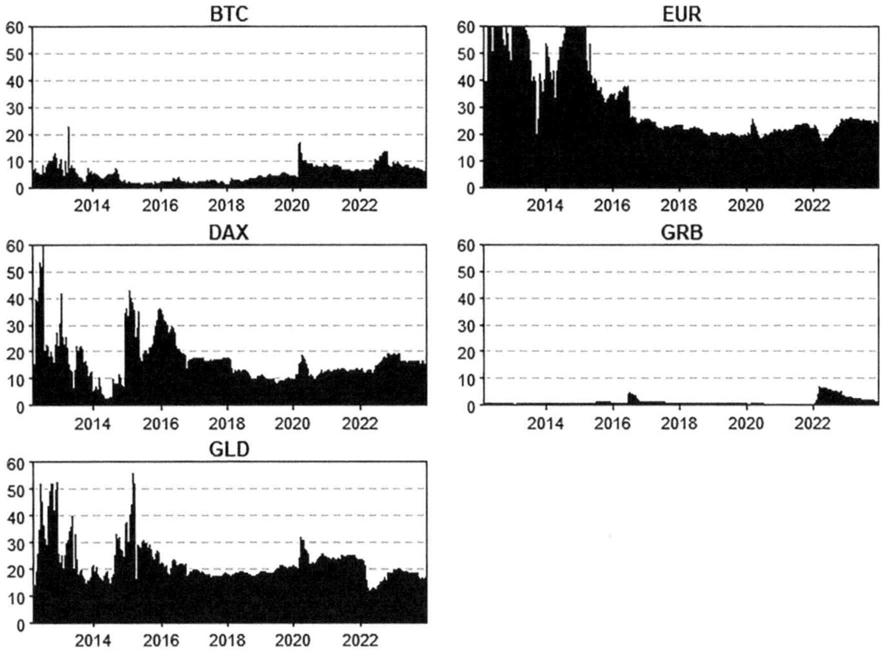

Fig. 4.14 Spillovers received from the German network by Bitcoin (BTC), the euro, gold, the DAX index, and German bonds (GRB)

4.2.1.5 Empirical Findings Summary

Considering the empirical results obtained for the economies of the United States, the United Kingdom, Germany, and Japan, we found supporting evidence for the theoretical literature reviewed in Chap. 1. The strengths and weaknesses of the target markets can position them as substitutes or complements to one another, thereby influencing money flows among them. Accordingly, connections between the target markets, reflected in the flow of money, are not merely academic constructs, but rather observable phenomena in real-world markets. This highlights a meaningful convergence between theoretical academic frameworks and actual market behavior.

Although connections between markets do exist, the intensity of these connections varies, as clearly observed in the empirical results. A key deviation from the theoretical expectations discussed in Chap. 1 pertains to the relatively low level of mutual sensitivity between Bitcoin and the other markets. Given the shared competitive advantages among Bitcoin, gold, and the major currencies—the U.S. dollar, British pound, euro, and Japanese yen—particularly in terms of their potential roles as payment means and stores of value, a higher degree of mutual sensitivity with Bitcoin was anticipated.

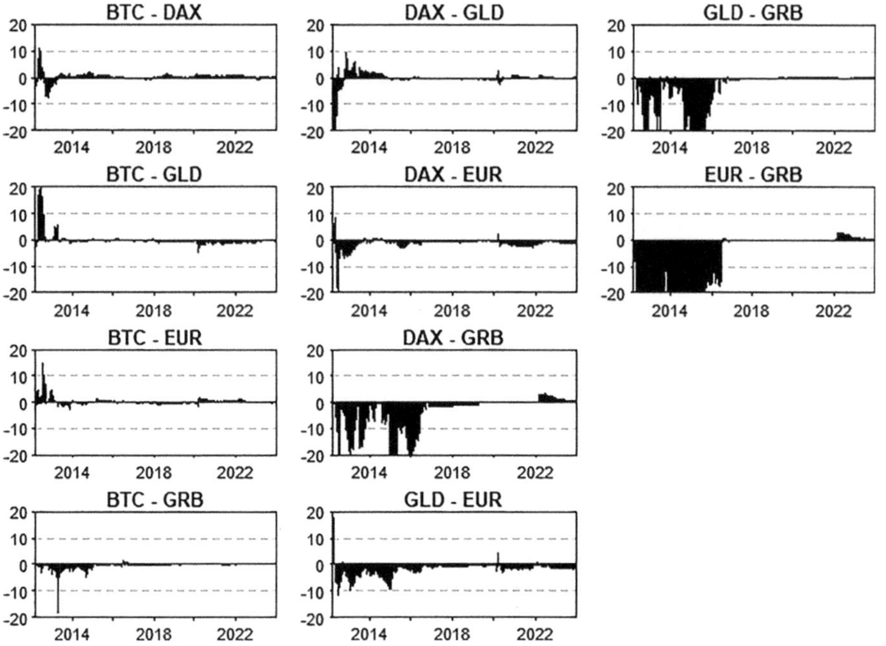

Fig. 4.15 Dynamic net pairwise connectedness within a German network of five markets: Bitcoin (BTC), the Euro, gold, the DAX index, and German bonds (GRB)

Fig. 4.16 Dynamic total connectedness within a Japanese network of five markets: Bitcoin (BTC), the yen, gold, the Nikkei index, and Japanese bonds (JPB)

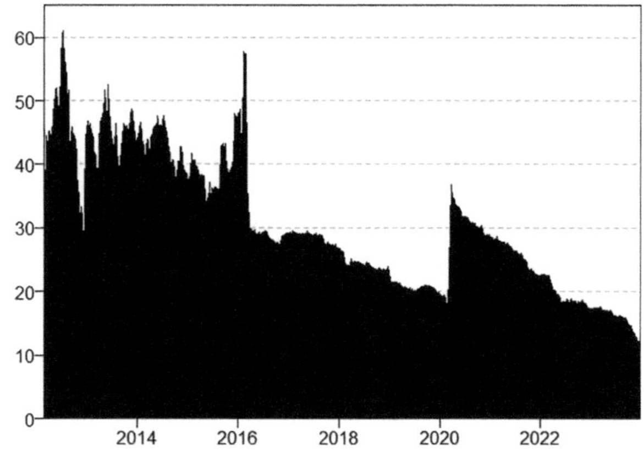

This expectation was also extended to Bitcoin's interaction with the stock market and the banking network. As discussed in Chap. 1, one of the most significant innovations associated with the crypto market is its potential to transform the current intermediary-based structure of conventional economies through the removal of various intermediaries from the economic environment. Although the results show

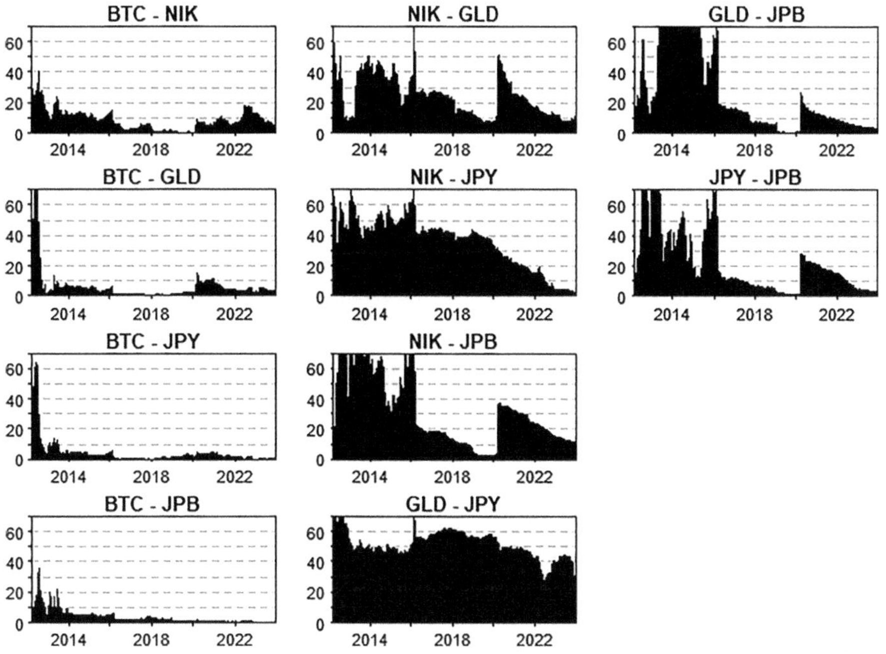

Fig. 4.17 Dynamic pairwise connectedness within a Japanese network of five markets: Bitcoin (BTC), the yen (JPY), gold, the Nikkei index (NIK), and Japanese bonds (JPB)

that Bitcoin exhibits more sensitivity to stock markets than to any other market, the degree of this sensitivity falls short of expectations.

One plausible explanation for this inconsistency is the emerging nature of the crypto market. While the official launch of Bitcoin dates back to 2009, the competitive innovations that distinguish this market have only started to emerge more clearly since 2020, and the market has experienced rapid development up until the present day (October 2025). Therefore, despite its competitive potential and its technological innovations, the crypto market may require more time to fully realize its capabilities and establish stronger interconnections with traditional financial market.

4.3 Speculation, Interest Rate Policy, and Financial Markets

After the empirical investigation of the connections among target markets within the financial networks of the United States, the United Kingdom, Germany, and Japan, based on the literature reviewed in Chap. 1, this section of the chapter aims to explore the grounds for speculative motivations, and potential relationships between the target

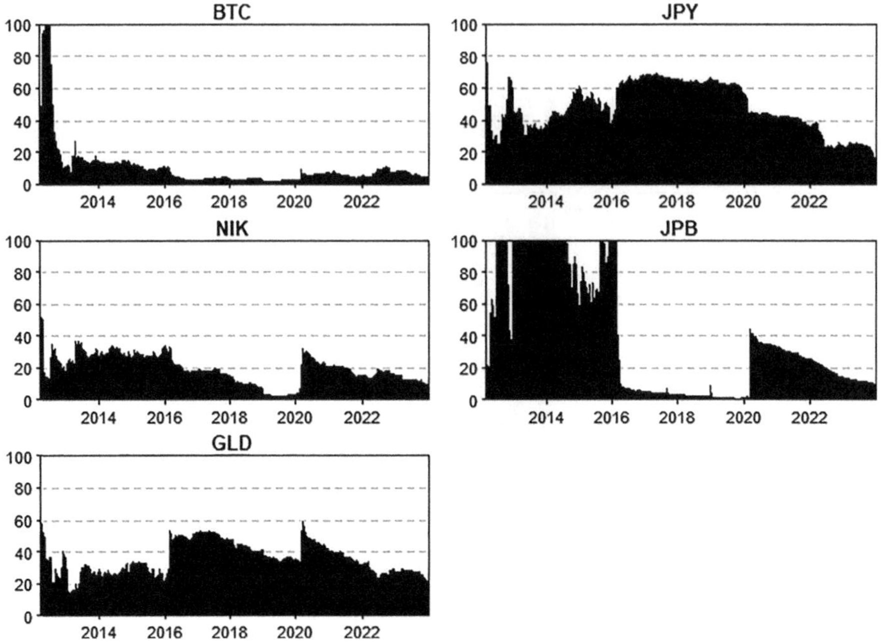

Fig. 4.18 Spillovers transmitted to the Japanese network by Bitcoin (BTC), the yen (JPY), gold, the Nikkei index (NIK), and Japanese bonds (JPB)

markets and interest rate policy within the financial networks of the aforementioned economies, grounded in the literature presented in Chap. 3.

To achieve this goal and simplify the understanding of these relationships, we begin by employing vector autoregression (VAR) models and conducting historical variance decomposition to examine the contribution of interest rates to the fluctuations in the target markets and to find out the degree of price volatility in each of them over time. The advantage of these findings is that they provide readers with a clear and accessible understanding of possible speculative motivations and the sensitivity of each target market to interest rate policies over an extended time period. The approach adopted in the previous section is continued here. The empirical analyses are carried out separately and sequentially for each market within the financial networks of the selected economies, enabling comparative analysis.

The specification of the VAR models, as mentioned, is aimed at identifying the share of interest rate policy in the historical fluctuations associated with each target market. In this context, a VAR model with P lags is specified as follows:

$$Y_t = C_0 + \sum_{i=1}^{P} C_i Y_{t-i} + \varepsilon_t, \quad t = 1, \ldots, T \tag{4.8}$$

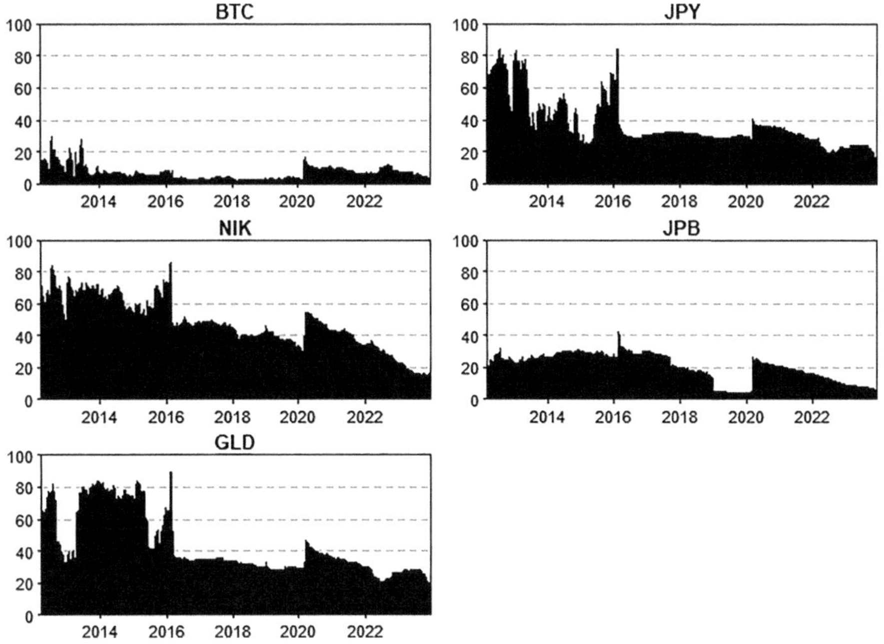

Fig. 4.19 Spillovers received from the Japanese network by Bitcoin (BTC), the yen (JPY), gold, the Nikkei index (NIK), and Japanese bonds (JPB)

where Y_t, C_0, C_i, Y_{t-i}, and ε_t represent respectively, the vector of endogenous variables defined in the system, the intercept coefficients, the coefficients of the lags of the endogenous variables, the lags of the endogenous variables, and the residuals with zero mean and serially uncorrelated errors. For simplicity, if it is assumed that there are two endogenous variables, x and y, with p lags, a vector autoregression model is defined as follows:

$$Y_t = B_{10} + B_{11}\ Y_{t-1} + \ldots + B_{1p}\ Y_{t-p} + b_{11}\ X_{t-1} + \ldots + b_{1p}\ X_{t-p} + U_{1t} \quad (4.9)$$

$$X_t = B_{20} + B_{21}\ Y_{t-1} + \ldots + B_{2p}\ Y_{t-p} + b_{21}\ X_{t-1} + \ldots + b_{2p}\ X_{t-p} + U_{2t} \quad (4.10)$$

where each of the endogenous variables considered in the system is a function of its lags, as well as the lags of other endogenous variables introduced into the system. In this way, the interactions between the system's variables are measured simultaneously. For simplicity, considering a one-period lag $t - 1$, the Eqs. (4.9) and (4.10) can be written in matrix form as follows:

$$\begin{bmatrix} \mathrm{Y_t} \\ \mathrm{X_t} \end{bmatrix} = \begin{bmatrix} \mathrm{B_{10}} \\ \mathrm{B_{20}} \end{bmatrix} + \begin{bmatrix} \mathrm{B_{11}} & \mathrm{b_{11}} \\ \mathrm{B_{21}} & \mathrm{b_{21}} \end{bmatrix} + \begin{bmatrix} \mathrm{Y_{t-1}} \\ \mathrm{X_{t-1}} \end{bmatrix} + \begin{bmatrix} \mathrm{U_{1t}} \\ \mathrm{U_{2t}} \end{bmatrix} \quad (4.11)$$

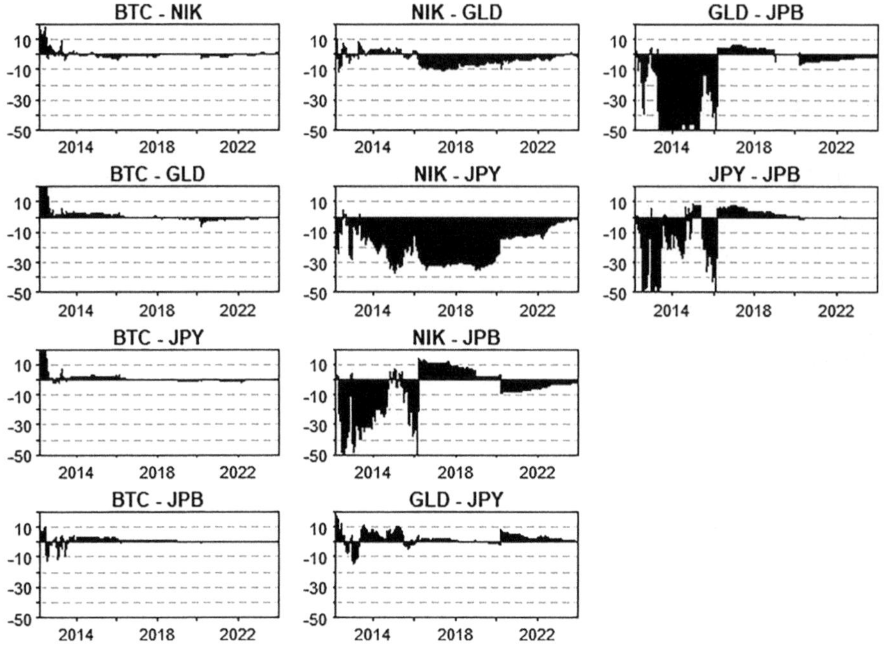

Fig. 4.20 The Japanese network. Dynamic net pairwise connectedness in a network of five market, including BTC, yen (JPY), gold, Nikkei index (NIK) and Japanese bonds (JPB)

Table 4.4 Spillover measures in a Japanese network of five markets

	BTC	NIK	GLD	JPY	JPB	From
BTC	93.45	3.06	1.49	0.93	1.06	6.55
NIK	3.07	53.13	7.99	21.08	14.72	46.87
GLD	2.70	4.99	57.53	19.50	15.28	42.47
JPY	1.93	2.11	21.60	63.99	10.36	36.01
JPB	1.94	8.76	3.87	5.47	79.96	20.04
TO	9.65	18.92	34.95	46.98	41.43	151.93
NET	3.10	−27.95	−7.52	10.97	21.40	30.39

Note: Spillovers among the five markets, including Bitcoin (BTC), the Yen (JPY), gold, the Nikkei index (NIK), and Japanese bonds (JPB). Spillovers that each of these five markets receives from (columns) and transmits to (rows) one another

Given the introduction of six endogenous variables into the system, the vector of endogenous variables is expressed as:

$$Y = [IR, \quad B, \quad EX, \quad GLD, \quad BTC, \quad STO] \tag{4.12}$$

where IR, B, EX, GLD, BTC, and STO respectively represent interest rates, bonds, major currencies, gold, cryptocurrencies, and stock markets.

In the next stage, some complexity is added to the empirical analysis, and as a strong complement to the results of the historical variance decomposition of the vector autoregression models, the dynamic correlation between each of the target markets and interest rates is assessed using corrected Conditional Dynamic Correlation–Generalized Autoregressive Conditional Heteroskedasticity (cDCC-GHARCH). One of the advantages of the cDCC-GARCH models is that they provide a clear and comprehensible depiction of the dynamic correlations between target markets and interest rate policies over time, in a way that is straightforward and easy to understand, allowing readers to engage with the correlations with clarity. Furthermore, the ability to introduce a large number of variables into the network is another advantage of these models, which can assist us in achieving the objectives we are pursuing.

A cDCC model, initially introduced by Engle (2002) and later revised by Aielli (2013), is specified as follows:

$$Y_t = B + \sum_{S=1}^{P} C_S Y_{t-S} + \varepsilon_t, \quad t = 1, \ldots, \quad T, \quad \varepsilon_t | \, INF_{t-1} \sim N(0, H_t) \tag{4.13}$$

$$Y_t \;\; or \;\; \varepsilon_t = H_t^{1/2} Z_t \tag{4.14}$$

where Y_t is a $k \times 1$ vector of observed returns at time t. H_t is a positive definite conditional covariance matrix with dimensions $k \times k$, and Z_t is a $k \times 1$ vector of standardized errors with zero mean. Equation (4.13) can be written in matrix form as follows (for simplicity, assuming 3 variables):

$$\begin{bmatrix} Y_{1,t} \\ Y_{2,t} \\ Y_{3,t} \end{bmatrix} = \begin{bmatrix} Y_1 \\ Y_2 \\ Y_3 \end{bmatrix} + \sum_{S=1}^{P} \begin{bmatrix} C_{11} & C_{12} & C_{13} \\ C_{21} & C_{22} & C_{23} \\ C_{31} & C_{32} & C_{33} \end{bmatrix} \begin{bmatrix} Y_{1,t-s} \\ Y_{2,t-2} \\ Y_{3,t-s} \end{bmatrix} + \begin{bmatrix} \varepsilon_1 \\ \varepsilon_2 \\ \varepsilon_3 \end{bmatrix} \tag{4.15}$$

Next, the conditional covariance matrix and a univariate GARCH model can be written as Eqs. (4.16) and (4.17) as follows:

$$H_t = D_t R_t D_t \tag{4.16}$$

$$\sigma_{i,t}^2 = w_i + a_i \, y_{i,t-1}^2 + B_i \, \sigma_{i,t-1}^2, \quad i = 1, \ldots, k \tag{4.17}$$

where D_t is a $k \times k$ diagonal matrix containing the conditional standard deviations from the univariate GARCH models, as described in Eq. (4.17), and based on the foundational GARCH (1,1) models by Engle (1982) and Bollerslev (1986). The diagonal elements of D_t correspond to these conditional standard deviations, so the number of diagonal elements equals the number of variables introduced into the system. R_t represents the $k \times k$ conditional correlation matrix.

To estimate the Conditional Dynamic Correlation GARCH model, in the first step, a univariate GARCH model is estimated, and then the standardized residuals $\eta_{i,t} = \varepsilon_{i,t} / \sqrt{\sigma_{i,t}}$ are obtained. Next, the conditional correlation matrix is derived as follows:

$$R_t = diag\left(c_{11,t}^{-1/2}, \ldots, c_{33,t}^{-1/2}\right) Q_t \, diag\left(c_{11,t}^{-1/2}, \ldots, c_{33,t}^{-1/2}\right) \tag{4.18}$$

where diag represents the diagonal elements, and $Q_t = \left(c_{ij,t}\right)$ is a positive definite matrix. Additionally, it is assumed that the matrix Q_t follows the univariate GARCH model as shown in Eq. (4.17):

$$Q_t = (1 - \theta_1 - \theta_2)\overline{Q} + \theta_1 \, \eta_{t-1} \, \eta_{t-1}' + \theta_2 \, Q_{t-1}, \quad \theta_1 \; and \; \theta_2 > 0, \quad \theta_1 + \theta_2 < 1 \tag{4.19}$$

The parameters θ_1 and θ_2 represent the effects of shocks and previous conditional correlations on the current conditional correlation. $\overline{Q}$ is the unconditional variance matrix of the standardized residuals $\eta_{i,t}$. The estimators of the correlation in Eq. (4.19) are given as follows:

$$P_{ij,t} = \frac{C_{ij,t}}{\sqrt{C_{ii,t} C_{ij,t}}} \tag{4.20}$$

In Conditional Dynamic Correlation GARCH (DCC-GARCH) models, the issue of $\overline{Q}$ is unclear, as neither the conditional correlation nor the conditional variance is specified. Aielli (2008) states that there is a possibility that the parameters may not be consistent and may exhibit some bias in these models. In this regard, the parameters are estimated to be small, such that θ_1 is close to zero, and the sum of the two parameters θ_1 and θ_2 is less than one. Therefore, Aielli introduces a revised version of the DCC-GARCH model, the cDCC-GARCH, which retains the same specification as the DCC-GARCH model but modifies Eq. (4.19) as follows:

$$Q_t = (1 - \theta_1 - \theta_2)\overline{Q} + \theta_1 \, \eta_{t-1}^{*} \, \eta_{t-1}^{*\prime} + \theta_2 \, Q_{t-1} \tag{4.21}$$

where η^* is equal to: $diag\{Q_t\}^{1/2} \eta_t$.

4.3.1 Empirical Results-Historical Volatility

Given the employment of monthly time series, it is necessary to test for the presence of unit roots before estimating vector autoregression (VAR) models. Table 4.14 shows that the null hypothesis of the Augmented Dickey-Fuller (ADF) test with a minimum t-statistic, which indicates the presence of a unit root, is not confirmed for any of the variables. Considering that growth rates were used for the variables defined in the system, their stationarity was as expected. The results of the unit root test, to maintain coherence and focus more on the outputs related to the theoretical literature, are moved to the end of this chapter.

After ensuring the stationarity of the United States, Britain, the European Union, and Japan's time series, one lag is set based on the Schwarz and Akaike criteria to separately estimate the VAR models for each of the four countries.

4.3.1.1 The U.S. Financial Network

First, the estimation of the VAR model is initially carried out for the United States network, which includes national currency, gold, bonds, stocks, bank deposits, Bitcoin, and interest rates.

The model is first applied to the United States financial network. As shown in Fig. 4.21, interest rates have played a significant role in the fluctuations of the U.S. bond market. An interesting observation is that the sensitivity of the bond market to interest rates is greater than its sensitivity to fluctuations in other markets, which aligns with the literature in Chap. 3. This is because the attractiveness of bonds is largely tied to the interest rates they offer, which can increase opportunity costs for investments in competing markets.

A comparison of Figs. 4.22, 4.23, 4.24, and 4.25 reveals that, after the bond market, the gold and stock markets show the highest sensitivity to interest rates, which is not unexpected in light of the literature in Chap. 3. This is because the attractiveness of the gold market, which benefits from its store-of-value feature in inflationary environments with high liquidity, is considerably influenced by interest rates. The stock market's dependency on financing and borrowing costs, both of which are influenced by interest rate policies, also supports this finding.

As noted in Fig. 4.23, an interesting point is that the role of interest rates in the fluctuations of the U.S. Dollar Index is relatively low. As discussed in the literature in Chaps. 1 and 3, one potential weakness of major currencies like the U.S. dollar is that, considering the possibility of fiscal policy dominance and unlimited money printing, it may exhibit considerable weakness in inflationary environments, undermining its store-of-value capacity. This may explain why its sensitivity to interest rates was expected to be higher. A plausible explanation for this is that inflation-targeting monetary policies, which keep inflation within a specified range, have mitigated this weakness, thereby increasing the dollar's store-of-value capacity.

In contrast, as seen in Fig. 4.24, the sensitivity of the gold price index to interest rates is expectedly very high. Bitcoin shows very low sensitivity to interest rates, as illustrated in Fig. 4.25, which contradicts the literature in Chaps. 1 and 3. Given Bitcoin's store-of-value advantage in inflationary environments and its significant need for financing to further develop competitive innovations, it was expected that its sensitivity to interest rate policies would be considerable. A plausible explanation for this contradiction is that, due to the emerging nature of the crypto market, its

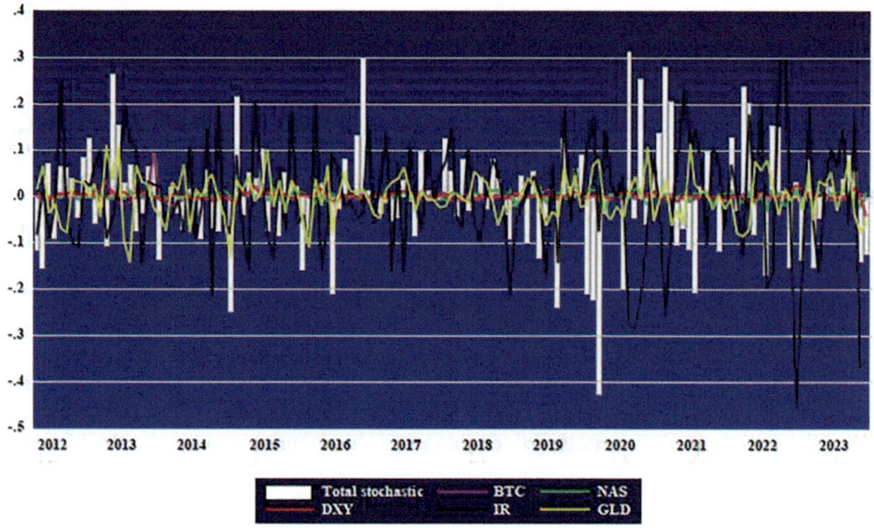

Fig. 4.21 Historical volatility of the bond market in the U.S. financial network, monthly time series from March 2012 to December 2023. (*Note*: The historical volatility of the 10-year U.S. Treasury bond yield [USB] is highlighted with white bars. The percentage changes in the Bitcoin price index [BTC], the U.S. stock market index, the NASDAQ-100 price index [NAS], the gold price index [GLD], the U.S. Dollar Index [DXY], and interest rates [IR] are also depicted. The contributions of interest rate policy and each market to the volatility in the bond market are distinguished by different colors in the ranges marked with white. Time series for the markets and interest rates are sourced from www.investing.com and www.data.oecd.org, respectively)

competitive capacities and technological innovations are more attractive to investors than its long-term response to interest rate policies. In other words, these competitive capacities carry more weight in investors' decisions to enter the crypto market.

Regarding the underlying factors for speculative motivations stemming from price fluctuations in the markets, the highest volatility is observed in the Bitcoin market, which is consistent with the literature and statistical analyses in Chap. 1. In contrast, volatility in the currency, stock, and bond markets, which play a crucial role in providing financial resources and maintaining stability in both the real and nominal sectors of the economy, and are therefore of significant importance to governments and central banks, remains low and relatively similar across these markets, aligning with the theoretical literature in Chap. 1.

Considering the historical volatility of the target markets, the gold market and the U.S. Dollar Index show the highest sensitivity to each other and low sensitivity to Bitcoin. On the other hand, Bitcoin is most sensitive to the stock market, which is also consistent with the results from the TVP-VAR models.

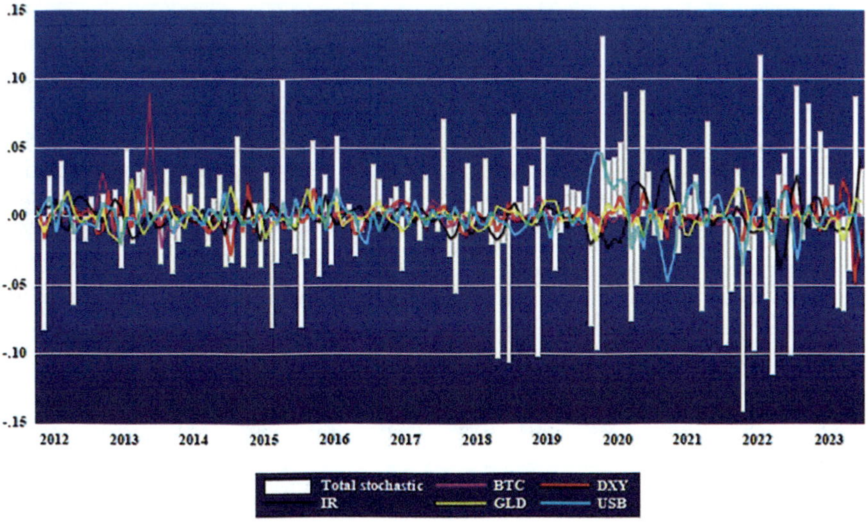

Fig. 4.22 Historical volatility of the stock market in the U.S. financial network, monthly time series from March 2012 to December 2023. (*Note*: The historical volatility of the NASDAQ-100 price index [NAS] is highlighted with white bars. The percentage changes in the Bitcoin price index [BTC], the 10-year bond yield [USB], the gold price index [GLD], the U.S. Dollar Index [DXY], and interest rates [IR] are also depicted. The contributions of interest rate policy and each market to the volatility in the stock market index are distinguished by different colors in the ranges marked with white. Time series for the markets and interest rates are sourced from www.investing.com and www.data.oecd.org, respectively)

4.3.1.2 The U.K. Financial Network

The U.K. financial network is the second network that is examined. It is important to determine whether the results related to the sensitivity of target markets to interest rates, particularly the contradictions observed in the U.S. financial network, are also seen in the U.K. financial network. A comparison of Figs. 4.21, 4.22, 4.23, 4.24, and 4.25, which were dedicated to the U.S. financial network, with Figs. 4.26, 4.27, 4.28, 4.29, and 4.30, which focus on the U.K. financial network, reveals very similar results between the two networks. The most significant sensitivity to interest rates is found in the bond market, followed by the gold and stock markets, which aligns with the literature in Chap. 3. Similar to the U.S. Dollar index, the major currency of the British pound also exhibits low sensitivity to interest rates, indicating that the store-of-value capacities of the U.S. dollar and the British pound, both of which have the largest share in the global economy, could be enhanced due to inflation-targeting monetary policies, which maintain inflation rates within limited and specific ranges.

Another similarity is that the share of interest rates in Bitcoin price fluctuations is considerably low. Therefore, the paradox seen in the U.S. financial network, regarding the low sensitivity of the crypto market to interest rates, is also observed in the U.K. financial network, strengthening the credibility of these empirical findings.

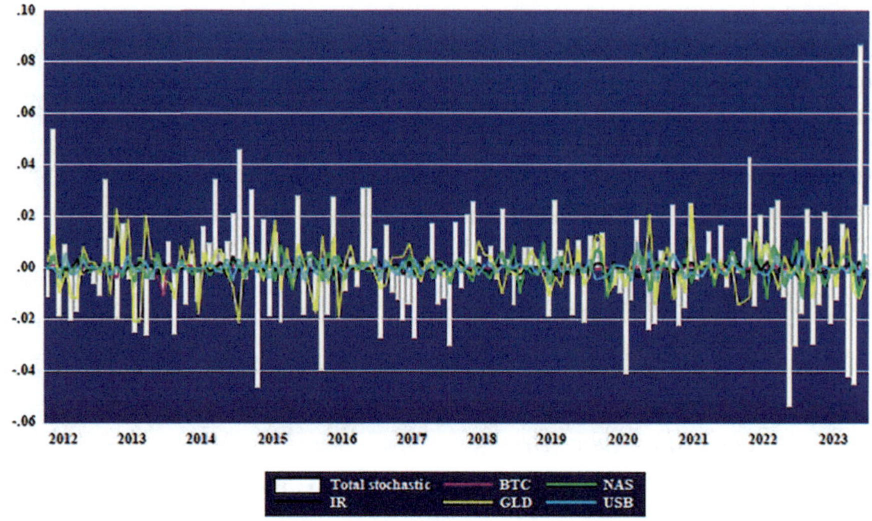

Fig. 4.23 Historical volatility of the U.S. dollar index in the U.S. financial network, monthly time series from March 2012 to December 2023. (*Note*: The historical volatility of the Dollar Index [DXY] is highlighted with white bars. The percentage changes in the Bitcoin price index [BTC], the 10-year bond yield [USB], the gold price index [GLD], the NASDAQ-100 price index [NAS], and interest rates [IR] are also depicted. The contributions of interest rate policy and each market to the volatility in the dollar index are distinguished by different colors in the ranges marked with white. Time series for the markets and interest rates are sourced from www.investing.com and www.data.oecd.org, respectively)

On the other hand, in both the U.S. and U.K. financial networks, the highest volatility is found in the crypto market, while volatility in major currencies, bonds, and stock markets—critical for securing financial resources and ensuring the stability of both real and nominal sectors of the economy, as discussed in Chap. 1—remains low. This aligns with the literature in Chap. 1, highlighting their importance for governments and central banks.

Additionally, like the U.S. financial network, the major currency of the British pound and gold share a notable sensitivity to one another and exhibit low sensitivity to Bitcoin. Besides, an interesting similarity in both networks is that the highest sensitivity of Bitcoin is to the stock market. These results are consistent with the empirical findings of the TVP-VAR models.

4.3.1.3 The German Financial Network

The third financial network examined in terms of the sensitivity of target markets to interest rate policies is dedicated to Germany. According to Figs. 4.31, 4.32, 4.33, 4.34, and 4.35, the similarities observed in the financial networks of the United States and the United Kingdom are also present in Germany's financial network.

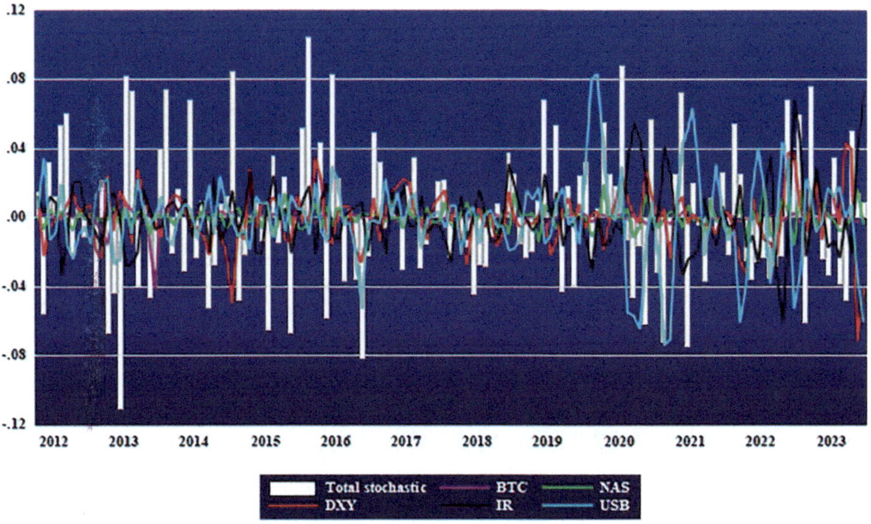

Fig. 4.24 Historical volatility of the gold price index in the U.S. financial network, monthly time series from March 2012 to December 2023. (*Note*: The historical volatility of the gold price index [GLD] is highlighted with white bars. The percentage changes in the Bitcoin price index [BTC], the 10-year bond yield [USB], the NASDAQ-100 price index [NAS], the Dollar Index [DXY], and interest rates [IR] are also depicted. The contributions of interest rate policy and each market to the volatility in the gold price index are distinguished by different colors in the ranges marked with white. Time series for the markets and interest rates are sourced from www.investing.com and www.data.oecd.org, respectively)

Specifically, interest rates play the most significant role in bond market volatility. After bonds, the gold and stock markets exhibit the highest sensitivity to interest rates. Similar to the major currencies of the U.S. dollar and the British pound, the share of interest rates in the volatility of the euro is low. This suggests that the inflation-targeting monetary policies of the European Central Bank, like those of the U.S. Federal Reserve and the Bank of England, have been successful in preserving the euro's store of value.

Bitcoin, like in the financial networks of the United States and the United Kingdom, shows a low sensitivity to interest rates. These similarities add credibility to the empirical results. Therefore, it seems that in Germany's financial network, the competitive potential of the crypto market has also had a greater influence on decision-making than the interest rate policies of the European Central Bank. Considering the novelty of this market, and as discussed in Chap. 1, the capacities that have primarily been introduced and matured over the past five years since 2020, this is not surprising.

Regarding price volatility and speculative motivations, similar to the financial networks of the United States and the United Kingdom, these price volatility in the stock, bond, and currency markets have remained within limited ranges, which has reduced speculative motivations in these markets, leading to greater stability. At the

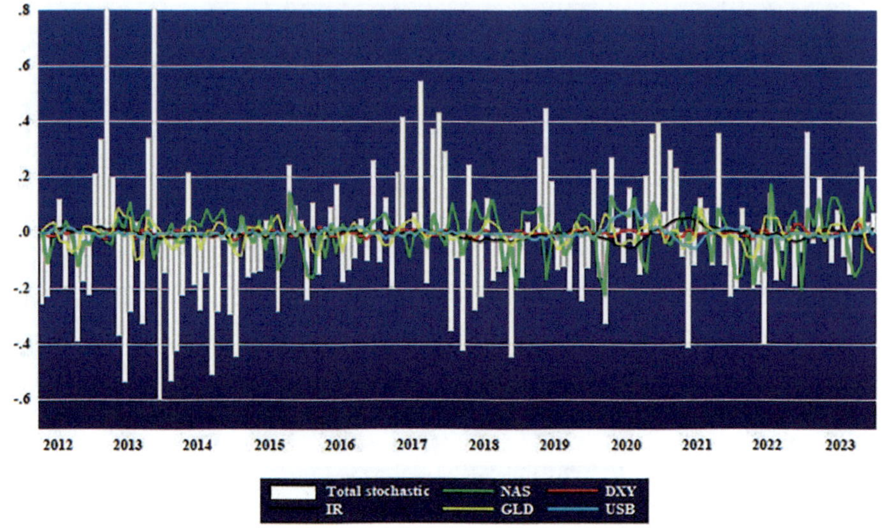

Fig. 4.25 Historical volatility of the Bitcoin price index in the U.S. financial network, monthly time series from March 2012 to December 2023. (*Note*: The historical volatility of the Bitcoin price index [BTC] is highlighted with white bars. The percentage changes in the NASDAQ-100 price index [NAS], the 10-year bond yield [USB], the gold price index [GLD], the U.S. Dollar Index [DXY], and interest rates [IR] are also depicted. The contributions of interest rate policy and each market to the volatility in the Bitcoin price index are distinguished by different colors in the ranges marked in white. Time series for the markets and interest rates are sourced from www.investing.com and www.data.oecd.org, respectively)

same time, the results show significant price volatility in the crypto market, resulting in speculative motives for short-term profits.

4.3.1.4 The Japanese Financial Network

The last financial network in which the historical volatility of target markets is analyzed using Vector Autoregressive (VAR) models to understand the sensitivity of target markets to central bank interest rate policies is Japan's financial network. The results are presented in Figs. 4.36, 4.37, 4.38, 4.39, and 4.40.

As shown in Fig. 4.36, similar to the financial networks of the United States, United Kingdom, and Germany, interest rates have a significant share in the volatility of bonds. After bonds, as illustrated in Figs. 4.37 and 4.39, the gold and stock markets display the highest level of sensitivity to interest rates. Compared to major currencies like the U.S. dollar, the British pound, and the euro, the Japanese yen shows greater sensitivity to interest rates. This sensitivity is not unexpected, considering that the Bank of Japan has followed a negative interest rate policy since 2016, which has reduced borrowing costs and, as a result, boosted borrowing incentives.

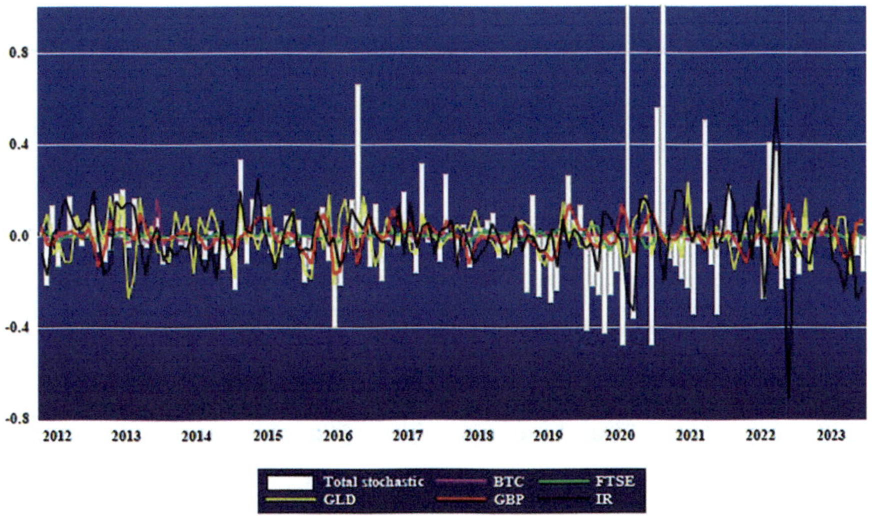

Fig. 4.26 Historical volatility of the bond market in the U.K. financial network, monthly time series from March 2012 to December 2023. (*Note*: The historical volatility of the 10-year U.K. bond yield [UKB] is highlighted with white bars. The percentage changes in the Bitcoin price index [BTC], the U.K. stock market price index FTSE100 [FTES], the gold price index [GLD], the British pound exchange rate against the U.S. dollar [GBP], and interest rates [IR] are also shown. The contributions of interest rate policy and each market to the volatility in the bond market are distinguished by different colors in the ranges marked in white. Time series for the markets and interest rates are sourced from www.investing.com and www.data.oecd.org, respectively)

Regarding price fluctuations and speculative motivations that follow, like the financial networks of the United States, United Kingdom, and Germany, these fluctuations in the stock, bond, and currency markets are largely contained within limited ranges. This containment is supported by governments and central banks due to their significant role in financing and shaping both nominal and real sectors of the economy, which has reduced speculative incentives and contributed to greater stability in these markets, which is in line with the literature from Chap. 1. Moreover, the results also indicate significant price volatility in the crypto market, which contrasts sharply with the fluctuations seen in the equity markets, major currencies, and bonds. As discussed in Chap. 1, the price volatility has led to speculative motives for short-term profits in the crypto market.

Another similarity between Japan's financial network and those of the other three countries is the notable sensitivity between gold and the major currency, the yen. Additionally, both gold and the yen show low sensitivity to Bitcoin. Bitcoin exhibits the highest sensitivity to the stock market, a trend also observed in the financial networks of Germany, the United Kingdom, and the United States.

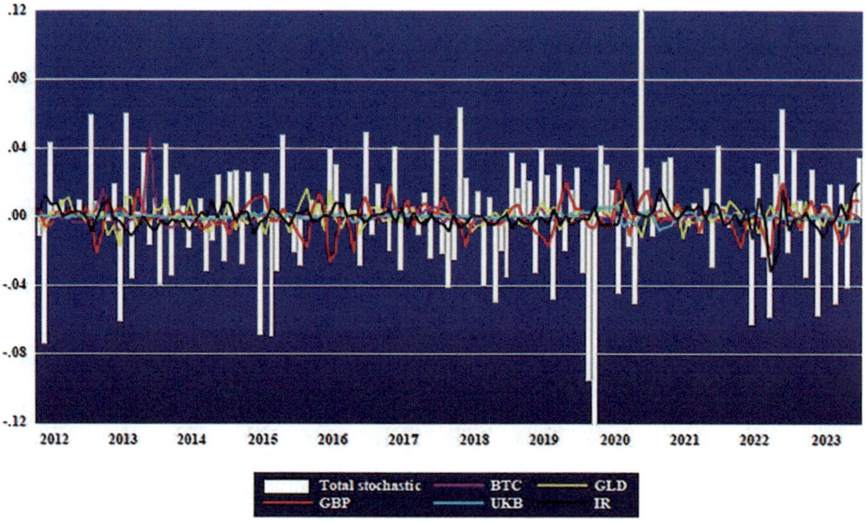

Fig. 4.27 Historical volatility of the stock market in the U.K. financial network, monthly time series from March 2012 to December 2023. (*Note*: The historical volatility of the stock market price index, FTSE100 [UKB], is highlighted with white bars. The percentage changes in the Bitcoin price index [BTC], the U.K. bond yield [UKB], the gold price index [GLD], the British pound exchange rate against the U.S. dollar [GBP], and interest rates [IR] are also shown. The contributions of interest rate policy and each market to the volatility in the stock market are distinguished by different colors in the ranges marked in white. Time series for the markets and interest rates are sourced from www.investing.com and www.data.oecd.org, respectively)

4.3.1.5 Empirical Findings Summary

The empirical results for the economies of the United States, the United Kingdom, Germany, and Japan provide strong support for the theoretical literature discussed in Chaps. 1 and 3.

The summary of the results indicates that price volatility in the crypto market is notably significant compared to other target markets, which has fueled speculative motives for short-term profits in this market. In contrast, markets that play a key role in financing, the conditions of the nominal and real sectors of the economy, and their attractiveness to foreign investors—bond, stock, and currency markets—price volatility is relatively low. This results in reduced speculative incentives in these markets, which is reflected in the stability of these markets under government fiscal policies and central bank monetary policies.

The findings also provide strong evidence regarding the low sensitivity of the crypto market to interest rate policies, while, in line with the theoretical literature in Chap. 3, the bond, gold, and stock markets showed high sensitivity to interest rates. Another observation, highlighting the success of inflation-targeting monetary policies by the Federal Reserve, the Bank of England, the European Central Bank, and the Bank of Japan, is that these policies have successfully kept inflation within a

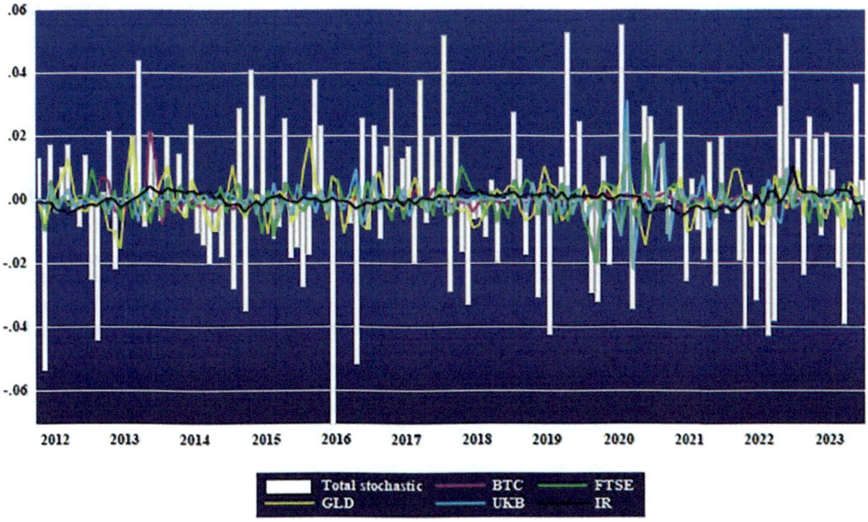

Fig. 4.28 Historical volatility of the British Pound in the U.K. financial network, monthly time series from March 2012 to December 2023. (*Note*: The historical volatility of the British pound exchange rate against the U.S. dollar [GBP] is highlighted with white bars. The percentage changes in the Bitcoin price index [BTC], the U.K. bond yield [UKB], the gold price index [GLD], the stock market price index [FTSE], and interest rates [IR] are also shown. The contributions of interest rate policy and each market to the volatility in the British pound exchange rate are distinguished by different colors in the ranges marked in white. Time series for the markets and interest rates are sourced from www.investing.com and www.data.oecd.org, respectively)

specified range. This has led to a low sensitivity of major currencies, the U.S. dollar, the British pound, the euro, and the Japanese yen, to changes in interest rates, thus reinforcing their role as stores of value. Confirming these results in the financial networks of the United States, the United Kingdom, Germany, and Japan indicates that if these inflation-targeting policies are followed effectively and central bank independence is respected, the store-of-value capacity of these major currencies will remain intact. In such cases, there will be no need for major global economies to suppress the crypto market in order to maintain the high share of their currencies in the global economy.

While the need for financial resources in the crypto market to develop productive projects and its advantage as a store of value would normally create high sensitivity of the crypto market to interest rate changes, the very short lifespan of this industry, whose competitive capacity and technological innovations have mostly developed since 2020, has led to these factors having a greater weight in the decision-making of crypto market investors compared to the impact of monetary policies.

Therefore, the empirical results support the theoretical framework presented in Chaps. 1 and 3 and suggest the possibility of predicting market sensitivity to one another and to interest rate policies with low error based on this literature. The alignment of the empirical results with the theoretical framework shows that the

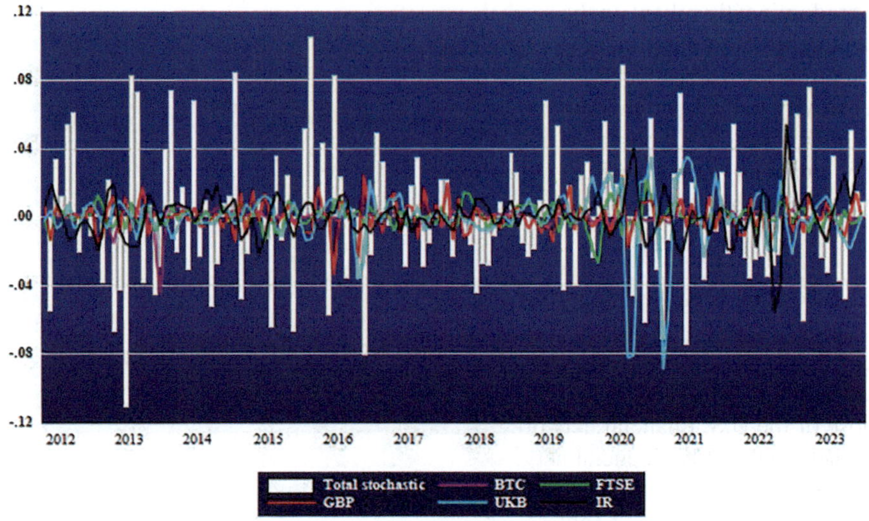

Fig. 4.29 Historical volatility of the gold price index in the U.K. financial network, monthly time series from March 2012 to December 2023. (*Note*: The historical volatility of the gold price index [GLD] is highlighted with white bars. The percentage changes in the Bitcoin price index [BTC], the U.K. bond yield [UKB], the stock market price index [FTSE], the British pound exchange rate against the U.S. dollar [GBP], and interest rates [IR] are also shown. The contributions of interest rate policy and each market to the volatility in the gold price index are distinguished by different colors in the ranges marked in white. Time series for the markets and interest rates are sourced from www.investing.com and www.data.oecd.org, respectively)

theoretical literature is not limited to academic and theoretical contexts but also has practical relevance in the real world.

The overall results show, on the one hand, a high level of sensitivity among the target markets, confirming the existence of money flows between them, and on the other hand, a considerable sensitivity of these markets to interest rate changes. Therefore, it is feasible for central banks to manage money flows between the target markets in line with policy objectives by implementing appropriate interest rate policies. This management of money flows between markets is particularly important for controlling and moderating speculative incentives, as well as supporting markets with the potential to foster productive investment development.

4.3.2 Empirical Results-Dynamic Correlations

After examining the contribution of interest rates to the historical volatility of target markets using variance decomposition, which identified the sensitivity of each market to interest rate policies over time, this section aims to provide a complement to the historical volatility results by analyzing the dynamic correlation between interest

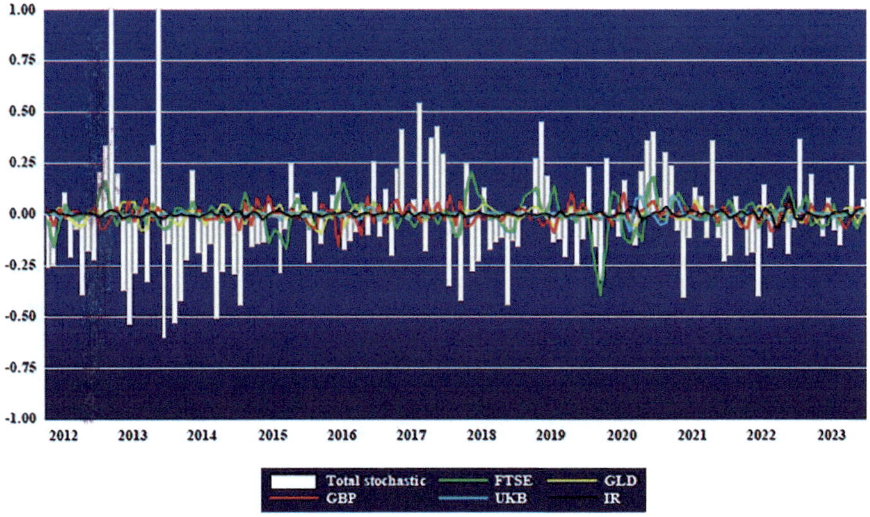

Fig. 4.30 Historical volatility of the Bitcoin price index in the U.K. financial network, monthly time series from March 2012 to December 2023. (*Note*: The historical volatility of the Bitcoin price index [BTC] is highlighted with white bars. The percentage changes in the U.K. bond yield [UKB], the gold price index [GLD], the stock market price index [FTSE], the British pound exchange rate against the U.S. dollar [GBP], and interest rates [IR] are also shown. The contributions of interest rate policy and each market to the volatility in the Bitcoin price index are distinguished by different colors in the ranges marked in white. Time series for the markets and interest rates are sourced from www.investing.com and www.data.oecd.org, respectively)

rates and target markets. For this section, following the approach used in previous sections, the analysis is conducted separately for each of the networks of the United States, the United Kingdom, Germany, and Japan using cDCC-GARCH models. This approach aims to provide a clearer and more straightforward understanding of the dynamic correlations between interest rate policies and target markets through comparative analysis.

To use these models, it is first necessary to examine whether there is significant short-term volatility, and if this volatility remains stable in the long term. The results in Table 4.15 confirm that significant volatility exists in the short term and its persistence in the long term. Therefore, the use of conditional dynamic correlation cDCC-GARCH models is feasible. To maintain continuity and focus on the empirical results and their analysis, Table 4.15 is moved to the end of this chapter.

4.3.2.1 The U.S. Financial Network

First, the cDCC-GARCH model is applied to the United States network, which includes national currency, gold, bonds, stocks, bank deposits, Bitcoin, and interest rates. As shown in Fig. 4.41, there are significant correlations on the one hand between

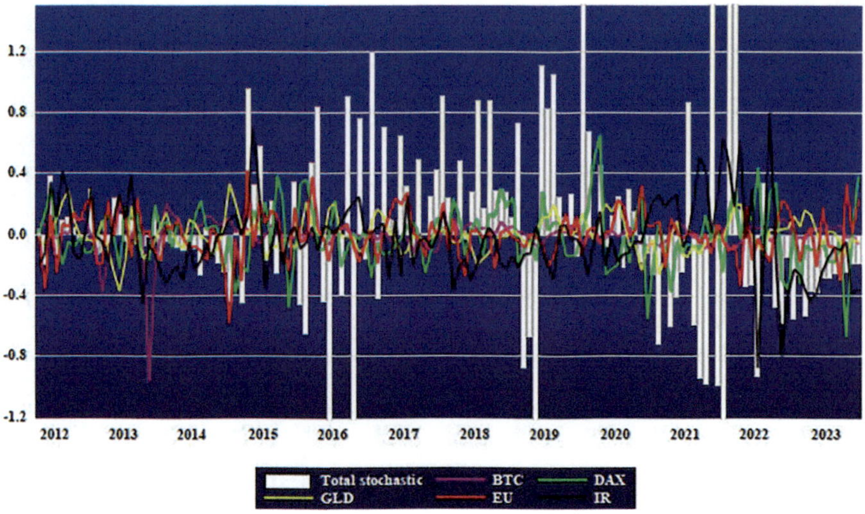

Fig. 4.31 Historical volatility of the bond market in the German financial network, monthly time series from March 2012 to December 2023. (*Note*: The historical volatility of the 10-year German government bond yield [GRB] is highlighted with white bars. The percentage changes in the Bitcoin price index [BTC], the German stock market price index [DAX], the gold price index [GLD], the euro exchange rate against the U.S. dollar [EU], and interest rates [IR] are also shown. The contributions of interest rate policy and each market to the volatility in the bond yield are distinguished by different colors in the ranges marked in white. Time series for the markets and interest rates are sourced from www.investing.com and www.data.oecd.org)

the target markets, in line with the literature of Chap. 1, and on the other hand, between the markets and interest rates, which is consistent with the literature of Chap. 3.

The differences in the correlations between interest rate policies and markets are related to both the severity and direction. Correlations between Bitcoin, gold, and stock markets have been positive. This positive correlation between gold and Bitcoin, based on the literature of Chap. 1 and the common competitive advantages related to their store-of-value potential, was expected. The stock market, in export-oriented economies such as the United States, which also has a low dependency on imported raw materials, is typically seen as an inflation hedge. Therefore, part of the money flow in inflationary environments tends to mobilize toward this market, along with gold and Bitcoin markets.

These three markets—gold, Bitcoin, and stock market—show negative correlations with the U.S. Dollar Index, as was anticipated based on the literature of Chaps. 1 and 3. A depreciation of national currencies increases the competitiveness and attractiveness of export goods in international markets; hence, the negative correlation between the national currency and the stock market, particularly in export-oriented economies like the United States with low reliance on imported raw materials, is in line with expectations. According to the literature of Chap. 1, the common competitive advantages that gold and Bitcoin share with major currencies like the U.S. dollar,

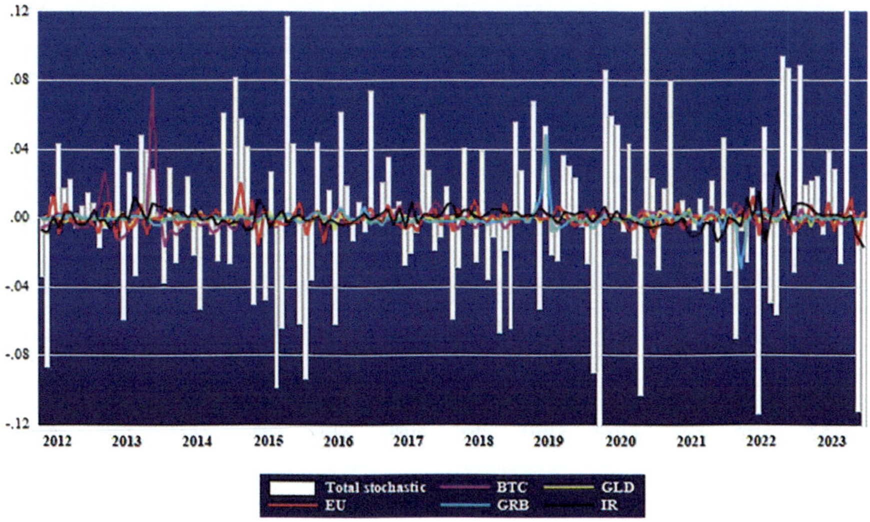

Fig. 4.32 Historical volatility of the stock market in the German financial network, monthly time series from March 2012 to December 2023. (*Note*: The historical volatility of the German stock market price index [DAX] is highlighted with white bars. The percentage changes in the Bitcoin price index [BTC], the 10-year German bond yield [GRB], the gold price index [GLD], the euro exchange rate against the U.S. dollar [EU], and interest rates [IR] are also shown. The contributions of interest rate policy and each market to the volatility in the stock market price index are distinguished by different colors in the ranges marked in white. Time series for the markets and interest rates are sourced from www.investing.com and www.data.oecd.org)

and their differing sensitivity to liquidity volume and inflation rates, also make the negative correlation between them unsurprising. In fact, the expectations derived from the theoretical literature in Chaps. 1 and 3 are confirmed by the empirical results.

Regarding the correlation between interest rates and target markets, interest rates show a positive correlation with the U.S. dollar and bonds and a negative correlation with gold and Bitcoin, which aligns with the literature of Chaps. 1 and 3. On the other hand, the correlation the bond market shows with the U.S. dollar has generally been positive, while with gold has been negative, and with no specific trend observed with other markets. According to the literature in Chaps. 1 and 3, since bonds pay interest to their holders, in environments with high interest rates, low liquidity, and lower inflation, the value of national currencies and bonds tends to rise simultaneously, while the attractiveness of markets that act as stores of value, like gold and cryptocurrencies, diminishes in high-inflation, high-liquidity environments.

These findings align with the theoretical literature and also appear in the empirical results, indicating the depth and validity of the theoretical literature for predicting money flow between markets and their sensitivity to monetary policies.

To provide a clearer understanding of this concept, further details are provided. Contractionary monetary policies, i.e., interest rate hikes, raise the opportunity cost

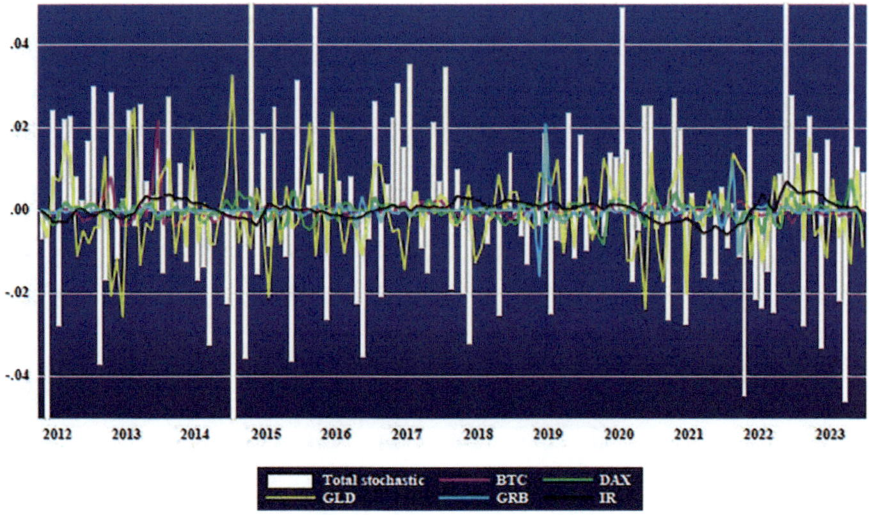

Fig. 4.33 Historical volatility of the euro in the German financial network, monthly time series from March 2012 to December 2023. (*Note*: The historical volatility of the euro exchange rate against the U.S. dollar [EU] is highlighted with white bars. The percentage changes in the Bitcoin price index [BTC], the 10-year German bond yield [GRB], the DAX price index [DAX], the gold price index [GLD], and interest rates [IR] are also shown. The contributions of interest rate policy and each market to the volatility in the euro are distinguished by different colors in the ranges marked in white. Time series for the markets and interest rates are sourced from www.investing.com and www.data.oecd.org)

of holding cash and reduce borrowing incentives, leading to a decrease in liquidity and, consequently, a reduction in inflation, which drives up the value of national currencies. Moreover, with higher interest rates and lower inflation, the attractiveness of bond yields increases, while the opportunity cost of not holding assets such as bonds, which yield interest, also rises.

In contrast, contractionary monetary policies, which reduce liquidity and inflation and therefore increase the value of national currencies, diminish the attractiveness of gold and crypto markets. This is because a large portion of the appeal of gold and Bitcoin comes from their role as a store of value in inflationary environments. Additionally, since holders of gold and Bitcoin do not earn interest, the opportunity cost of holding them rises, leading to further reduced attractiveness. This negative impact from high interest rates on Bitcoin is more pronounced, as Bitcoin is still an emerging industry that relies heavily on financial resources to fund its projects. Therefore, contractionary monetary policies, which raise borrowing costs for financing, can have a more significant negative impact on this industry.

The correlation between interest rates and the stock market has been positive in some periods and negative in others, but it shows an overall downward trend across the entire time period. According to the literature of Chap. 3, interest rates can have a dual effect on stock markets. Interest rate hikes can enhance the attractiveness of

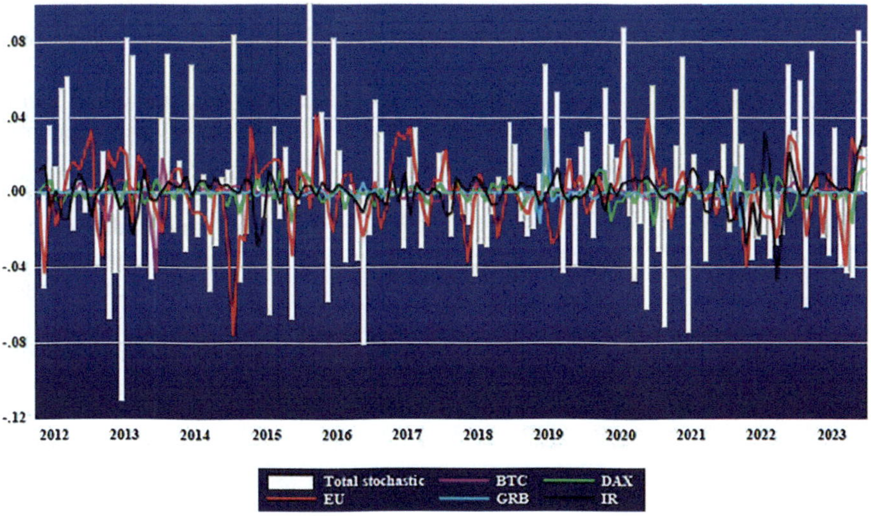

Fig. 4.34 Historical volatility of the gold price index in the German financial network, monthly time series from March 2012 to December 2023. (*Note*: The historical volatility of the gold price index [GLD] is highlighted with white bars. The percentage changes in the Bitcoin price index [BTC], the 10-year German bond yield [GRB], the DAX price index [DAX], the euro currency unit against the U.S. dollar [EU], and interest rates [IR] are also shown. The contributions of interest rate policy and each market to the volatility in the gold price index are distinguished by different colors in the ranges marked in white. Time series for the markets and interest rates are sourced from www.investing.com and www.data.oecd.org)

depositing funds in the banking network, which has a positive impact on the ability of corporations listed in the stock market to access financial resources for implementing and expanding productive investments. On the other hand, higher interest rates also increase borrowing costs, which negatively affects the performance and profitability outlook of corporations. Therefore, the overall effect of interest rates, as discussed in Chap. 3, depends on the net outcome of the positive effects of increased access to financial resources and the negative effects of higher borrowing costs. As such, the positive and negative correlations between this market and interest rates over time are consistent with the theoretical literature in Chap. 3.

The crypto market indicates a very low correlation with interest rates, typically ranging between zero and −0.1 in most years. This aligns with the empirical results from the TVP-VAR models in the first section of this chapter, as well as the findings from the historical variance decomposition in the second section, both of which highlight the market's minimal sensitivity to interest rates.

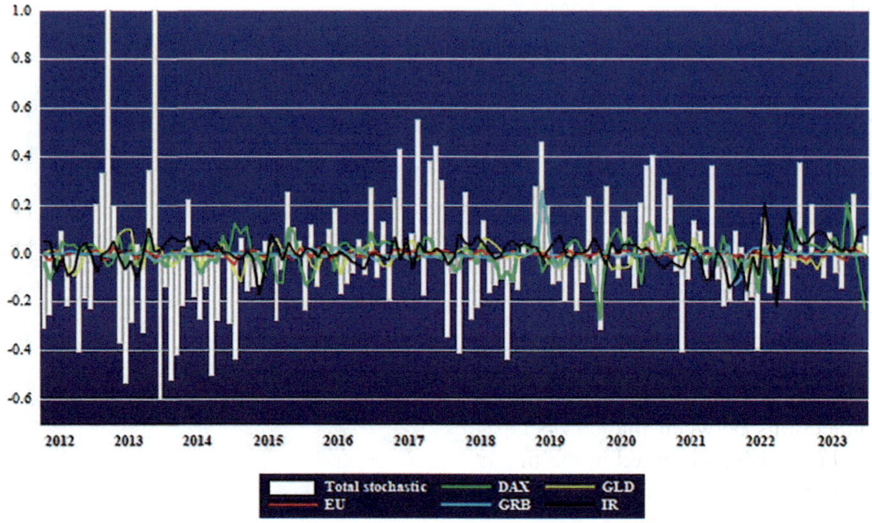

Fig. 4.35 Historical volatility of the Bitcoin price index in the German financial network, monthly time series from March 2012 to December 2023. (*Note*: The historical volatility of the Bitcoin price index [BTC] is highlighted with white bars. The percentage changes in the DAX price index [DAX], the 10-year German bond yield [GRB], the gold price index [GLD], the euro currency unit against the U.S. dollar [EU], and interest rates [IR] are also shown. The contributions of interest rate policy and each market to the volatility in the Bitcoin price index are distinguished by different colors in the ranges marked in white. Time series for the markets and interest rates are sourced from www.investing.com and www.data.oecd.org)

4.3.2.2 The U.K. Financial Network

As shown in Fig. 4.42, there are very close similarities between the results in the U.K. and U.S. financial networks. Similar to the U.S. financial network, the dynamic correlation among gold, crypto, and stock markets is positive in the U.K. financial network. However, unlike the U.S. financial network, where the U.S. dollar showed a negative correlation with the gold, crypto, and stock markets, the British pound shows a positive correlation with these markets. One plausible explanation for this difference is that major currencies like the pound are classified as commodity or risky currencies in financial markets, which leads to significant co-movements between the Pound and gold, crypto, and stock markets. In contrast, the U.S. dollar, categorized as a non-risky currency, shows a negative correlation with gold, crypto, and stock markets.

Similar to the U.S. financial network, the bond market and the British pound show a positive correlation with interest rates. In this regard, the positive correlation with bonds has been particularly notable, fluctuating between positive ranges of 0.6% to 0.62% over a significant portion of the time series. The correlation between interest rates and the gold market has also been negative as expected, aligning with the results in the U.S. financial network and the literature in Chap. 3.

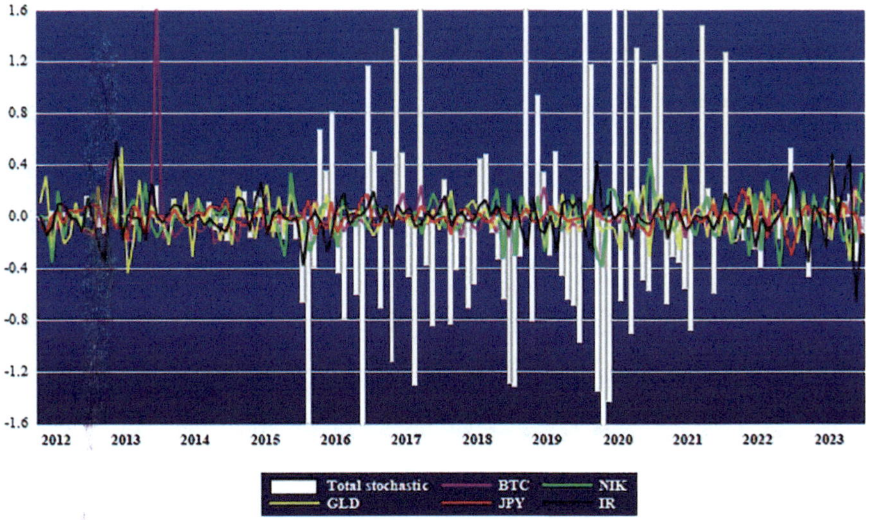

Fig. 4.36 Historical volatility of the bond market in the Japanese financial network, monthly time series from March 2012 to December 2023. (*Note*: The historical volatility of the 10-year Japanese government bond yield [JPB] is highlighted with white bars. The percentage changes in the Bitcoin price index [BTC], the Japanese stock market price index, Nikkei [NIK], the gold price index [GLD], the Japanese yen exchange rate against the U.S. dollar [EU], and interest rates [IR] are also shown. The contributions of interest rate policy and each market to the volatility in the bond yield are distinguished by different colors in the ranges marked in white. Time series for the markets and interest rates are sourced from www.investing.com and www.data.oecd.org)

The stock market and interest rates exhibit fluctuating correlations between positive and negative ranges, which has followed a general downward trend over the entire time period. This is consistent with the empirical results of the U.S. financial network and the literature in Chap. 3 regarding the dual effects of interest rates on stock markets. The correlation between interest rates and Bitcoin also includes both positive and negative ranges, showing a downward trend across the entire time period, which is in line with the literature of Chap. 3.

Like the stock market, Bitcoin can indicate a dual sensitivity to interest rate policies: on the one hand, a positive effect from greater access to financial resources for developing productive projects, and on the other, a negative effect from higher borrowing costs. The crypto market, like the financial network in the United States, exhibits very low correlation with interest rates, fluctuating between zero and 0.06 in most years. This is consistent with the empirical results from the TVP-VAR models in the first section of this chapter, as well as the results from the historical variance decomposition in the second section, both of which indicate a very low sensitivity of the crypto market to interest rates.

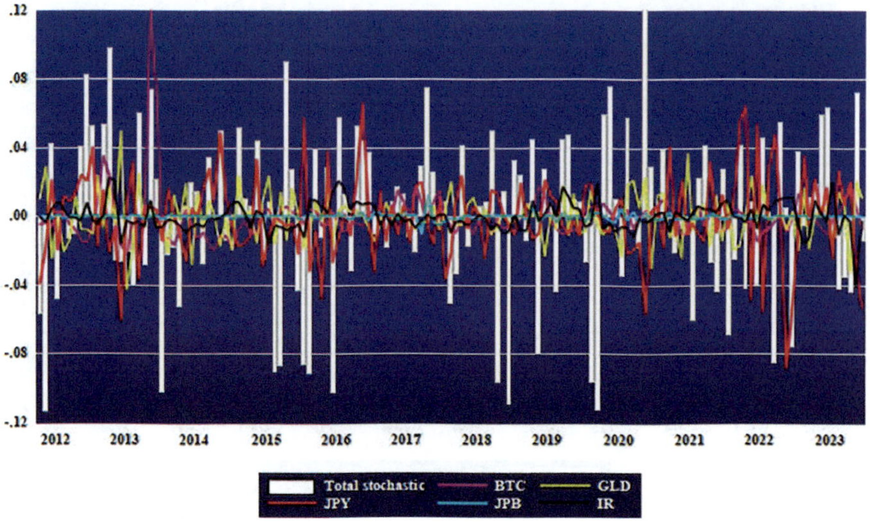

Fig. 4.37 Historical volatility of the stock market in the Japanese financial network, monthly time series from March 2012 to December 2023. (*Note*: The historical volatility of the Japanese stock market price index, Nikkei [NIK], is highlighted with white bars. The percentage changes in the Bitcoin price index [BTC], the gold price index [GLD], the 10-year Japanese government bond yield [JPB], the Japanese yen exchange rate against the U.S. dollar [EU], and interest rates [IR] are also shown. The contributions of interest rate policy and each market to the volatility in the stock market price index are distinguished by different colors in the ranges marked in white. Time series for the markets and interest rates are sourced from www.investing.com and www.data.oecd.org)

4.3.2.3 The German Financial Network

According to Fig. 4.43, similar to the U.K. financial network, there is a positive correlation between the euro, gold, and Bitcoin in the German financial network. Given that the euro, similarly to the pound, is classified in commodity or risky currencies, its positive correlation with gold and Bitcoin is not unexpected. The correlation between the stock market and Bitcoin is positive, which also holds true for the United Kingdom and the United States. If we consider the literature from Chap. 1, the potential of the crypto market to eliminate the role of various intermediaries within the current conventional economy, which is heavily dependent on intermediaries, a negative correlation of the crypto market with the stock market should be expected. However, since these potentials have not yet materialized and smart contracts, which can potentially eliminate intermediaries, are very emerging, having only started developing seriously in 2020, it appears that the co-movements between the stock and crypto markets, observed in the financial networks of the United States, United Kingdom, and Germany, are more influenced by the competitive capacity of both markets to hedge inflation risk.

Interest rates show a positive correlation with bonds and the euro, and a negative correlation with gold, which aligns with empirical findings in the U.S. and U.K.

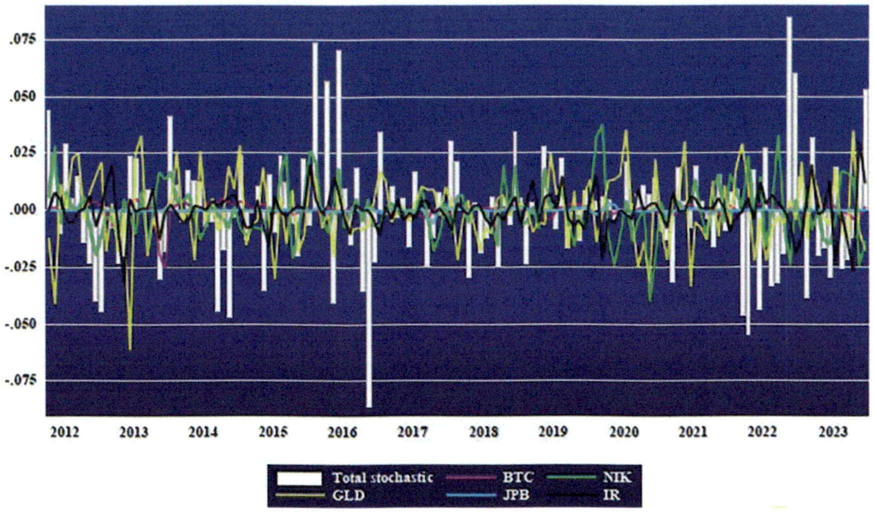

Fig. 4.38 Historical volatility of the yen in the Japanese financial network, monthly time series from March 2012 to December 2023. (*Note*: The historical volatility of the Japanese yen currency unit against the U.S. dollar [JPY] is highlighted with white bars. The percentage changes in the Bitcoin price index [BTC], the gold price index [GLD], the Nikkei price index [NIK], the 10-year Japanese government bond yield [JPB], the Japanese Yen exchange rate against the U.S. dollar [EU], and interest rates [IR] are also shown. The contributions of interest rate policy and each market to the volatility in the Japanese yen currency unit are distinguished by different colors in the ranges marked in white. Time series for the markets and interest rates are sourced from www.investing.com and www.data.oecd.org)

financial networks and is consistent with the literature from Chaps. 1 and 3. In environments with high interest rates, low liquidity, and inflation, the attractiveness of national currencies and bonds increases. Since interest is paid to bondholders, contractionary monetary policies, which raise interest rates, can increase the real interest rate received by bondholders over time and, simultaneously, reduce inflation and liquidity, thereby increasing the value of the national currency. On the other hand, contractionary monetary policies, which decrease liquidity and inflation, reduce the attractiveness of markets that serve as stores of value in high liquidity, inflationary environments, such as crypto and gold.

In the German financial network, the stock market shows a positive correlation with interest rates. Therefore, the positive impact of increased access to financial resources in the stock market seems to have outweighed the negative effects of rising borrowing costs.

The crypto market, like in the financial networks of the United States and United Kingdom, shows a very low correlation with interest rates, fluctuating between 0 and −0.1 in most years. This is consistent with the empirical results of TVP-VAR models in the first part of this chapter, as well as the historical variance decomposition results in the second part of this chapter, which showed a very low sensitivity of the crypto market to interest rates.

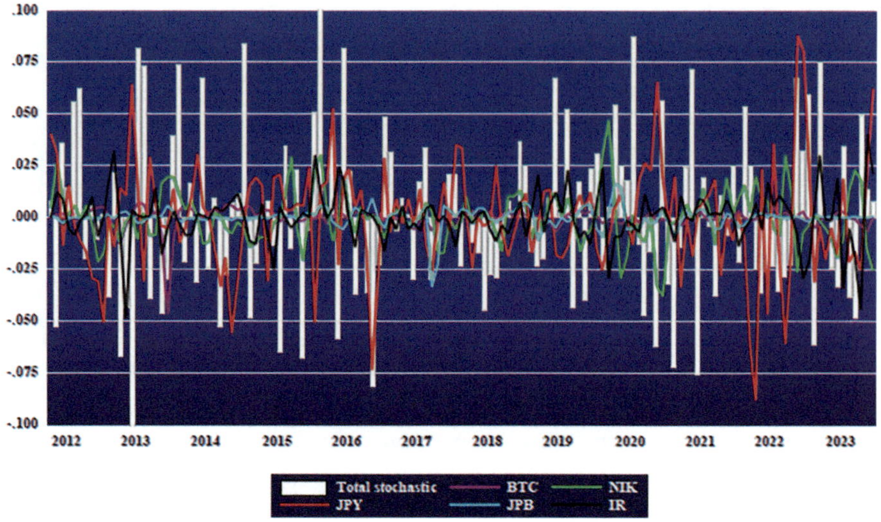

Fig. 4.39 Historical volatility of the gold price index in the Japanese financial network, monthly time series from March 2012 to December 2023. (*Note*: The historical volatility of the gold price index [GLD] is highlighted with white bars. The percentage changes in the Bitcoin price index [BTC], the Nikkei price index [NIK], the 10-year Japanese government bond yield [JPB], the Japanese yen exchange rate against the U.S. dollar [EU], and interest rates [IR] are also shown. The contributions of interest rate policy and each market to the volatility in the gold price index are distinguished by different colors in the ranges marked in white. Time series for the markets and interest rates are sourced from www.investing.com and www.data.oecd.org)

4.3.2.4 The Japanese Financial Network

The last financial network examined is Japan. According to Fig. 4.44, there is a positive correlation between Bitcoin, gold, and the yen, a result similar to what was observed in the financial networks of the United States, United Kingdom, and Germany. In this context, the positive correlation between the yen and gold is particularly notable. As discussed in Chap. 1, due to its store of value, gold is considered a safe-haven asset, with demand for it increasing during global instability and inflationary environments. The yen is also recognized as a safe-haven currency in financial markets, and its co-movement with gold further supports this notion.

The correlation between the stock market and Bitcoin is positive in Japan, similar to the other three countries. The negative correlation between interest rates and gold, and the positive correlation between interest rates and bonds, was expected and aligns with the findings from the financial networks of the United States, United Kingdom, and Germany, as well as the literature in Chap. 3. The positive correlation between bonds and interest rates is especially notable, with a positive correlation of 0.7%.

In contrast to the positive correlation between major currencies like the pound, euro, and U.S. dollar with interest rates, which is in line with the theoretical literature discussed in Chap. 3, the yen shows a negative correlation with interest rates. Yet, this

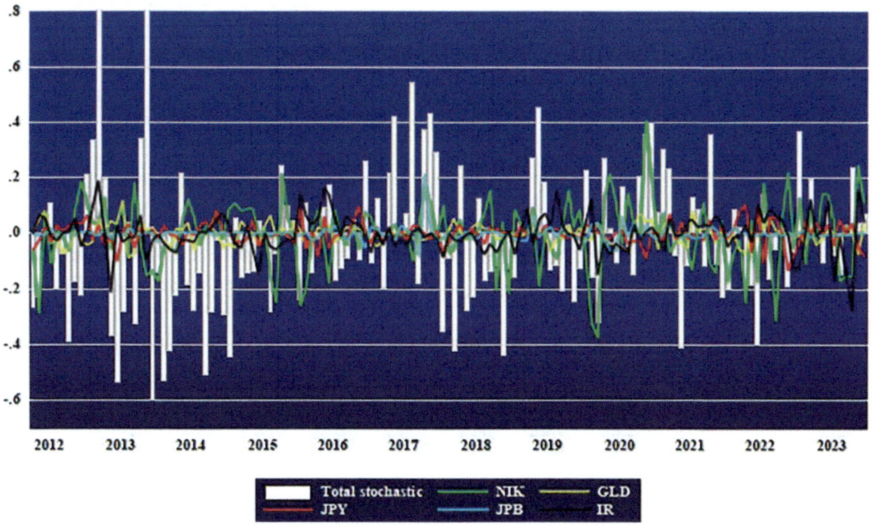

Fig. 4.40 Historical volatility of the Bitcoin price index in the Japanese financial network, monthly time series from March 2012 to December 2023. (*Note*: The historical volatility of the Bitcoin price index [BTC] is highlighted with white bars. The percentage changes in the Nikkei price index [NIK], the gold price index [GLD], the 10-year Japanese government bond yield [JPB], the Japanese yen exchange rate against the U.S. dollar [EU], and interest rates [IR] are also shown. The contributions of interest rate policy and each market to the volatility in the Bitcoin price index are distinguished by different colors in the ranges marked in white. Time series for the markets and interest rates are sourced from www.investing.com and www.data.oecd.org)

is not surprising. Due to the inflation reduction caused by contractionary monetary policies, i.e., interest rate hikes, as well as the increase in borrowing costs and the opportunity cost of holding cash that follows these policies, it is expected that there is a positive correlation between the value of national currencies and interest rates. In the case of the yen, since Japan's central bank has followed a policy of negative interest rates since 2016, a negative correlation between the yen and interest rates is not unexpected.

The stock market shows a positive correlation with interest rates. Negative interest rates may have played a key role in fostering this positive correlation by reducing the cost of accessing financial resources through borrowing.

The crypto market, like in the financial networks of the United States, United Kingdom, and Germany, indicates a very low correlation with interest rates, fluctuating between 0 and −0.1 in most years. This aligns with the empirical results from TVP-VAR models in the first part of this chapter, as well as the historical variance decomposition results in the second part, which indicate that the crypto market is not highly sensitive to interest rates. In fact, given the very short lifespan of the technologies offered by the crypto market, which, as previously mentioned, have seen serious development since 2020, investor attention to the Bitcoin market is more influenced by its competitive capabilities and industrial innovations rather than by

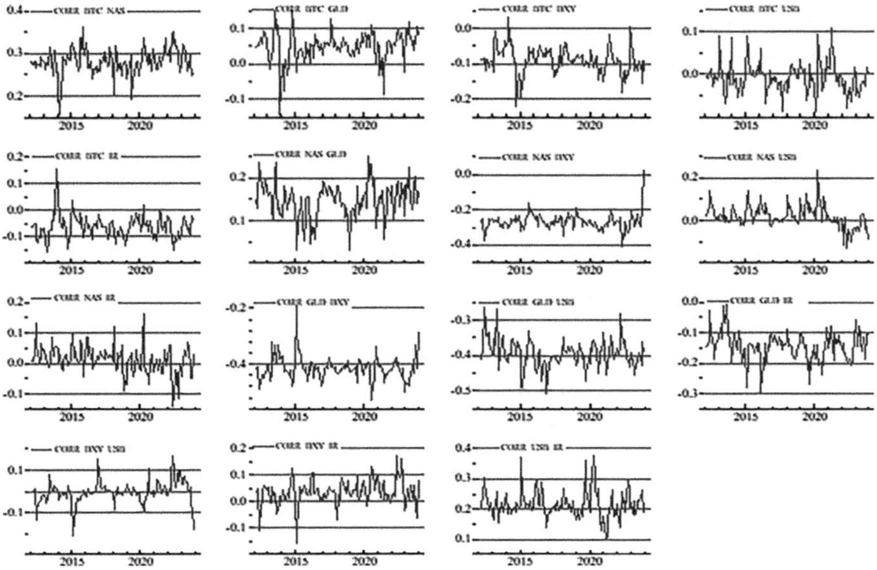

Fig. 4.41 Dynamic correlations between target markets in the U.S. financial network, monthly time series from March 2012 to December 2023. (*Note*: The dynamic correlations between the 10-year U.S. Treasury bond yield [USB], Bitcoin price index [BTC], the NASDAQ-100 price index [NAS], gold price index [GLD], U.S. Dollar Index [DXY], and interest rates [IR] are shown. Time series for the markets and interest rates are sourced from www.investing.com and www.data.oecd.org)

interest rate policies. Similar empirical results obtained in the financial networks of all four countries further strengthen the validity of these findings.

4.3.2.5 Empirical Findings Summary

Based on the empirical results for the United States, the United Kingdom, Germany, and Japan, there is strong supporting evidence for the theoretical framework discussed in Chaps. 1 and 3.

The empirical findings in this section serve as a complement to those presented earlier. On the one hand, they highlight the existence of strong correlations among bond markets, stock markets, major currencies, and gold. On the other hand, they reveal significant correlations between these markets and the interest rate policies of the central banks of major global economies. Therefore, the high degree of correlation between these markets and interest rates complements the high sensitivity of these markets to interest rate changes observed in the historical volatility decomposition of the previous section. These complementary results strengthen the credibility of the empirical findings, which are consistent with the theoretical literature discussed in Chaps. 1 and 3.

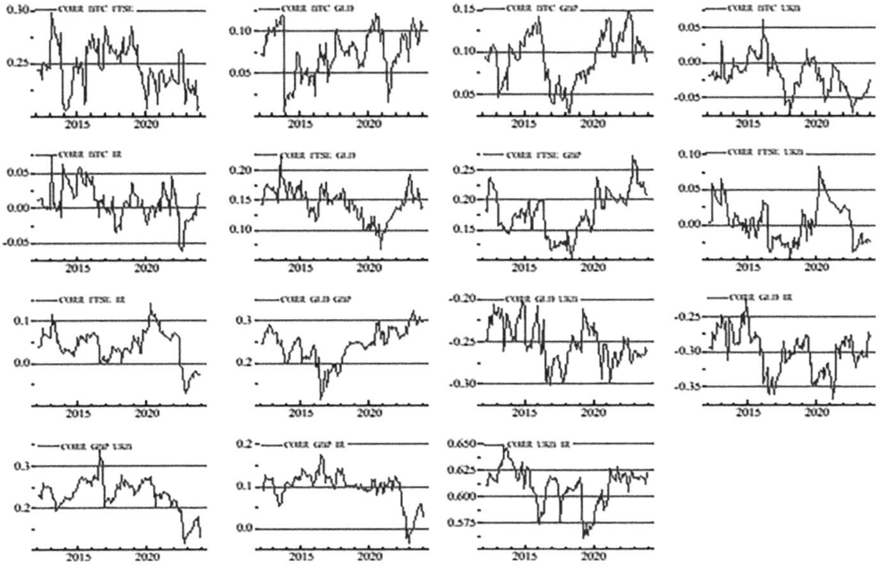

Fig. 4.42 Dynamic correlations between markets in the U.K. financial network, monthly time series from March 2012 to December 2023. (*Note*: The dynamic correlations between the 10-year U.K. government bond yield [UKB], Bitcoin price index [BTC], the FTSE-100 price index [FTSE], gold price index [GLD], British pound exchange rate against the U.S. dollar [GBP], and interest rates [IR] are shown. Time series for the markets and interest rates are sourced from www.investing.com and www.data.oecd.org)

Furthermore, the empirical results of this section indicate a very low correlation between the crypto market and interest rate policies. This is in line with the variance decomposition presented earlier, which showed that the contribution of interest rates to historical volatility in the crypto market was significantly lower compared to the other target markets.

Another key finding, also consistent with the theoretical literature in Chaps. 1 and 3, is the positive correlation observed among gold, stock markets, the yen as a safe-haven currency, and the pound and the euro as the major (risk-sensitive) commodity currencies. The U.S. dollar has acted as a substitute market for stock markets, gold, and major currencies (yen, euro, and pound), displaying a notable negative correlation with them. Bond markets have shown a positive correlation with national currencies, while simultaneously exhibiting a negative correlation with gold and crypto markets, again aligning with the theoretical framework presented in Chaps. 1 and 3.

Bringing these results together, it becomes evident that the significant positive and negative correlations among the markets, indicating strong money flows between them, along with the varying degrees of their sensitivity to interest rate changes, suggest that central banks can influence these money flows through interest rate policies. This allows them to manage such flows in alignment with defined policy objectives.

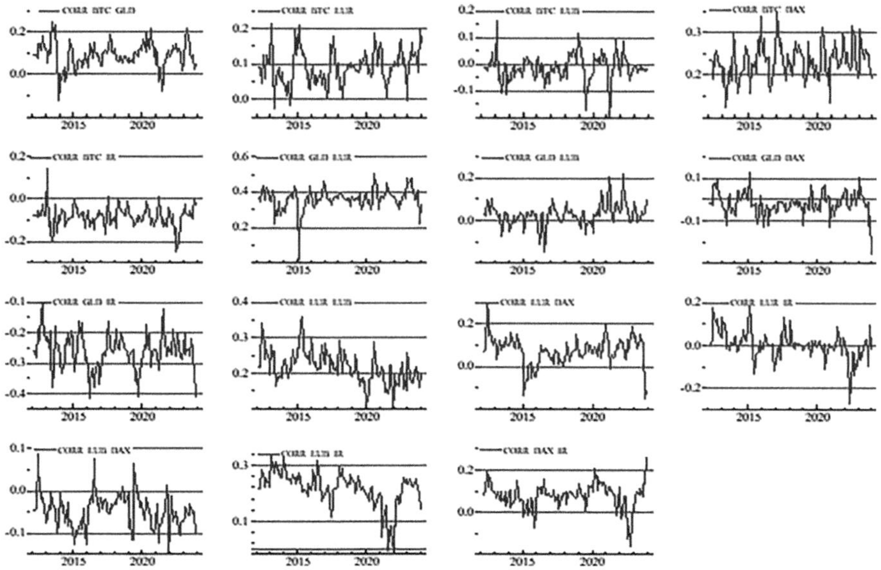

Fig. 4.43 Dynamic correlations between markets in the German financial network, monthly time series from March 2012 to December 2023. (*Note*: The dynamic correlations between the 10-year German government bond yield [GRB], Bitcoin price index [BTC], the DAX stock price index [DAX], gold price index [GLD], the Euro exchange rate against the U.S. dollar [EUR], and interest rates [IR] are shown. Time series for the markets and interest rates are sourced from www.investing.com and www.data.oecd.org)

4.4 Economic Development and Financial Markets

An empirical examination of the connections between target markets, including major global currencies, bonds, gold, stocks, and cryptocurrencies, conducted for the financial networks of the United States, the United Kingdom, Germany, and Japan in the first section of this chapter, using TVP-VAR models based on the literature from Chap. 1. The second section of this chapter explored the conditions for speculative incentives and the sensitivity of the target markets to interest rate policies using historical variance decomposition and cDCC-GARCH models, underpinned by the literature of Chap. 3.

In this section, which constitutes the final empirical appendix of this chapter, the influence of financial markets on indicators representing economic development is examined, based on the literature of Chap. 2. For this purpose, macroeconomic indicators representing economic development, inflation rates, and GDP growth are used. Then, the effects of the target markets on these indicators are analyzed using Markov Switching models.

In summary, as discussed in Chap. 2, economic development is defined as achieving sustainable growth in investment and gross domestic product, where

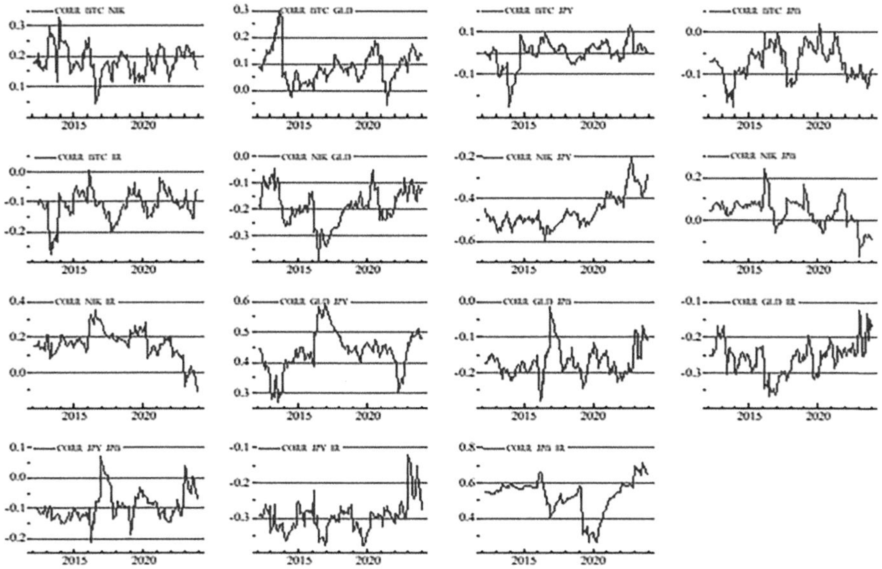

Fig. 4.44 Dynamic correlations between markets in the Japanese financial network, monthly time series from March 2012 to December 2023. (*Note*: The dynamic correlations between the 10-year Japanese government bond yield [JPB], Bitcoin price index [BTC], the Nikkei stock price index [NIK], gold price index [GLD], Japanese Yen exchange rate against the U.S. dollar [JPY], and interest rates [IR] are shown. Time series for the markets and interest rates are sourced from www.investing.com and www.data.oecd.org)

continuous access to financial resources is a key prerequisite. Financial intermediaries, including the stock market and the banking network, alongside the bond market, can play a significant role in ensuring the availability of these resources. Furthermore, since the United States, the United Kingdom, Germany, and Japan are export-oriented economies, fluctuations in their currency value can be a fundamental factor in determining the competitiveness of their export products in global markets. The relative advantages of production within a country or the costliness of domestic production, which may diminish the relative advantage in domestic production and thereby influence the level of imports, are also affected by the national currency market. Thus, the national currency market, along with financial intermediaries and bonds, is recognized as a market with the potential to drive economic development.

In addition to sustained and favorable economic growth, inflation is another key indicator in development literature, as discussed in Chap. 2. The level of uncertainties in economic environments, the impact on purchasing power—which influences human capital development through incentives and productivity—lending and borrowing motivations, and consequently, access to financial resources and borrowing costs, financial market conditions and money flows between them, as well as production costs and labor market expenses, are among the most critical areas through which inflation impacts the economic development process. Therefore, inflation and GDP growth are considered as our variables representing economic development.

To select target markets whose impacts on economic growth and inflation are examined, it is necessary to consider several points. One of these relates to the crypto market. As observed in previous empirical results and discussed in the literature of Chap. 1, this market is very emerging, and most of its competitive advantages have been significantly developed since 2020. Therefore, since economic development is a long-term process, examining the empirical effects of this market on development indicators currently seems irrational for this short period of time. The impact of this market on economic development is more indirect, primarily occurring through the flow of money between markets. Therefore, in this section, the target markets whose impact on development indicators are empirically examined include major currencies, bonds, banking networks, and stock markets. For this, the following models, based on the theoretical literature of Chap. 2, are defined (for simplicity in writing, a one-period lag is considered for the target variables, which are economic growth and inflation rates):

$$\begin{aligned} \text{GDP } t = b_1 + b_{2.st} \ \text{GDP } t - 1 + b_{3.st} \ \text{STO } t + b_{4.st} \ \text{DEP } t + b_{5.st} \ \text{Bond} \\ + b_{6.st} \ \text{EX } t + b_7 \ \text{INF } t + b_8 \ \text{INV } t \end{aligned} \quad (4.22)$$

$$\begin{aligned} \text{INF } t = b_1 + b_{2.st} \ \text{INF } t - 1 + b_{3.st} \ \text{STO } t + b_{4.st} \ \text{DEP } t + b_{5.st} \ \text{Bond} \\ + b_{6.st} \ \text{EX } t + b_7 \ \text{INV } t \end{aligned} \quad (4.23)$$

where GDP, STO, DEP, Bond, EX, INF, and INV respectively represent: economic growth, the value of shares traded in stock markets, the ratio of bank deposits to GDP, the yield on 10-year bonds, major currencies, inflation, and fixed capital formation as investment rates.

To empirically examine these models, we use frameworks that account for the different conditions that development variables may experience, such as recessionary and boom periods or high and low inflationary environments. This approach allows us to assess the impact of target markets on development variables under varying conditions. On the other hand, time series data may experience sudden changes at certain points, referred to in econometrics as regime changes or shifts, which can occur gradually or abruptly. Therefore, Markov Switching models, which possess these advantages, have been chosen for empirical analysis in this section.

Regime shifts are typically assumed to be exogenous according to Hamilton's study (1989). Markov Switching models were initially developed by Goldfeld and Quandt (1973) and later extended by Hamilton (1989, 1994). These models, depending on the dependence of a specific part of the model on the regime, include various types such as Mean Shift (MSM), Intercept Shift (MSI), Autoregressive Coefficient Shift (MSA), Variance Shift (MSH), or combinations of these.

Below, a brief specification is provided to familiarize with the space and framework of these models. Assuming that changes in dependent variables occur under two regimes:

$$R_t = \begin{cases} B_1 Z_t + £_{t,} & if\ S_t = 1 \\ B_2 Z_t + £_{t,} & if\ S_t = 2 \end{cases} \tag{4.23}$$

where R_t is a vector of endogenous variables, which is assumed to change over two regimes during the specified time period. Z_t is a vector of exogenous variables, whose effect on the dependent variable may be regime-dependent. S_t is the unobserved regime variable that follows a first-order Markov process. £t represents the error terms.

The transition probability matrix, which indicates the probability of remaining in a regime and not transitioning to another (P_{11}, P_{22}), and the probability of transitioning between regimes (P_{12}, P_{21}), is given as follows:

$$P = \begin{bmatrix} P_{11} & P_{21} \\ P_{12} & P_{22} \end{bmatrix} \tag{4.25}$$

$$P_{ij} = Pr\,(S_t = j / S_{t-1} = i) \tag{4.26}$$

$$\sum_{j=1}^{2} P_{ij} = 1 \ \ for \ \ all \ \ i, j = 1{,}2 \tag{4.27}$$

Markov Switching models are estimated using the maximum likelihood estimation process:

$$\eta_{i,t} = f\,(y_t | s_t = i,\ \psi_{t-1};\ \theta) = \frac{1}{\sqrt{2\pi\sigma^2}} exp\left(-\frac{\left(y_t - B_0 - X_t'\ B_i\right)^2}{2\sigma_i^2} \right) \tag{4.28}$$

where ψ_{t-1} represents the information from the previous period, and θ is the vector of estimated parameters.

4.4.1 Empirical Results-Markov Switching Models

Given the use of annual time series data, it is necessary to examine the stationarity of the variables before estimating the Markov Switching models. According to Table 4.16, the results of the augmented Dickey-Fuller minimum t-test, which also accounts for structural breaks, indicate that most variables are stationary at the first difference, while some are stationary at level. To maintain the coherence of the discussion and focus on the consistency of the analytical results, the unit root test results are presented at the end of this chapter.

After assessing the stationarity of the variables, based on the significance of regime coefficients, the Akaike and Schwarz information criteria, and the explanatory power of the models, determined by the maximum likelihood estimator, one of the Markov Switching models is selected for empirical analysis. The approach previously adopted to separately conduct empirical analyses for each of the financial networks of the United States, the United Kingdom, Germany, and Japan, which enabled comparative analysis, is also pursued in this section. Initially, the effects of the target financial markets, including bonds, national currencies, and stock markets, and the banking sector, on the indicators representing economic development, which are the inflation rate and GDP growth, are examined for the United States.

4.4.1.1 The U.S. Financial Network

According to Table 4.5, Regime 0 (with a lower mean) and Regime 1 (with a higher mean) correspond to periods of recession and boom, respectively. According to Tables 4.5 and 4.6, the target markets in the U.S. show statistically significant effects on development indicators, inflation, and economic growth, which is consistent with the literature discussed in Chap. 2.

During recessionary periods, the bond market and financial intermediaries, including the stock market and banking sector, show significant positive effects on U.S. economic growth. These three markets, due to their potential in providing

Table 4.5 Estimation results of the Markov Switching model for U.S. economic growth (1975–2023)

Variables Regimes	Coefficient		Std. error		Prob	
	Reg (0)	Reg (1)	Reg (0)	Reg (1)	Reg (0)	Reg (1)
Constant	−0.208	0.415	0.014	0.02	0.000	0.000
USSTO	0.018	−0.009	0.001	0.001	0.000	0.000
USDEP	0.08	−0.299	0.004	0.018	0.000	0.000
USB	0.319	−0.501	0.019	0.05	0.000	0.000
DXY	0.012	0.141	0.005	0.01	0.025	0.000
INF	−0.004	−0.037	0.002	0.014	0.897	0.017
INV	0.341	0.246	0.006	0.062	0.000	0.000
AR-1	0.089	−2.7	0.11	0.349	0.000	0.000
AR-2	−0.032	−1.55	0.071	0.393	0.000	0.001

Note: The Markov Switching model used is of the MSMA type, which allows both the mean and lag coefficients to vary across regimes. AR-1 and AR-2 correspond to the lagged coefficients of GDP growth. The variables Constant, USSTO, USDEO, USB, DXY, INF, and INV represent, respectively, regime-specific constants, the value of shares traded in the U.S. stock market, bank deposits, the 10-year U.S. government bond yield, the U.S. Dollar Index, the inflation rate, and gross fixed capital formation. Except for DXY, which is sourced from www.investing.com, all variables are based on World Bank time series data

Table 4.6 Estimation results of the Markov Switching model for U.S. inflation rate (1975–2023)

Variables Regimes	Coefficient		Std. error		Prob	
	Reg (0)	Reg (1)	Reg (0)	Reg (1)	Reg (0)	Reg (1)
Constant	2.47	0.215	0.154	0.058	0.000	0.001
USSTO	0.114	−0.045	0.022	0.012	0.000	0.001
USDEP	−1.39	−0.065	0.065	0.021	0.000	0.005
USB	1.21	0.166	0.097	0.113	0.000	0.150
DXY	−0.203	−0.049	0.031	0.027	0.000	0.078
INV	2.19	0.607	0.24	0.099	0.000	0.000
AR-1	−0.084	0.054	0.242	0.116	0.000	0.064

Note: The Markov Switching model used is of the MSMA type, which allows both the mean and lag coefficients to vary across regimes. AR-1 refers to the lag coefficient of the inflation rate. The variables Constant, USSTO, USDEO, USB, DXY, and INV represent, respectively, regime-specific constants, the value of shares traded in the U.S. stock market, bank deposits, the 10-year U.S. government bond yield, the U.S. Dollar Index, and gross fixed capital formation. Except for DXY, which is sourced from www.investing.com, all variables are based on World Bank time series data

and mobilizing financial resources, which is an essential prerequisite for achieving economic development, receive institutional support from governments and central banks, as detailed in Chaps. 1 and 2. Therefore, as evidenced by the results, they play a determining role as stimulants in facilitating recovery from economic downturns.

In both boom and recessionary regimes, the U.S. dollar shows a positive impact on economic growth. The limited reliance of the U.S. economy on imported raw materials, along with the high quality of its export products, which are in strong demand globally, neutralizes the typically negative effects of a strong dollar on net exports and, consequently, on U.S. economic growth.

According to Table 4.6, where Regime 0 represents periods of high inflation and Regime 1 represents periods of low inflation, unlike bank deposits, which act as a stabilizing factor by reducing inflation during both high- and low-inflation periods, the stock market shows an inflationary effect during high-inflation periods and a deflationary effect during low-inflation periods. In contrast, the impact of the bond market on the inflation rate is only statistically significant and positive during high-inflation periods.

Meanwhile, the U.S. dollar demonstrates a deflationary effect on inflation in both high- and low-inflation regimes. The positive impact of the U.S. dollar on GDP growth, alongside its deflationary effects on inflation, indicates its overall positive contribution to the U.S. economic development. Therefore, based on the results discussed, the targeted financial markets in the U.S., in line with the theoretical framework presented in Chap. 2, exhibit significant effects on the indicators that represent economic development.

4.4.1.2 The U.K. Financial Network

Next, the effects of the target financial markets on the indicators representing economic development, the inflation rate and GDP growth, are examined for the United Kingdom's financial network. According to Table 4.7, similar to the U.S. financial network, the stock and bond markets show positive effects during periods of economic recession, acting as stimulants for recovery, which aligns with the expectations based on the literature in Chap. 2.

One difference observed in the U.K. financial network compared to that of the U.S. lies in the banking sector. Unlike in the U.S., the British banking sector does not exhibit a positive impact during recessionary periods. Another notable similarity between the U.S. and U.K. financial networks is the effect of their major currencies. The euro, similar to the U.S. dollar, demonstrates a positive influence on economic growth during both boom and recessionary periods.

According to Tables 4.7 and 4.8, as with the U.S. financial network, the target markets in the U.K. show statistically significant effects on development indices, the inflation rate and economic growth, which is line with the literature in Chap. 2. As shown in Table 4.8, The British pound, like the U.S. dollar, acts as an inflation-moderating factor during inflationary periods. Additionally, the inflation-hedging role of the stock market is another common finding observed in both financial systems.

Table 4.7 Estimation results of the Markov Switching model for U.K. economic growth (1975–2023)

Variables Regimes	Coefficient		Std. error		Prob	
	Reg (0)	Reg (1)	Reg (0)	Reg (1)	Reg (0)	Reg (1)
Constant	0.106	−0.451	0.02	0.082	0.000	0.000
UKSTO	0.024	0.535	0.009	0.017	0.016	0.000
UKDEP	−0.097	−0.177	0.012	0.035	0.000	0.000
UKB	−0.081	3.477	0.064	0.097	0.222	0.000
GBP	0.087	2.401	0.024	0.071	0.001	0.000
INF	−0.671	−1.083	0.067	0.021	0.000	0.000
INV	0.435	0.368	0.055	0.164	0.000	0.034
AR-1	−0.319	−4.681	0.171	0.096	0.075	0.000
AR-2	0.002	−8.714	0.172	0.316	0.098	0.000

Note: The Markov Switching model applied is of the MSMAH type, which allows the mean, lag coefficients, and variance to vary across regimes. AR-1 and AR-2 correspond to the lagged coefficients of GDP growth. The variables Constant, UKSTO, UKDEO, UKB, GBP, INF, and INV represent, respectively, regime-specific constants, the value of shares traded in the U.K. stock market, bank deposits, the 10-year U.K. government bond yield, the value of the British pound exchange rate against the U.S. dollar, the inflation rate, and gross fixed capital formation. Except for GBP and UKSTO, which are sourced from www.investing.com and www.fred.stlouisfed.org, all variables are based on World Bank time series data

Table 4.8 Estimation results of the Markov Switching model for U.K. inflation rate (1975–2023)

Variables Regimes	Coefficient		Std. error		Prob	
	Reg (0)	Reg (1)	Reg (0)	Reg (1)	Reg (0)	Reg (1)
Constant	−3.593	0.357	0.046	0.018	0.000	0.000
UKSTO	−0.092	−0.024	0.014	0.007	0.000	0.004
UKDEP	−0.072	0.11	0.017	0.012	0.001	0.000
UKB	0.177	0.238	0.068	0.05	0.018	0.000
GBP	0.28	−0.083	0.016	0.02	0.000	0.001
INV	0.335	−0.044	0.004	0.0002	0.000	0.000
AR-1	−0.79	0.132	0.168	0.175	0.000	0.459
AR-2	−0.542	−0.631	0.104	0.178	0.000	0.002
AR-3	0.4	−0.244	0.105	0.173	0.001	0.17
AR-4	−0.088	−0.557	0.071	0.198	0.228	0.010

Note: The Markov Switching model applied is of the MSMAH type, which allows the mean, lag coefficients, and variance to vary across regimes. AR-1, AR-2, AR-3, and AR-4 refer to the lagged coefficients of the inflation rate. The variables Constant, UKSTO, UKDEO, UKB, GBP, and INV represent, respectively, regime-specific constants, the value of shares traded in the U.K. stock market, bank deposits, the 10-year U.K. government bond yield, the value of the British pound exchange rate against the U.S. dollar, and gross fixed capital formation. Except for GBP and UKSTO, which are sourced from www.investing.com and www.fred.stlouisfed.org, all variables are based on World Bank time series data

4.4.1.3 The German Financial Network

The next economy is Germany, where we examine the effects of target markets on representative indices of economic development using Markov-switching models. According to Tables 4.9 and 4.10, the results show very similar effects of these markets in Germany compared to their effects in the United States and the United Kingdom. Target markets in Germany, like in the United States and the United Kingdom, have a significant impact on development indices, inflation and economic growth, which aligns with the expectations based on the literature in Chap. 2.

As indicated in Table 4.8, stock and bond markets show significantly positive effects during periods of economic recession. Therefore, like the U.S. and U.K. economies, stock and bond markets have acted as strong drivers for Germany's recovery from recessionary periods, which is consistent with the literature in Chap. 2. The impact of bank deposits during recessions has also been positive, which mirrors the effect of bank deposits in the United States. The major currency, the euro, also shows a positive effect during recession periods, similar to the U.S. dollar and the British pound.

According to Table 4.10, Germany's stock market, like the U.K. stock market, has acted as an inflation hedge. Regardless of periods of high or low inflation, its

Table 4.9 Estimation results of the Markov Switching model for the German economic growth (1975–2023)

Variables Regimes	Coefficient		Std. error		Prob	
	Reg (0)	Reg (1)	Reg (0)	Reg (1)	Reg (0)	Reg (1)
Constant	−0.295	0.145	0.059	0.042	0.000	0.002
GRSTO	0.022	0.03	0.005	0.0057	0.001	0.000
GRDEP	0.203	−0.213	0.018	0.025	0.000	0.000
GRB	0.47	0.224	0.086	0.058	0.000	0.001
EUR	0.036	−0.076	0.009	0.006	0.001	0.000
INF	−0.062	0.105	0.0226	0.017	0.011	0.000
INV	0.285	0.593	0.0222	0.011	0.000	0.000
AR-1	−0.735	−1.39	0.115	0.173	0.000	0.000
AR-2	−0.499	−0.022	0.129	0.105	0.001	0.834

Note: The Markov Switching model used is of the MSMA type, which allows the mean and lag coefficients to vary across regimes. AR-1 and AR-2 correspond to the lagged coefficients of GDP growth. The variables Constant, GRSTO, GRDEO, GRB, EUR, INF, and INV represent, respectively, regime-specific constants, the value of shares traded in the German stock market, bank deposits, the 10-year German government bond yield, the value of the euro exchange rate against the U.S. dollar, the inflation rate, and gross fixed capital formation. Except for EUR, which is sourced from www.investing.com, all variables are based on World Bank time series data

Table 4.10 Estimation results of the Markov Switching model for the German inflation rate (1975–2023)

Variables Regimes	Coefficient		Std. error		Prob	
	Reg (0)	Reg (1)	Reg (0)	Reg (1)	Reg (0)	Reg (1)
Constant	−0.85	−0.689	0.008	0.074	0.000	0.000
GRSTO	−0.027	−0.016	0.002	0.005	0.000	0.004
GRDEP	0.209	−0.07	0.005	0.036	0.000	0.069
GRB	0.625	−0.034	0.021	0.112	0.000	0.760
EUR	0.098	0.045	0.01	0.011	0.000	0.001
INV	0.044	0.072	0.083	0.0006	0.000	0.000
AR-1	−1.865	0.078	0.28	0.104	0.000	0.459
AR-2	−1.839	0.44	0.413	0.096	0.000	0.000
AR-3	1.962	0.196	0.438	0.084	0.000	0.029

Note: The Markov Switching model used is of the MSMA type, which allows the mean and lag coefficients to vary across regimes. AR-1, AR-2, and AR-3 correspond to the lagged coefficients of the inflation rate. The variables Constant, GRSTO, GRDEO, GRB, EUR, and INV represent, respectively, regime-specific constants, the value of shares traded in the German stock market, bank deposits, the 10-year German government bond yield, the value of the euro exchange rate against the U.S. dollar, and gross fixed capital formation. Except for EUR, which is sourced from www.investing.com, all variables are based on World Bank time series data effect on the inflation rate has been decreasing. Bank deposits and bonds also show a moderating effect during inflationary conditions. Meanwhile, the euro has had a decreasing effect during low-inflation periods and an increasing effect during high-inflation periods.

4.4.1.4 The Japanese Financial Network

Japan is the final economy, where we empirically analyze the effects of target markets on indices representing economic development using Markov-switching models. As shown in Tables 4.11 and 4.12, the effects observed in Japan closely mirror those found in the United States, the United Kingdom, and Germany. Similar to these economies, target markets in Japan show a significant influence on development indicators, inflation and economic growth, which is consistent with the theoretical literature outlined in Chap. 2.

As shown in Table 4.11, similar to the cases of the U.K. and Germany, government bonds in Japan have a strong positive impact on economic growth, regardless of whether the economy is in a recession or boom. This positive effect is considerably stronger than the effects of the stock market, the banking sector, or the Japanese yen on economic growth. The banking sector have acted as a stronger driver than the stock market in pulling the Japanese economy out of recessions. This finding becomes

Table 4.11 Estimation results of the Markov Switching model for the Japanese economic growth (1985–2023)

Variables Regimes	Coefficient		Std. error		Prob	
	Reg (0)	Reg (1)	Reg (0)	Reg (1)	Reg (0)	Reg (1)
Constant	0.762	−0.126	0.094	0.038	0.000	0.005
JPSTO	0.101	−0.023	0.018	0.007	0.000	0.006
JPDEP	−0.201	0.037	0.015	0.005	0.000	0.000
JPB	1.57	1.262	0.221	0.135	0.000	0.000
JPY	−0.545	0.214	0.033	0.023	0.000	0.000
INF	2.477	−0.198	0.132	0.094	0.000	0.052
INV	1.752	−1.264	0.115	0.131	0.000	0.000
AR-1	−0.836	0.577	0.189	0.072	0.000	0.000
AR-2	0.987	−0.148	0.115	0.067	0.000	0.000

Note: The Markov Switching model applied is of the MSMA type, which allows the mean and lag coefficients to vary across regimes. AR-1 and AR-2 correspond to the lagged coefficients of GDP growth. The variables Constant, JPSTO, JPDEO, JPB, JPY, INF, and INV represent, respectively, regime-specific constants, the value of shares traded in the Japanese stock market, bank deposits, the 10-year Japanese government bond yield, the yen exchange rate against the U.S. dollar, the inflation rate, and gross fixed capital formation. Except for JPY and JPB, which are sourced from www.investing.com and www.fred.stlouisfed.org, all variables are based on World Bank time series data

Table 4.12 Estimation results of the Markov Switching model for the Japanese inflation rate (1985–2023)

Variables Regimes	Coefficient		Std. error		Prob	
	Reg (0)	Reg (1)	Reg (0)	Reg (1)	Reg (0)	Reg (1)
Constant	−0.28	−0.073	0.029	0.032	0.000	0.042
JPSTO	−0.194	0.02	0.004	0.002	0.001	0.005
JPDEP	−0.05	−0.016	0.011	0.004	0.005	0.004
JPB	−0.769	−0.331	0.175	0.102	0.001	0.006
JPY	0.102	−0.043	0.024	0.021	0.001	0.055
INV	0.65	0.64	0.169	0.102	0.002	0.000
AR-1	0.467	0.148	0.185	0.157	0.019	0.361
AR-2	−0.553	−0.449	0.175	0.142	0.006	0.006
AR-3	0.64	−0.405	0.143	0.136	0.000	0.009

Note: The Markov Switching model applied is of the MSMA type, which allows the mean and lag coefficients to vary across regimes. AR-1, AR-2, and AR-3 correspond to the lagged coefficients of the inflation rate. The variables Constant, JPSTO, JPDEO, JPB, JPY, and INV represent, respectively, regime-specific constants, the value of shares traded in the Japanese stock market, bank deposits, the 10-year Japanese government bond yield, the yen exchange rate against the U.S. dollar, and gross fixed capital formation. Except for JPY and JPB, which are sourced from www.investing.com and www.fred.stlouisfed.org, all variables are based on World Bank time series data

particularly important when considering the dominant role of the banking system in financing the Japanese economy, as discussed in Chap. 2. The major currency, the yen, shows a positive effect during recessionary periods, similar to the U.S. dollar, the British pound, and the euro.

According to Table 4.12, the banking sector and bond market show a decreasing effect on the inflation rate during both high- and low-inflation periods in Japan. The inflation-hedging role of the stock market is observed only during periods of low inflation. In contrast, the yen indicates a moderating effect on inflation only during periods of high inflation.

4.4.1.5 Empirical Findings Summary

This section was dedicated to the empirical examination of the theoretical literature discussed in Chap. 2, which focused on the relationships between economic development and financial markets.

The summary of the findings indicates that the banking sector, along with stock and bond markets, which play a key role in financing and mobilizing financial resources, affect economic development under various economic and inflationary conditions, as expected. These results were confirmed across all four major economies: the United States, the United Kingdom, Germany, and Japan, each of which holds a significant share in global economic development. In addition, the national currency market, which was expected to influence development due to its potential impact across different sectors of the economy, also showed statistically significant effects under varying economic and inflationary regimes.

As discussed in Chaps. 1, 2, and 3, the stability of these markets is often supported by government policies and central bank monetary policies. The empirical results provide further confirmation of why these institutional supports exist, particularly because the findings show strong evidence of the positive role these markets play during recessionary periods, acting as drivers for recovery and as stabilizers under inflationary pressure.

Therefore, as in previous empirical sections, this analysis further confirms that the theoretical foundations are not limited to academic or abstract frameworks. Rather, they manifest in real-world dynamics and, more importantly, help shape expectations in actual economic environments.

4.5 Supplementary Results

See Tables 4.13, 4.14, 4.15, and 4.16.

Table 4.13 ADF min-t unit root tests

Variables	*t*-Statistic	Critical values	Results
BTC	23.77	4.443649	Stationary
GLD	25.67	4.443649	Stationary
DXY	27.51	4.443649	Stationary
GBP	26.22	4.443649	Stationary
EUR	26.36	4.443649	Stationary
JPY	25.41	4.443649	Stationary
NAS	27.68	4.443649	Stationary
FTSE	27.33	4.443649	Stationary
DAX	26.56	4.443649	Stationary
NIK	26.06	4.443649	Stationary
USB	29.79	4.443649	Stationary
UKB	30.09	4.443649	Stationary
GRB	37.60	4.443649	Stationary
JPB	32.83	4.443649	Stationary

Note: In the ADF min-t unit root test, the null hypothesis indicates that the variables are non-stationary at the 5% level of significance

Table 4.14 ADF min-t unit root tests

Variables	t-Statistic	Critical values	Results
BTC	20.66	4.443649	Stationary
GLD	12.71	4.443649	Stationary
DXY	13.45	4.443649	Stationary
GBP	12.76	4.443649	Stationary
EUR	12.85	4.443649	Stationary
JPY	11.05	4.443649	Stationary
NAS	13.87	4.443649	Stationary
FTSE	15.50	4.443649	Stationary
DAX	12.57	4.443649	Stationary
NIK	12.07	4.443649	Stationary
USB	11.88	4.443649	Stationary
UKB	14.41	4.443649	Stationary
GRB	20.05	4.443649	Stationary
JPB	13.43	4.443649	Stationary
IRUS	8.76	4.443649	Stationary
IRUK	10.00	4.443649	Stationary
IREU	8.82	4.443649	Stationary
IRJP	12.17	4.443649	Stationary

Note: In the ADF min-t unit root test, the null hypothesis indicates that the variables are non-stationary at the 5% level of significance

Table 4.15 cDCC-GHARCH Models for the United States, United Kingdom, Germany, and Japan

	Coefficient	Std. error	t-Statistic	Prob
The United States (α)	0.037	0.020	1.82	0.0502
The United States (β)	0.534	0.016	3.32	0.0012
The United Kingdom (α)	0.247	0.115	2.13	0.0345
The United Kingdom (β)	0.888	0.062	14.33	0.0000
Germany (α)	0.219	0.095	2.28	0.0240
Germany (β)	0.598	0.136	4.37	0.0000
Japan (α)	0.021	0.011	1.94	0.0527
Japan (β)	0.030	0.014	2.06	0.0413

Note: α and β represent short-term volatility and the persistence of that volatility in the long term, respectively. If these coefficients are statistically significant, the presence of short-term volatility and its long-term persistence cannot be rejected

Table 4.16 ADF min-t unit root tests

Variables	*t*-Statistic	Critical values	Results
USGDP (L)	7.12	4.443649	Stationary
USSTO (L)	2.52	4.443649	Non-stationary
USSTO (D1)	9.007	4.443649	Stationary
USDEP (L)	2.30	4.443649	Non-stationary
USDEP (D1)	7.59	4.443649	Stationary
USB (L)	3.15	4.443649	Non-stationary
USB (D1)	7.04	4.443649	Stationary
DXY (L)	3.61	4.443649	Non-stationary
DXY (D1)	6.43	4.443649	Stationary
USINF (L)	4.78	4.443649	Stationary
USINV (L)	8.06	4.443649	Stationary
UKGDP (L)	9.41	4.443649	Stationary
UKSTO (L)	3.79	4.443649	Non-stationary
UKSTO (D1)	8.54	4.443649	Stationary
UKDEP (L)	4.70	4.443649	Stationary
UKB (L)	3.16	4.443649	Non-stationary
UKB (D1)	5.76	4.443649	Stationary
GBP (L)	3.71	4.443649	Non-stationary
GBP (D1)	7.90	4.443649	Stationary
UKINF (L)	6.64	4.443649	Stationary
UKINV (L)	5.96	4.443649	Stationary
JPGDP (L)	7.05	4.443649	Stationary
JPSTO (L)	3.75	4.443649	Non-stationary
JPSTO (D1)	12.64	4.443649	Stationary
JPDEP (L)	3.52	4.443649	Non-stationary
JPDEP (D1)	10.93	4.443649	Stationary
JPB (L)	7.29	4.443649	Stationary
JPY (L)	4.68	4.443649	Stationary
JPINF (L)	5.13	4.443649	Stationary
JPINV (L)	4.25	4.443649	Non-stationary
JPINV (D1)	5.76	4.443649	Stationary
GRGDP (L)	7.53	4.443649	Stationary
GRSTO (L)	3.11	4.443649	Non-stationary
GRST (D1)	8.38	4.443649	Stationary
GRDEP (L)	1.84	4.443649	Non-stationary
GRDEP (D1)	9.10	4.443649	Stationary
GRB (L)	2.75	4.443649	Non-stationary
GRB (D1)	5.59	4.443649	Stationary

(continued)

Table 4.16 (continued)

Variables	*t*-Statistic	Critical values	Results
EUR (L)	4.00	4.443649	Non-stationary
EUR (D1)	5.45	4.443649	Stationary
GRINF (L)	4.12	4.443649	Non-stationary
GRINF (D1)	7.03	4.443649	Stationary
GRINV (L)	5.89	4.443649	Stationary

Note: In the ADF min-t unit root test, the null hypothesis indicates that the variables are non-stationary at the 5% level of significance. (L) and (D1) denote the level and the first difference, respectively. GDP, STO, DEP, B, INF, and INV refer, respectively, to Gross Domestic Product, the value of shares traded in the stock market, bank deposits, 10-year government bond yield, inflation rate, and gross fixed capital formation. US, UK, JP, and GR represent the economies of the United States, the United Kingdom, Japan, and Germany, respectively. DXY is the U.S. Dollar Index, while GBP, EUR, and JPY indicate the values of the British pound, euro, and Japanese yen against the U.S. dollar, respectively

References

Aielli, G. P. (2008). Consistent estimation of large scale dynamic conditional correlations (Working Paper No. 47). *Department of Economics, Statistics, Mathematics, and Sociology, University of Messina, Messina.*

Aielli, G. P. (2013). Dynamic conditional correlation: On properties and estimation. *Journal of Business & Economic Statistics, 31*(3), 282–299.

Antonakakis, N., Chatziantoniou, I., & Gabauer, D. (2020). Refined measures of dynamic connectedness based on time-varying parameter vector autoregressions. *Journal of Risk and Financial Management, 13*(4), 84.

Bollerslev, T. (1986). Generalized autoregressive conditional heteroskedasticity. *Journal of Econometrics, 31*(3), 307–327.

Dai, Z., & Zhu, H. (2022). Time-varying spillover effects and investment strategies between WTI crude oil, natural gas and Chinese stock markets related to belt and road initiative. *Energy Economics, 108,* Article 105883.

Diebold, F. X., & Yilmaz, K. (2012). Better to give than to receive: Predictive directional measurement of volatility spillovers. *International Journal of Forecasting, 28*(1), 57–66.

Diebold, F. X., & Yilmaz, K. (2014). On the network topology of variance decompositions: Measuring the connectedness of financial firms. *Journal of Econometrics, 182*(1), 119–134.

Engle, R. (2002). Dynamic conditional correlation: A simple class of multivariate generalized autoregressive conditional heteroskedasticity models. *Journal of Business & Economic Statistics, 20*(3), 339–350.

Engle, R. F. (1982). Autoregressive conditional heteroscedasticity with estimates of the variance of United Kingdom inflation. *Econometrica: Journal of the Econometric Society,* 987–1007.

Goldfeld, S. M., & Quandt, R. E. (1973). A Markov model for switching regressions. *Journal of Econometrics, 1*(1), 3–15.

Hamilton, J. (1994). *Time series econometrics.* Princeton University Press.

Hamilton, J. D. (1989). A new approach to the economic analysis of nonstationary time series and the business cycle. *Journal of the Econometric Society,* 357–384.

Chapter 5
Conclusion and Policy Implications

5.1 Introduction

In this book, the connection among financial markets, speculative motivations, monetary policy, and economic development has been examined. The approach taken throughout the book includes a discussion of theoretical literature, the use of real-world examples for a clearer and more intuitive understanding of the concepts, and the inclusion of empirical appendices alongside theoretical discussions to provide a more comprehensive and accessible picture for readers. Moreover, in order to enhance generalizability, ensure broader geographical coverage, and enable comparative analyses, the book considers various economies, developed, developing, and emerging, across different regions including the United States, Europe, and Asia.

The writing of this book has taken into account the diversity of its potential audience, which may include academic environments, institutional players such as governments and central banks, financial and monetary institutions, as well as various investors in financial markets. Therefore, an effort has been made to minimize the complexity of the concepts discussed, making them easier to grasp and more relatable for the book's target audiences. The inclusion of real-world examples and empirical appendices to support the theoretical frameworks serves this purpose.

The structure of the book is organized as follows: Chaps. 1 through 3 are devoted to theoretical literature, covering the following topics, respectively:

- Financial markets and speculative motives: the banking sector, bonds, gold, major currencies, crypto, and stock markets
- Relationship between financial markets and economic development
- Relationship between financial markets and monetary policies

Each theoretical chapter includes in-text real-world examples to enhance the connection between the reader and the conceptual content.

Chapter 4 complements each of the theoretical Chaps. 1, 2, and 3 with empirical appendices, utilizing appropriate models for empirical investigation. A summary of

A. Sadeghi et al., *Financial Markets, Speculation, and Development*,
https://doi.org/10.1007/978-981-95-5895-7_5

empirical findings is presented at the end of each appendix corresponding to the respective theoretical chapter.

Chapter 5, the present and final chapter of the book, offers a synthesis of the theoretical discussions from Chaps. 1, 2, and 3 and the empirical findings presented in Chap. 4. It concludes with a summary, key findings, and practical policy implications,

5.2 Conclusion

Economic development is the central focus of long-term planning in various economies. Achieving this goal requires the fulfillment of certain prerequisites that, if met, can facilitate and smooth the path toward development. One of the key prerequisites is the continuous availability of financial resources necessary to attain a sustainable and desirable rate of investment and GDP growth.

Given that financial resources serve as a fundamental requirement, financial markets, where such resources can be attracted and mobilized, gain significant importance. As discussed in the theoretical literature in Chap. 1, each financial market, including bonds, gold, major currencies, crypto, and stock markets, has its own advantages and weaknesses that may either attract or deter the flow of money. In other words, the strengths or vulnerabilities associated with each market can redirect money flows from one market to another.

Considering the empirical results obtained for the economies of the United States, the United Kingdom, Germany, and Japan, we found the strong connections among the target markets, which reflects the flows of money between them. Depending on their strengths and weaknesses, these markets can act as either substitutes or complements to one another, influencing how money flows across them.

Regarding the crypto market, the empirical results indicated a relatively weak connection with the other target markets, which was somewhat surprising. However, considering external real-world factors, this outcome was not entirely unexpected. A plausible explanation for this inconsistency lies in the emerging nature of the crypto market. Although Bitcoin was officially launched in 2009, the distinctive innovations driving this market have only become more apparent since around 2020, with rapid development continuing through to October 2025. Consequently, despite its competitive potential and technological advancements, the crypto market may need more time to fully develop its capabilities and build stronger links with traditional financial markets.

After the empirical investigation of the connections among target markets within the financial networks of the United States, the United Kingdom, Germany, and Japan, based on the literature in Chap. 1, the second section of Chap. 4 explored the grounds for speculative motivations and potential relationships between the target markets and interest rate policy within the financial networks of the aforementioned based on the literature of Chap. 3.

Following the empirical analysis of the connections among the target markets within the financial networks of the United States, the United Kingdom, Germany, and Japan, as discussed in Chap. 1, the second section of Chap. 4 examined price volatility driving speculative motives and potential links between the target markets and interest rate policies, as outlined in Chap. 3. The empirical results highlighted strong connections between the target markets and the interest rate policies of the central banks of major global economies, with these markets demonstrating high sensitivity to interest rate changes, aligning with the theoretical insights in Chap. 3.

Furthermore, the findings revealed that price volatility in the crypto market is significantly higher compared to the other target markets, fueling speculative behavior aimed at short-term profits. In contrast, markets critical for financing and the conditions of the nominal and real sectors of the economy, including bonds, stocks, and national currencies, exhibit significantly lower price volatility. This results in diminished speculative incentives in these markets, reflected in their stability.

Based on the empirical results presented in the final section of Chap. 4, in line with Chap. 2, the banking sector, along with stock and bond markets, plays a key role in financing and mobilizing financial resources and influences economic development under various economic and inflationary conditions. These findings were consistent across the four major economies, the United States, the United Kingdom, Germany, and Japan, all of which contribute significantly to global economic development. Additionally, the national currency market, expected to impact development due to its influence on multiple economic sectors, also demonstrated statistically significant effects under different economic and inflationary regimes. For this reason, as discussed in Chaps. 1, 2, and 3, the stability of these markets is often supported by government and central bank monetary policies. The empirical results further validate the reasons behind this institutional support, particularly as they demonstrate strong evidence of the positive role these markets play during recessionary periods, acting as drivers of recovery and moderators under inflationary pressure.

If we tie the theoretical literature from Chaps. 1, 2, and 3 with the empirical results related to these chapters in Chap. 4, summarized here:

- High level of sensitivity among the target markets, confirming the existence of money flows between them
- Sensitivity of the markets to interest rate changes
- The significant contributions of the target markets to sustainable economic development

This conclusion is obtained: central banks can influence sustainable economic development by managing money flows between target markets in alignment with policy objectives, particularly through appropriate interest rate policies, as illustrated in Fig. 5.1 in detail. This management of money flows is essential for controlling speculative incentives and supporting markets that have the potential to drive productive investment growth.

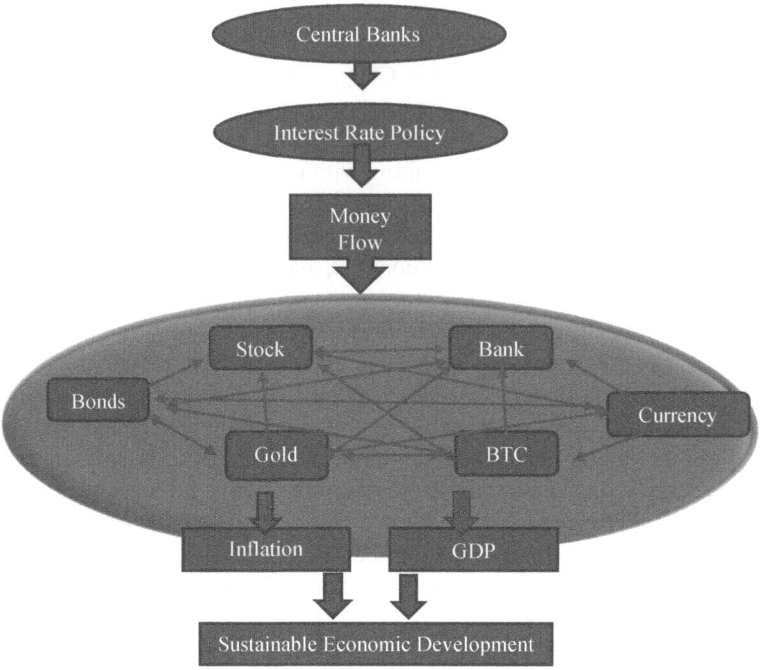

Fig. 5.1 Connection among financial markets, monetary policy, and economic development. (*Note*: The flow of money between financial markets, including bonds, major currencies, gold, crypto, and stock markets, is illustrated by the arrows within the ellipse. On the other hand, the conditions of each of these target markets are potentially influenced by central banks' interest rate policies, affecting the flow of money circulating between them. Considering the influence of financial markets and the banking sector on key indicators of economic development, GDP growth, and inflation, central banks can play a key role in sustainable development by appropriately using interest rate policies in response to inflation to manage speculative motives and money flows across the target markets)

5.3 Policy Implications

Given the theoretical literature discussed and the empirical results presented, the flow of money circulating between financial markets and its central role in sustainable development should hold special significance for central banks, governments, and their policies. In this context, several points must be taken into consideration:

A. **Active interest rate policies in response to inflation rate fluctuations**

   As discussed in the literature of Chaps. 1 and 3, much of the appeal and risks in financial markets are linked to how they are influenced by lending and borrowing motivations, liquidity volume, and inflation, all of which are impacted by interest rate policies. In this context, as highlighted in monetary literature, the response of central bank interest rate policies to inflation fluctuations, whether active or passive, is of critical importance. A passive central bank, failing to respond timely and appropriately to inflation, can reduce its influence over money flows between target markets.

B. **Managing speculative incentives**

Central banks have the ability to strengthen long-term investment appeal in markets that can effectively channel financial resources into developmental and productive investments through implementing active interest rate policies. This way, by reducing price volatility, which fosters short-term speculative incentives, central banks can reduce the likelihood of money flow diversion into speculative markets.

C. **The importance of the bond market for sustainable development**

In addition to its key role in financing governments and corporations, the growing importance of the bond market in financing clean energy projects, which can help reduce environmental and climate damage, is another area that must be considered in interest rate policies for managing money flows between markets, such as preferential interest rates. This is because one of the factors that determines the attractiveness of this market and drives money flow into it is the yield rates of bonds.

D. **The need for adaptation to the crypto industry and avoidance of suppressive approaches**

As discussed in detail in this book, the competitive potential of the crypto industry and its technological innovations, which have become more tangible since 2020, could lead to significant structural changes in the current conventional economy, which relies heavily on various intermediaries. The impact of these innovations, particularly in the areas of smart contracts and decentralized finance systems, could provide greater sustainable development opportunities for countries.

One distinctive feature of the crypto market, compared to other markets, is its potential to realize a world without intermediaries. Money inflow into the crypto market can accelerate the growth of this industry, whose positive impact on long-term economic development will become evident. This includes facilitating and expediting payments, reducing investment risks through suitable value storage, particularly in inflationary environments or during instability, and promoting business development without the involvement of intermediaries, especially for micro and individual enterprises.

E. **Strengthening the store of value of major currencies**

Given the importance of national currencies in the path toward sustainable development, as observed both in theoretical and empirical literature, it is essential to maintain the independence of central banks and continue inflation-targeting monetary policies, which have been significant in the last decade. As seen in part of the empirical results, changes in interest rates have not played a major role in the historical volatility of major currencies: the U.S. dollar, British pound, euro, and Japanese yen. This can be attributed to the independence of the central banks of these major economies and the success of their inflation-targeting monetary policies in keeping inflation rates within limited and defined ranges.

In this way, the store-of-value capacity of these major currencies, which could be severely affected by the lack of central bank independence and the possibility of unlimited money printing, would be preserved, maintaining their standing against markets with competitive capacities like gold and crypto. In turn, a large part of the concerns that could have led to an approach of suppressing the crypto market in favor of major global economies would also be alleviated. There has always been this concern that the increasing role of the crypto market in the global economy could reduce the share of major currencies, thereby strengthening the motivation to suppress this market.

The approach taken by the U.S. Federal Reserve in relation to its alignment with the crypto market, including listing Bitcoin as an asset on its balance sheet, indicates an improvement in the environment for this industry due to inflation-targeting monetary policies and the strengthening of the position of major currencies.

F. **Considering Bitcoin's competitive potential as a store of value**

Given Bitcoin's competitive potential as a store of value, stemming from its scarcity and defined supply ceiling, it presents a strong competitive capacity to gold. Hence, placing Bitcoin on the balance sheets of central banks can help mitigate economic risks in inflationary conditions, especially considering that Bitcoin's market cap is much smaller than gold's, which strengthens expectations for an upward trend in its value.

G. **Regulatory frameworks**

A current threat to the crypto market is the unequal distribution of coins, which has strengthened speculative motives for short-term profits. Individuals and institutions holding large amounts of coins can create artificial price volatility in the market, undermining Bitcoin's store-of-value potential. This has increased the risk of investment and the possibility of capital flight from the industry. Therefore, the presence of regulatory bodies in this market is essential to ensure its stability and mitigate these risks.

GPSR Compliance

The European Union's (EU) General Product Safety Regulation (GPSR) is a set of rules that requires consumer products to be safe and our obligations to ensure this.

If you have any concerns about our products, you can contact us on ProductSafety@springernature.com

In case Publisher is established outside the EU, the EU authorized representative is:

Springer Nature Customer Service Center GmbH
Europaplatz 3
69115 Heidelberg, Germany

Batch number: 10703869

Printed by Printforce, the Netherlands